BLUE CLOGS

William Heap, 1769-1833
Founder of the family firm of Samuel Heap and Son

BLUE CLOGS

THE LIVES AND TIMES OF THE
HEAP FAMILY OF CALDERSHAW, ROCHDALE

Derek Heap

ELSP

Published in 2011 by
ELSP
11 Regents Place
Bradford on Avon
Wiltshire   BA15 1ED

www.ex-librisbooks.co.uk

Typeset in 10/14 point Bembo

Cover design by Andy Heap and Emily Isles

Printed in Britain by
CPI Group (UK) Ltd
Croydon, CR0 4YY

ISBN 978-1-906641-35-1

This book is for Harry the Third
in the hopes that perhaps one day
he might wish to discover more
about the other two

CONTENTS

PREFACE

Every family, said the late Lord Lindsay, should have a record of its own. Each has its peculiar spirit running through the whole line and in more or less development, perceptible in almost every generation.

Rightly viewed as a powerful and much neglected instrument of education, I can imagine no study more rife with pleasure and instruction. Nor need our ancestors have been Scipios or Fabii to interest us in their fortunes.

We do not love our kindred for their glory or their genius, but for those domestic affections and private virtues that, unobserved by the world, expand in confidence towards ourselves, like the banion of the east, and flourish with independent vigour in the heart to which kind providence has guided them.

And why should we not derive an equal benefit from the study of the virtues of our forefathers? An affection to regard for their memory is natural to the heart, it is an emotion totally distinct from pride, an ideal love, free from that of consciousness of requited affection and reciprocal esteem which constitutes so much of the satisfaction we derive from the love of living.

They are denied it is true to our personal acquaintance, but the light they shed during their lives survives within their tombs, and will reward our search if we explore them.

from Palatine Notebook vol one

ACKNOWLEDGEMENTS

I am grateful to the many people who have helped me in the writing of this book and to those many relatives who have responded to my incessant demands for information and photographs. Particular thanks to Peter Heap in Canada for the colour reproduction of the portrait of William Heap 'The Founder' which hung in the board room of Samuel Heap and Son at Caldershaw; my cousin Richard Heap for the chapter on the Greaves family and for doing much of the leg-work on the ground up in Lancashire; Julian Jefferson and the staff of the Touchstones Local Studies Centre in Rochdale and for permission to publish photographic material from their archive; Jean Matthews and her fellow librarians at the Bradford on Avon library who never failed to find obscure publications in equally obscure locations.

My thanks to Negley Harte for his interest and support and his permission to quote from his unpublished history of Samuel Heap and Son; to my son in law, Phillip Lecomber, for charting my footsteps through the computer jungle and manipulating my data into a readable format; and to Roger Berthoud for reading the text and correcting my grammar and syntax.

But above all, to my dear wife for her patience, understanding, encouragement and constant support over many years as gradually the history began to unfold.

INTRODUCTION

This is the story of one family who lived in south-east Lancashire. It begins in about 1720 and continues to the present day. There are about four hundred members of this family, some of whom are just names on a chart, others about whom we know a great deal. There are probably at least a further hundred or so about whom we know nothing. Some would have it that the family can be traced as far back as the 13thC and we refer to this in one of our opening chapters

These were not important people, there are no Lords or Knights of the Realm, no explorers or great scientists, they were just ordinary people such as you might have found anywhere in the United Kingdom; but each in their own way contributed something to our way of life. They began as humble workers in what was primarily an agricultural context, working the fulling mills which provided an essential service to the woollen industry. They ended up running a highly successful Dyeing and Finishing business, leaders in their field and owning six mills. By the end of the 19thC they would have been proud to call themselves members of what became known as the upper middle class, although it is unlikely they would have seen this as a necessary or meaningful stratification of the society in which they lived. They would play a leading role in the new municipalities which were emerging in this part of the country and faced with tackling the problems of social deprivation and poor housing, they devoted their talents to improving the life in the new textile towns. There was nothing unusual about this, there were countless other families following the same path, but they would all adopt the entrepreneurial approach which was the cause of their success and the source of their new found wealth.

They lived through one of the more exciting periods in the history of our country, beginning with the final closure of the American Colonial problem with the defeat of our armies in North America. Although seen as an unmitigated disaster at the time, it was to have the opposite effect of strengthening relations between the Americans and ourselves – that 'special relationship' which we are told still exists to this day and proved to be of immense benefit to the development of the textile industry in Lancashire. They lived through three Revolutions, they watched first with amazement and then with fear and doubts as the French Revolution took hold across the Channel and stood back aghast when its leaders chopped off the heads of their reigning monarchs. The Napoleonic wars which followed brought an increase in trade and an increased demand for finished flannels and cotton goods very much to their financial advantage. They watched as the effects of the enclosure acts altered the pattern of the countryside in which they lived, driving a predominantly agricultural labour force into the new towns in search of work, thus providing them with the labour to work their factories and mills. They lived through the Industrial Revolution as one of the many architects responsible for the changes which it brought about and which gave birth to their increasing prosperity and riches. They watched warily the demands for change from their workforce and endured the Chartists riots and strikes and plug riots which followed. Whilst sympathising with many of their demands they deplored the effect this might have on the success of their business ventures.

They lived through three major wars and innumerable smaller contests as their rulers carved out an Empire – all of which benefited their trade but otherwise left them unmoved. It was not until the first Great War of 1914-18 that they would really become involved, although much to our surprise the family appears to have escaped almost unscathed. The same could not be said for the 1939/45 war which followed during which a young man probably destined to become Chairman of the Board of the family firm was killed in Normandy shortly after D-Day.

But this is not just the story of our family. It is also part of the history of the textile industry in south-east Lancashire. The family were primarily engaged in the wool and flannel trade, only later were they to diversify into cotton. Through the history of the family firm of Samuel Heap and Son we can chart the spectacular rise in their fortunes and their ultimate demise in 1964 when they were bought out by Courtaulds. By then the writing was on the wall and with it the virtual end of the textile industry as they had known it.

We could not have attempted this book without the support and help of many members of the family who were pestered for dates of birth and other information about their forbears. In most cases the information was willingly given, in some cases less so. Some will be disappointed to find they have no mention other than a listing in one of the appendices or their names featuring on one of the many family trees included in the text. The very volume of the information available has of necessity meant that some events and some people have had to be left out. Furthermore we decided somewhat reluctantly to draw a line at the end of the 1939–45 war although of necessity one or two have jumped that barrier.

Provided there is a basis of truth you can say what you like about those who are dead, the dead cannot be libelled and there is added interest when activities and lives can be associated with events occurring in the outside world. The same cannot be said for those who are still living. They are entitled to their privacy. Their story is not yet complete and it will be for future generations to chronicle the story of their lives.

We hope this book will find a place on the shelves of many members of the family and they will find therein something of interest, even perhaps learn something about themselves. This book is not just about the family but offers a window through which we can look back on the social and historical changes which affected this part of Lancashire in the 19thC mainly as a result of the Industrial Revolution and as such it may be of interest to a wider audience.

1

WHO DO WE THINK WE ARE?

Perhaps that's what I wanted to find out, who are we? Who were our ancestors? Questions which go straight to the heart of that ever increasing band of people who spend their leisure hours digging through the records searching for their ancestors. Does it matter? – probably not though those troublesome genes must come into it somewhere. The discovery that one of our ancestors was killed in Normandy shortly after D-Day may prompt a brief surge of pride that we too played our part in defeating the Nazi scourge, delight perhaps when one unearths a connection with minor Royalty (not that we did), or less so on learning one of our ancestors was claiming Poor Law relief in the early part of the 18thC.

I know who I am. I am a Lancastrian, born and bred, who raises his glass to drink the health of the Duke of Lancaster. But do we really know who we are? It used to be enough just to have a name but even that can raise difficulties, different spellings, people change their names. Add a Christian or 'given' name, or better still two of them, and identification should become easier as you narrow the field of search – but does it? At least one member of each generation of our family was called William which can be confusing. The same applies to Herbert, and when they are referred to as 'Bert' do you mean Herbert or Albert?

The further back you trace the history of the family the more likely it becomes that you can assume an ethnic origin restricted to these islands of ours, be it Celtic, Norman, Roman or whatever, but heaven help the researcher of the future whose enquiries will probably take him or her to all the quarters of the globe in parts of which not even surnames are recognisable as such. The greater mobility of peoples, the rapidity of travel and an ever increasing immigration quota, have changed for ever the make-up of the people who live in our country and such changes will become more marked as each year goes by as they intermarry and procreate the next generation.

Although it is the outcome of my more recent researches which has persuaded me to attempt this book, it has been sparked off in part at least by the recent surge in interest in the subject. I first began delving into the history of our family some fifty-five years ago when I was a penniless medical student in London. At that time I accumulated a wealth of information and documents all laboriously copied out in longhand. Although the source material is the same today as it was fifty years ago the methodology is very different. Computers hadn't been invented and a web site was a pond inhabited by ducks! Everything was written either on quarto size paper or foolscap. It did however have one big advantage, everything was accessible without cost, apart from the odd crossing the palm of the Verger, and you could actually lay your hands on the original documents. Census returns were all viewable at the Public Records Office where you would be handed the original books in which the hand written enumerators returns were bound in book form. There is a satisfying thrill in reading the entries made by one of your three times great uncles acting as enumerator who took the opportunity to make an additional note of the number of employees in his mill. Although the more recent census returns offer us a mass of detail not available in earlier years, I doubt today's enumerator would get away with such a gratuitous entry.

But there is another reason for attempting this book. I am now the sole depository of a vast wealth of information about some of the closer members in our family, most of whom are now dead. I was there, I attended the twenty-fifth wedding anniversary party of Leslie and Ann Handley and was unwise enough to make some cryptic written comments at the time. I lived through the thirties as a child growing up in the Practice house at 70 Spotland Road which gave me an insight into what life was like for an upper middle class child growing up in a cotton town. Although I spent my war years away at school, they have left an indelible memory. Those years were to have a dramatic effect on the lives of some of our relatives, and ushered in social changes which would alter the very fabric of the society within which we had all been born and brought up.

❉

The Society of Genealogists offices and library in Harrington Gardens was but a short step from the flat which I shared with two other medical students in Thurloe Square, a very up-market address for an impecunious medical student.

Our landlady was the widow of the late Bishop of Norwich and attendance of at least one of us at the monthly religious gathering or prayer meeting was obligatory. The Librarian at the Society of Genealogists welcomed me with open arms and offered me every facility and help in my researches. I discovered a treasure trove of books, plans, documents, registers and lists included amongst which were the published volumes of the Lancashire Parish Register Society which covered most of the parishes in which I was interested. I was hooked from that moment on…

❋

Although the methodology may have changed, research into the history of one's family is much the same now as it was fifty years ago. Enquiries fall quite simply and easily into five separate parts.

Firstly, what is already known? What can you remember? Have you any ancient relatives whose memory must be tapped before they die? I was lucky to enlist the help of my Aunt Kathleen whose memory on family matters was prodigious. All the names that appear on the main family tree after the birth of William Tweedale Heap in 1832, ending with Richard and Patricia Heap – some two hundred relatives and ancestors in all – are almost entirely the product of Kathleen's memory. Kathleen would talk and sup her gin while I would try to keep up, scribbling away, writing it all down. It had the added attraction that her remarks were peppered with additional comments about the individuals concerned which became increasingly outrageous as the level of gin in the bottle decreased.

Her information has stood the test of time and most of it has proved to be accurate. Her memory of the generations prior to William Tweedale Heap proved to be less so, although subsequent enquiries and researches have enabled us to fill this gap. Not only did I come to rely on Kathleen's memory, but she would accompany me on my forays into the wilds of Lancashire to access the Parish records of the various churches and chapels on our list, digging into the parish chests and sifting through their dusty content and on occasion bribing the Verger for even greater access.

The second and much valued resource are the documents, Wills, newspaper cuttings etc. associated with the events taking place in the lives of the participants in our story. The history of the family revolves around the fortunes (and subsequent misfortune) of the dyeing and finishing firm of Samuel Heap and Son in Caldershaw. I have a copy of the Will of the Founder of the firm,

William Heap, and various other documents relating to the firm, copies of letters to a cousin in America written in 1833[1] which afford a fascinating glimpse of the historical events taking place at that time and which reveal their ardent Wesleyan Methodist approach to life in general which had a considerable influence on the way they brought up their families. We also have copies of what have come to be known as the Lye-Stamm papers.[2] There is still some doubt as to their origin, but they have provided a mass of data about members of the family in the early part of the 19th century and detailed family trees of other related families.

The third source available to the researcher is the official record of births, deaths and marriages held by the General Register Office in Southport. After 1837 all persons were required by law to register any birth, death or marriage. It is simple and easy to access and can provide much detailed and supportive information about relatives which may have been lacking – albeit now at an astronomical cost.

Another similar but even more helpful resource are the ten yearly Census Returns which began in 1841. The 1841 Census is somewhat limited in the information provided but each subsequent ten-year return offered more and more detail and can open a window, as in the case of Dr Samuel Heap, into just what was going on inside the family on the night in question.

The Census also provided an introduction to the return for each area. For example we learn that there were 84,718 persons resident in the district of Rochdale in 1841 which consisted of some 58,620 acres. The figure had fallen to 34,545 persons by 1858 but the area covered was different and related to the new County Borough. Nevertheless they make the point that the population of the town had fallen and the number of uninhabited houses had increased due to the depression in trade.

This figure of 84,718 in 1841 is staggering as, as far as I can recall, the population of Rochdale had only risen to 90,000 by the 1950s. This was due to the rapid expansion of the Cotton Industry – if you have mills, you must have operatives to man the machines. Labour must have flooded into the town, all of whom required some form of living accommodation, albeit much of it squalid back to back houses with only primitive sanitation.[3] There were also numerous workhouses scattered throughout the town, each with some twenty or more inhabitants, a further indication of the social consequences of the rapid expansion of the town. If you couldn't work, if you couldn't pay the rent, if you suffered with chronic ill health, you ended up in the workhouse on Poor Law relief. There was also a barracks in Spotland with 125 men and

14 women! – presumably these were the wives of the soldiers. It was an Irish regiment. The barracks were empty in 1851. There were no officers listed but presumably the officers would have been boarded out in the town and would therefore have appeared on one of the house returns.

The decline in numbers attributed to a depression in trade is supported by the fact that the census records two mills had closed in 1841 and a further two in 1851 resulting in emigration of part of the labour force. The 1851 census also notes that part of the population decline could be accounted for by the fact that the railway workers had moved on by 1851 having completed their section of the line from Manchester to Leeds – the Rochdale section was opened in 1840.

Two of the enumerators in the 1841 census were John Heap and James Heap – both sons of William Heap, founder of the firm at Caldershaw. They had also insisted that the 1851 census return should show how many workers they employed. Samuel Heap employed 24 men and 10 boys at Caldershaw, James Heap – also at Caldershaw – employed 34 men and boys, whilst Thomas Heap – the eldest son, is shown as employing 70 men, 28 women, 28 boys and 25 girls in his Ogden Mill at Milnrow. The employment of large numbers of children in the mills was only too common and was to cause Parliament to introduce Factory Act after Factory Act in an endeavour to control the numbers, raise the minimum age of employment and require the employer to make some provision for their education.

The 1851 census returns also show that nearly all the large families had one or more domestic servants, many of whom had travelled considerable distances to find work in Rochdale. It was not just the large moneyed families whom you might have expected to employ servants to attend to their needs, not that there were many of these – the Gentry being conspicuous by their absence in and around Rochdale. The mill owning families all employed domestic staff as you would expect, but so did the retailers and shopkeepers. Even some of the larger families working in the mills employed servants. As far as the mill workers were concerned, these would have been relatives or older widows. With the whole family out at work in the mill including the older children, someone had to stay behind to look after the babies and those considered too young to work.

Much has been said[3] about the evils of employing children in the mills, but it did help forge a large family group in which each member was dependant on the others in the group. It was not uncommon to have five or six wage earners in one family. The older adult members would mainly be employed on piece work while the children were subcontracted by their parents to work with them and were paid by the hour by their parents. Working in this way the piece worker didn't have to waste time carrying out unproductive work such as cleaning around the machines or fetching and carrying. He or she would be able to concentrate on producing the pieces for which he got paid. It was working in this way that was the cause of so many of the accidents. A stopped machine is 'non productive' whilst it is not in operation, so the children were required to crawl under the machinery whilst it was still in motion to collect up the waste cotton or wool which had fallen out onto the floor. Accidents were inevitable and the list of horrific injuries sustained by some of the children beggars belief.

The next source available to the researcher is the Parish Registers. Prior to 1837 the only records of births deaths and marriages were those kept by the Church and it is these Parish Registers which provide the fourth source of information. The registers were often kept in a large oak chest in the vestry where they were liable to attack by mice, damp or fire. Hardly surprisingly many of them were incomplete although happily quite a number of the incumbents were required to send a copy to the Bishop, known as the Bishop's Transcripts, and these have filled some of the gaps. There is an added complication in that our Family were fervent Wesleyan Methodists and they kept their own registers of baptisms, births and deaths and burials in their Chapel records. However the State wouldn't recognise marriages carried out in the Methodist churches and so many of them had to go through some form of ceremony in the local Parish Church to have their marriage recognised.

Happily many of the Parish Records are now published in book form or on CD, microfiche or microfilm, the original registers held either in the National Archives Office at Kew or in the appropriate County Records Office which, so far as we are concerned, would be at Preston. The records are incomplete and the original copies are often difficult to read and decipher, but if you are lucky they may take you back as far as the middle of the 17thC. The records often contain small snippets of additional information which the recording incumbent has seen fit to include. One of the Lancaster records include a John Heap, a prisoner, who died on 7 April 1784; the Middleton registers record that in 1705 a Joseph Heap made a donation of one shilling towards the rebuilding of St Paul's and in the following year he gave sixpence towards the redemption of the English captives at Algiers.

After you have exhausted the Parish Registers and are still finding relatives you will need to start delving in the Court Rolls, the lists of those who paid the Hearth Tax, the Poor Law records and such like. Very few such records are indexed, many are difficult to read and often in Latin and the further back you go the greater the problems become.

Finally the International Genealogical Index contains literally millions of records of births and marriages but no death records or burials. The records have been collected and stored by the Mormons or the Church of Latter Day Saints. Most are stored on microfilm held in safe storage below ground at the Mormon Headquarters in Salt Lake City, Utah. The material is easily and readily available through any one of the hundreds of offices throughout the world attached to the Mormon Temples.

❖

Researching one's family history may be no different in theory today from what it was when I started back in 1954 but the practice has changed out of all recognition. Fifty years ago there was no internet, little of the subject matter was indexed, books and registers had to searched manually and the Heap entries extracted. There were no photocopiers and everything had to copied in longhand before being typed up.

Today documents can be photocopied or scanned, imported into ones filing system where it can be stored and then extracted and imported into the final word processed document as and when required. All the Census returns, the General Register of Births, deaths and marriages, nearly all the Parish and Non Conformist Registers are available on-line. In practice there is so much information and so many people in the field trying to sell you ways and means of accessing it that it becomes increasingly difficult and expensive to navigate your way round the web.

❖

So where do we begin: perhaps with Joseph, Harry and Harvey, the most recent additions to the tree, and incidentally all with given names which already feature on the tree, or with Robert son of John Heap of Worsthorne near Burnley born in 1713, the first name on our Tree? But which is the beginning and which the end? Logic suggests that you begin with the first person on the Tree and then work your way forwards until you get to the present day but practicality suggests that you start at the end and work your way backwards (or is it forwards?) until you arrive at the beginning ... or is it the end?

It is not really the names that are important. They appear in their multitude increasing with every generation, particularly in the early years of the 19thC, our ancestors were a fecund lot. The name of HEAP is the one and only constant link between them all. Richard and Charles Heape have provided us with a wealth of material about the possible derivation of the name Heap or Heape, and they have some interesting suppositions to make about the original place name from which they believe the surname is derived.[10]

There appear to be some twenty or more variants on the way the name is spelt, the further you go back in time the more peculiar some of them become. Charles and Richard Heape suggest that the earliest mention of the name 'de HEP' is way back in the 13thC when they were landholders in the Salford Hundred. In addition to HEAP and HEAPE, we have HEP or HEPE, HEIP, HEIPP, HEIPE, HEIPPE, HEYPE, HEYPPE, HEPPE, HEAPP, and finally HEEP of Dickensian fame, although this is the one spelling variant which has not so far appeared in the records. Our medieval scribes and even our 18th and 19thC parish clerks cannot be relied upon and it is not uncommon to find the same name written with different spellings on the same page. It is necessary to keep an open mind! An interesting footnote – when you book a table in a restaurant in France and write down the name of HEAP the French pronounce it as 'HEP'

Surnames did not really come into proper use until 12thC when the increasing numbers and diversity of the population made such a change necessary. Furthermore people started to move around and it became necessary to have a system which allowed people to be more easily identified and if necessary, traced. Levying taxes becomes much easier when people have names which can be put on lists.

Surnames fall into four groups, those derived from 'nicknames' such as Strong and Blunt; 'patronyms' originally assigned because of the name of the father such as Robin-son and Tomlin-son; 'metonyms' derived from trades or occupations such as Smith and Wright; and 'toponyms' where the persons name is associated with a geographical location and takes the name with them when they move.

The name of HEAP is thought to be a toponym. The name is of Anglo-Saxon derivation when it could mean a mass of irregularities in the land or a crowd or multitude. If a toponym, then where was the original geographical location? Richard Heape identifies this as 'Heap Fold', a small hamlet about a third of a mile outside Heap Bridge towards the south-east which he associates with the original land held by the de Hep family mentioned in a charter of 1210.

In those far off days people tended to stay in one place. Indeed their contract with the local Lord often forbade them to move. Such roads as there were, were often impassable particularly during the winter months. Even in later years before the advent of the railway, travel was either on horseback or by stage coach when a journey from Rochdale to Manchester could take up a whole day particularly if you had to walk or ride the whole way Our modern transport system enables us to move about the country at will and even to cross over the channel to Europe just for a days meeting and then be back home before nightfall. As we travel, so does our business … a very different situation to that which existed in southeast Lancashire as the cotton industry began its rapid expansion at the beginning of the 19thC. Raw cotton would be brought in on wagons after unloading at Liverpool, and the finished goods would travel out the same way or be taken down to London by cart before being loaded at the London docks for shipment to the burgeoning markets out east. The advent of the canals, shortly followed by the railways, revolutionised trade and dramatically reduced the time spent on travelling both for goods and for people. As a result the population started to move, if there was better money elsewhere – then move and take your family with you.

In spite of this increased movement the population remained remarkably static. A recent research project developed by University College London (UCL)[5] has investigated the distribution of surnames in Great Britain, both current and historic, in order to understand patterns of regional economic development, population movement and cultural identity. The survey is based on the 1881 census and more recent data collected in 1998. The names are 'counted' according to the postal districts in which they lived. In the 1881 census the name HEAP is almost entirely restricted to south-east Lancashire with the densest pockets in Blackburn (includes Burnley) and Oldham (includes Rochdale). A not dissimilar pattern is shown for the 1998 data. The densest pockets remain as before in south-east Lancashire with the highest incidence recorded in Blackburn, Burnley, Oldham, Rochdale and Manchester although the name has now spread outwards to include Yorkshire, up into Cumbria and down into the North Midlands.

The distribution pattern for HEAPE, whilst having elements in common with HEAP, is nowhere near as conclusive. The 1881 data shows a small dense area in the Rochdale and Oldham postal districts but not elsewhere, with a similar area in Leicestershire, presumably the branch referred to by Richard and Charles Heape. There is also a rather curious concentration in mid-Wales. In 1998 the figures for HEAPE were so small that they do not qualify for entry and there is therefore no distribution map available.

You can make statistics tell you anything you want to know, but I think all this tells us is that as a family we have been remarkably static. It may also tell us that either the HEAPEs have stopped breeding! … or, more likely, that custom and usage have caused the final 'e' to be dropped. You may place what interpretation you wish but the predominant spelling of the name today is HEAP and has probably been so for the last two hundred years. There is some support for this view in Hank's *Dictionary of American Family Names* (the data source for the population profiles referred to earlier) which lists HEAPE as being a variant of HEAP with a frequency of 267 for HEAPE as against 638 for HEAP. My case rests…

❖

But there is much more to family history than a list of names on a family tree with their dates of birth, marriage and death. Who were these people, what made them tick, what were the conditions under which they were living, what was going on in the outside world at the time? Clothe the names on our family tree with this sort of information and they come alive. In this respect we are lucky in that the history of our family is tied up with the history of the textile Industry in south east Lancashire. Rochdale had been a centre of the wool trade for over two hundred years. It was the centre of the flannel trade and was one of the largest and most successful of the cotton towns. Our family participated to the full and grew rich in the process.

Notes and references
1 see appendix IV
2 see appendix III
3 Hunt, Tristram: The Frock-coated Communist: a biography of Friedrich Engels. Penguin 2009. Chapters 3 and 4 relating to working and living conditions in Manchester
4 Heape, C and R. *Records of the Family of Heape.* Aldine Press, Rochdale 1905
5 Surname Profiler. CASA. UCL (London) 1999

2

EARLY DAYS: 1170 TO 1600
RECORDS OF THE FAMILY OF HEAPE

Recorded and proven history takes our family back to about 1720. Apocryphal stories point to a much earlier date but with little evidence to support such a proposition. However one source which cannot be ignored is a book privately printed and published in 1905 entitled *The Records of the Family of Heape* by Richard Heape and Charles Heape. It is a magnificent tome and clearly no expense was spared in its preparation. The cover is of white heavy parchment like material embossed with gold lettering and the family coat of arms in red. It is well illustrated with brown sepia photographs many of which are of water colour paintings of the various sites and properties occupied by the family. It is packed full of family trees of all the families connected by marriage, a treasure trove to any genealogist, or nightmare, depending on their accuracy. Richard Heape says that the whole exercise cost £1,700, a considerable sum in those days – perhaps £10,000 in today's money, researchers fees alone would be well into the thousands.

Part 1 deals with the history of the family before 1682 and is written by Charles Heape. It purports to take the story back as far as 1170 with the birth of a Robert de Hep. His name appears as a witness to a charter recording the gift by Roger de Montbegon of the Forest of Holcombe to 'God and St Mary Magdalene of Bretton and to the monks serving God there'. Charles employed professional researchers to assist him in his task and this section of the book is almost entirely dependant on names found in ancient charters, deeds of gift, lists of Jurors, Court Records and the like, most of which are difficult to access and almost unreadable to the mere amateur.

Part 2 deals with the history from 1682 onwards and is written by Richard Heape. This is based on the large collection of family papers in their possession and the same sources as we have made use of in the research into our branch of the family, *i.e.* birth, marriage and death registers, burial records, grave stone inscriptions and the like. It is much easier to read and understand and, where the various generations are proven, can be accepted as accurate.

Charles begins his account by stating that the original family home was the Vil of Heape which lay within the Salford Hundred. He suggests the location is that now occupied by Heap Fold which lies to the north of, and in close proximity to, Heap Bridge. *Heape* or *Hep* does not feature in the Domesday Book as the Salford Hundred belonged to the King and the King's lands were not listed. There were 21 berewicks (villages or hamlets) in the Salford Hundred each of which was held by a Thane at the time of Edward the Confessor. The first mention of the Vil of Heape was in deeds c.1200. The Family left their ancestral home in the first half of 15thC never to return. It was our branch of the family which returned to the area some time in the second half of the 18thC when they settled at Bridge Hall, a fact which seems to have escaped Charles Heape's notice although his notes on the Rossendale Branch of the family suggest he must have been aware of this

Charles then traces the descent of the family from Robert de Hep c.1170 through eight generations to John de Hepe, who married Margaret, and who is named in a witness enquiry in 1412. Each name, except one, is supported by an entry as Juror on a Court Roll or some other legal document.[2] There are no records of dates of birth or death etc as such events were not recorded at that time. The fact that their names appear at all is in itself an indication of their status within the community. They are all named as *de Hep* or *de Hepe* indicating they were all resident in the same place. In those early days if you moved away from the family home you did not take your 'surname' with you, you adopted a new name indicating where you had come to reside. There are very few siblings named, although there was a high birth-rate relatively few would survive to adulthood. The Vil of Hep would not support a large family and younger sons would be under pressure to move out, females would marry and also move out.

But then two events occurred which were to have a dramatic effect on the family and its future generations. In 1348 the Black Death swept through the country and, if we are to believe the chronicles, at least one third of the population died. Surprisingly after this date the number of members of the Heap families for whom we have some form of record increased! It would be pleasing to think this was the survival of the fittest but it is more likely this was due to improved record keeping and that from this time onwards people tended to retain their surname when they moved.

CHART 1

de Hep family
1170-1463

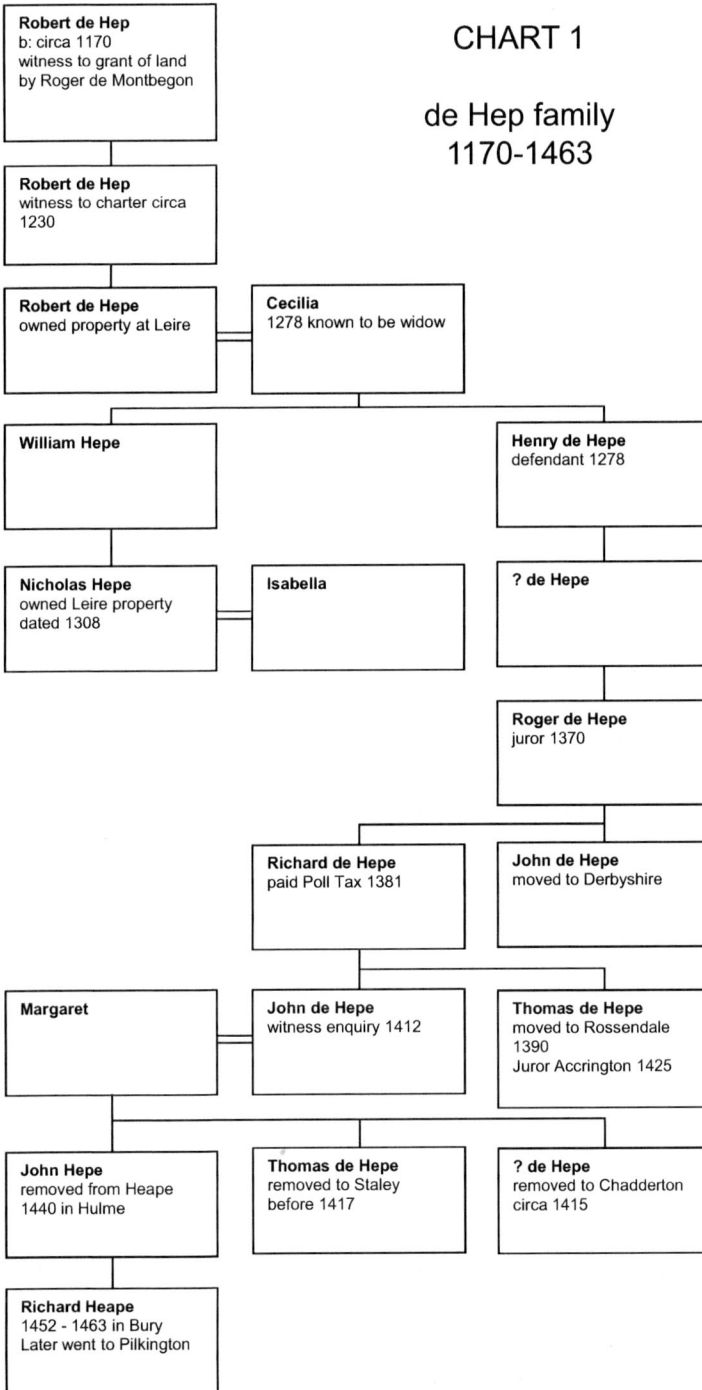

Robert de Hep
b: circa 1170
witness to grant of land
by Roger de Montbegon

Robert de Hep
witness to charter circa
1230

Robert de Hepe
owned property at Leire

Cecilia
1278 known to be widow

William Hepe

Henry de Hepe
defendant 1278

Nicholas Hepe
owned Leire property
dated 1308

Isabella

? de Hepe

Roger de Hepe
juror 1370

Richard de Hepe
paid Poll Tax 1381

John de Hepe
moved to Derbyshire

Margaret

John de Hepe
witness enquiry 1412

Thomas de Hepe
moved to Rossendale
1390
Juror Accrington 1425

John Hepe
removed from Heape
1440 in Hulme

Thomas de Hepe
removed to Staley
before 1417

? de Hepe
removed to Chadderton
circa 1415

Richard Heape
1452 - 1463 in Bury
Later went to Pilkington

The devastation which followed the Black Death meant that labourers were scarce and therefore the cost of labour was high. It also resulted in movement of labour in that much of the land had been left untilled. As a result land was up for grabs and such land as was bought and sold went for very low prices. These new land holders often became copy-holders holding their land by tenure from the Lord of the Manor.

The result, as far as the family was concerned, was that within a hundred years the whole family had moved out of the ancestral home. For the first time we find the siblings named and identified by the family name with the 'de' having been dropped. The first to go was a younger brother of Richard, named John, who went to Taddington in Derbyshire.[3] Richard's grandson, Thomas de Hepe, moved to Rossendale in 1390 and it is suggested that our branch of the family derives from this source (see below); John and Margaret's eldest son John Hepe moved in 1440 to Hulme; their second son Thomas de Hepe moved to Staley before 1417; their third son – de Hepe moved to Chaddderton *circa* 1415. The authors of the Records of Family of Heape trace their descent from the Thomas who moved to Staley

Before examining the Rossendale branch in greater detail we should ask ourselves what caused this apparent sudden mass exit from the ancestral home. There may have been similar 'migrations' of the younger sons before this date but in the absence of a retained surname they remain hidden. It is more unusual for a whole family to migrate, including the head of the family, vacating the ancestral home in the process and the land which went with it. Charles Heape has suggested that such a change must have resulted from 'a considerable force' and he offers either 'inducement' due to a favourable opening elsewhere, or by 'compulsion' the conditions at the old home having become too hard to permit a continuance. He offers no proof of this although it is suggested that the land at Heape or Hep was of poor quality and new pastures offered greater opportunities for profit. We have seen already that following the devastation of the Black Death there would have been ample opportunities open to them. The family were closely related to the Radcliffes[4] who were already farming in the same area and to whom they were connected by marriage. This could well have been the only inducement necessary for them to 'up-sticks' and leave.

We must now leave the main branch of the family who retained the 'e' on the end of their surname to the present day. They moved from Staley to Hartley just south of Rochdale but within the Castleton township. Clothiers by trade, they branch out into the wholesale grocery trade and improved their fortunes when one of their number emigrated to Australia where he set up a very successful business before returning to Lancashire. Thereafter the pattern of their lives was very similar to our own. Mayors of Rochdale and staunch Wesleyans Methodists, but curiously enough going out of their way to purchase a pew at the Parish Church of St Chad which they retained whilst continuing to worship at Baillie Street – nothing like backing both horses to win!

✻

The Rossendale branch of the Family

During the course of his research Charles Heape assembled a mass of data about the members of the family who had migrated to Rossendale and he summarises this information in his Appendix B.[5] He even goes so far as to structure the data in a family tree which is reproduced below. It begins with Thomas de Hepe, one of the younger sons of Richard de Hepe, who left the family home in 1390 and who is listed as a juror in Accrington in 1425. This first mention is recorded in the Court Rolls of Clitheroe which include the decisions of various lower courts including the Halmote of Accrington on which Thomas served as a Juror. This court recorded the changes in copyholder ownership of land and appointed the Grave or Greave of the Forest of Rossendale and the Fence Lookers of the district. Thomas is the last generation to use the 'de' in front of his surname.

No further entries are found until a Richard Hepe appears as a juror in 1465 at an inquest at Alnetham (today Altham six miles north of Haslingden). Richard could have been a grandson of Thomas. From 1496 onwards there are many mentions in the Court Rolls the details of which are shown on the tree. There is a Lawrence Heype of Haslingden in 1496, a Ralph of Wilpshire (three miles north of Blackburn). There are Heap's recorded at Wulfenden (two miles north of Newchurch), a Richard Heype appointed Grave of Rossendale for many years and tenant of the King, and many others. There are some twelve names in all living at some distance from each other which suggests that there was more than one family involved.[6]

A similar pattern is found in the Parish Registers of Burnley, Newchurch, and the surrounding towns for the 16thC and well into the 17thC. The majority spell their name as Heap. So many names are found that it is almost impossible to arrange them in any logical order other than to find the odd family which can be followed through several generations.

Another source of reference which becomes increasingly important in the 16th and 17thC is Newbigging.[7] He lists the copyholders in Rossendale

CHART 2

Heap of Rossendale
1390-1553

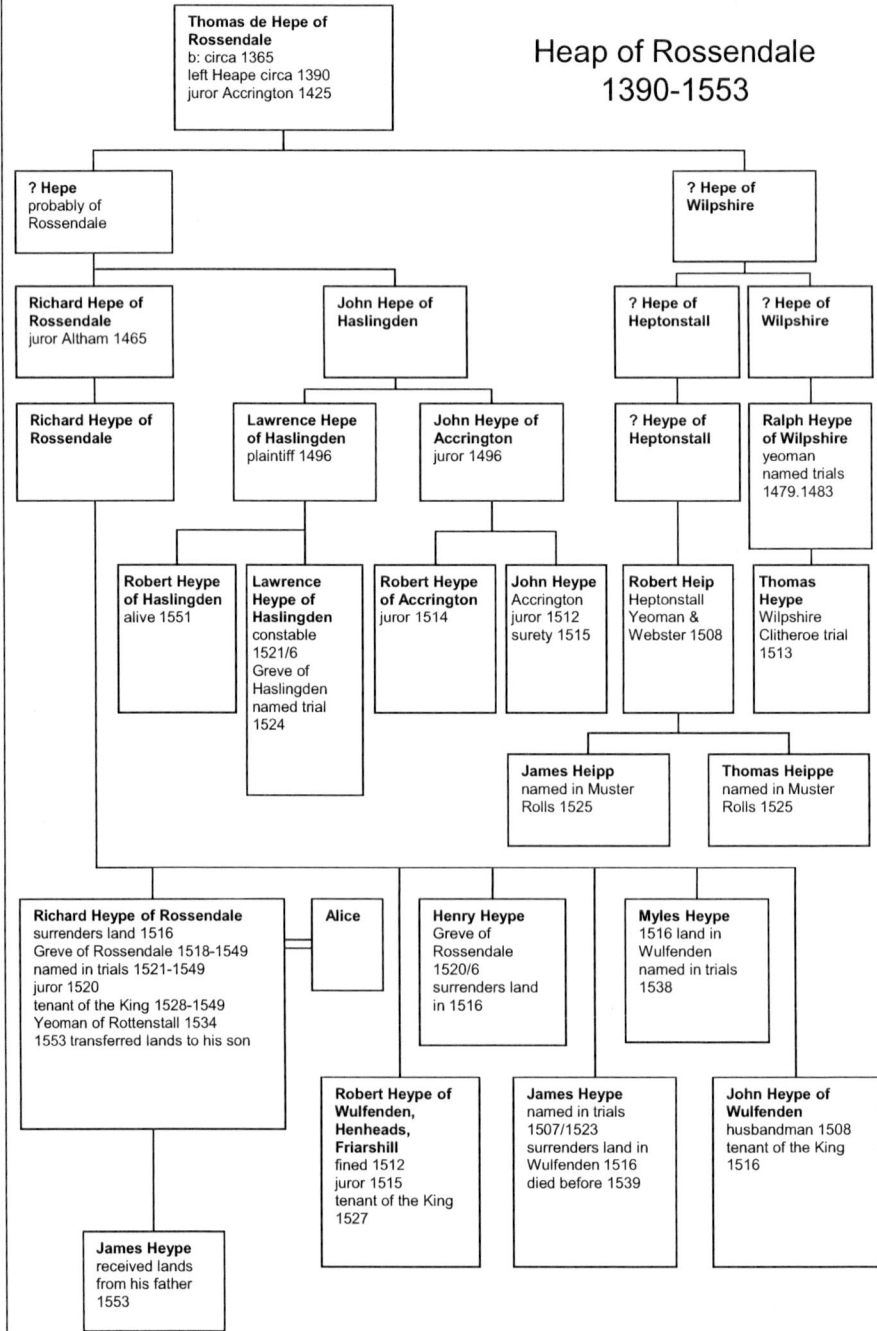

Thomas de Hepe of Rossendale
b: circa 1365
left Heape circa 1390
juror Accrington 1425

? Hepe
probably of Rossendale

? Hepe of Wilpshire

Richard Hepe of Rossendale
juror Altham 1465

John Hepe of Haslingden

? Hepe of Heptonstall

? Hepe of Wilpshire

Richard Heype of Rossendale

Lawrence Hepe of Haslingden
plaintiff 1496

John Heype of Accrington
juror 1496

? Heype of Heptonstall

Ralph Heype of Wilpshire
yeoman
named trials
1479.1483

Robert Heype of Haslingden
alive 1551

Lawrence Heype of Haslingden
constable 1521/6
Greve of Haslingden
named trial 1524

Robert Heype of Accrington
juror 1514

John Heype
Accrington
juror 1512
surety 1515

Robert Heip
Heptonstall
Yeoman & Webster 1508

Thomas Heype
Wilpshire
Clitheroe trial
1513

James Heipp
named in Muster Rolls 1525

Thomas Heippe
named in Muster Rolls 1525

Richard Heype of Rossendale
surrenders land 1516
Greve of Rossendale 1518-1549
named in trials 1521-1549
juror 1520
tenant of the King 1528-1549
Yeoman of Rottenstall 1534
1553 transferred lands to his son

Alice

Henry Heype
Greve of Rossendale
1520/6
surrenders land in 1516

Myles Heype
1516 land in Wulfenden
named in trials 1538

Robert Heype of Wulfenden, Henheads, Friarshill
fined 1512
juror 1515
tenant of the King 1527

James Heype
named in trials 1507/1523
surrenders land in Wulfenden 1516
died before 1539

John Heype of Wulfenden
husbandman 1508
tenant of the King 1516

James Heype
received lands from his father 1553

30

c.1603 amongst whom is Richard Heape of Rowtonstale and a further Richard (possibly the same man) owning land in Wulfenden. This should link up with the five Heype's shown as living at Wulfenden in the early part of 16thC. There are three Heap's listed as Overseers of the Poor between 1686 and 1714. Of greater interest was the appointment of three members of the Family as 'Greves' or 'Graves' of the Forest of Rossendale and also of Haslingden. Richard Heype held the post for ten years between 1518 and 1549 and Henry Heype between 1520-1526. Henry Heape of Rawtenstall held the post in 1654 and the heirs of Richard Heape of Bacup in 1696. Lawrence Heype was both Constable and Greve at Haslingden 1521-6.

The office of Greave is one of great antiquity and dates back to Saxon times. The Greave carried our numerous functions including that of Magistrate, taxing officer, 'Bang Beggar' whatever that might be, tracking down criminals, dealing with the poor, preparing returns of the able bodied capable of serving the King. The Precepts of the High Constable were addressed to the Greave who levied the rates and apportioned the share set aside for the repair of Lancaster Castle and the relief of prisoners. He was nominated by the principal landowners in the district and was appointed at the Halmot Court. He had several deputies to assist him in his duties. He appears to have been a senior local authority officer whose duties would overlap and control those of the Vestrymen, Constable and other officers whom we come to recognise as part of the Parish structure some years later.[7]

So where does this leave us as a family known to have moved in the early part of the 18thC from Burnley to Bridge Hall (Heap Bridge) and then to Caldershaw in Rochdale. Charles Heape had suggested that we originated from the Rossendale migration back in 13th and 14thC and I would see no reason to disagree with him but the evidence is far from complete. Charles has suggested that a more thorough search of the available records might provide some of the answers, but it would necessitate employing a qualified and professional researcher at very considerable cost and who knows, if we wait long enough all the relevant documents may be digitalised and available on-line!

If we feel we can 'buy-in' to the Rossendale descent, what of the earlier years? The first stumbling block is 'the migration years'. I find it difficult to accept that there was this sudden break-up of the family which left it's ancestral home and scattered to five quite separate locations with the only link being a 'surname' which itself has several variants. The earlier years from 1170 to 1400 are easier to accept. There were far fewer people around to confuse the issue and such as are recorded must have been of some status within the community. There would have been serfs or villains who worked the land but they would have been unlikely to feature on Court Rolls or to act as Jurors. We know that names tended to be associated with the place where that person resided and it is reasonable to assume that persons bearing the same name were related and therefore you can trace some form of descent.

I also have some difficulty over the variation in the spelling of the surname and this has been referred to elsewhere in the text.[1] This is a well recognised problem and similar difficulties have been experienced with many other families. It is perhaps made more difficult in that in later years the two spellings of Heape and Heap existed side by side and refer to two quite separate families although the pattern of their lives was very similar. It is not helped when Charles and Richard Heape seem to have change the spelling of a name or place to favour their own version. Very early on in my research, over fifty years ago, I met an elderly lady of the Heape family who lived at Healey whilst in search of information about the two families. I got a very frosty reception and was left in no doubt that as far as she was concerned the two families were not related in any way and that our family as mere mill owners were a long way down in the social order.

So there you have it – a possible descent from 1170 but there is more work to be done before anyone could accept it as being proven, a job for the next generation perhaps?

I cannot end this chapter without paying tribute to the talents of Charles and Richard Heape, the authors of *The Records of the Family of Heape*. This is a remarkable piece of work particularly as it was researched and written in the latter years of the 19thC before computers and digitalisation of records had even been thought of. There are of course some areas on which we would have to agree to differ but nevertheless it has been of great assistance to me in my own research.

Notes

1 see chapter 1 – Who do we think we are?
2 Records of the Family of Heap (R of FH) – pp. 23, 25 and 31
3 R of FH – p 28
4 R of FH – p. 34 Pedigree of the family of Radcliffe
5 R of FH – appendix B
6 R of FH – p 292. Pedigree Tree of Heap of Rossendale
7 Newbigging: *History of the Forest of Rossendale*. 2nd ed. 1893. p. 88 Duties of the Greave

3

THE FULLING MILLERS
STEPHEN AND WILLIAM HEAP

The history of the Heap Family of Caldershaw from 1750 and the prosperity of its members can be traced back to Stephen Heap and his son William who was later to found the firm which was to become Samuel Heap and Son. William and his father lie buried beneath great slabs of pennant stone outside the parish church of St Chad at Rochdale. The stones are engraved with their names, proudly recording their occupation of Fullers as befitting their status in the community. The two slabs lie close to each other just outside the porch to the south entrance to the church. Sadly, if you were to excavate below the slab you would find no evidence of a burial as in 1964 the Parish decided to lift all the flat gravestones in the old church yard which surrounds the church and re-lay them to form paved pathways running across the churchyard, thus ensuring that the tramp of many feet will inevitably over a period of time deface the inscriptions cut into the stone and a vital record of Rochdale's heritage will be lost for ever. Although there had been a detailed plan of the churchyard showing the exact location of the graves before this reorganisation – our two graves lay to the east of the church steps – no such plan or record was made at the time of the re-ordering of the churchyard and it was only by sheer chance that we were able to find our two family graves.

Stephen was the son of Robert Heap of Hurstwood and was born on 13th May 1739. Hurstwood is a small village lying a thousand metres to the south west of Worsthorne. Both villages lie within the present Civil Parish of Briercliffe and are situated 3½ kms to the east of the centre of Burnley. All the marriages, burials and baptisms were recorded in the parish registers of St Peter's church in Burnley and there are a surprising number of members of the Heap family shown as having lived or died in this small area, as there are in the

CHART 3

Descendant chart for
Robert Heap of Worsthorne

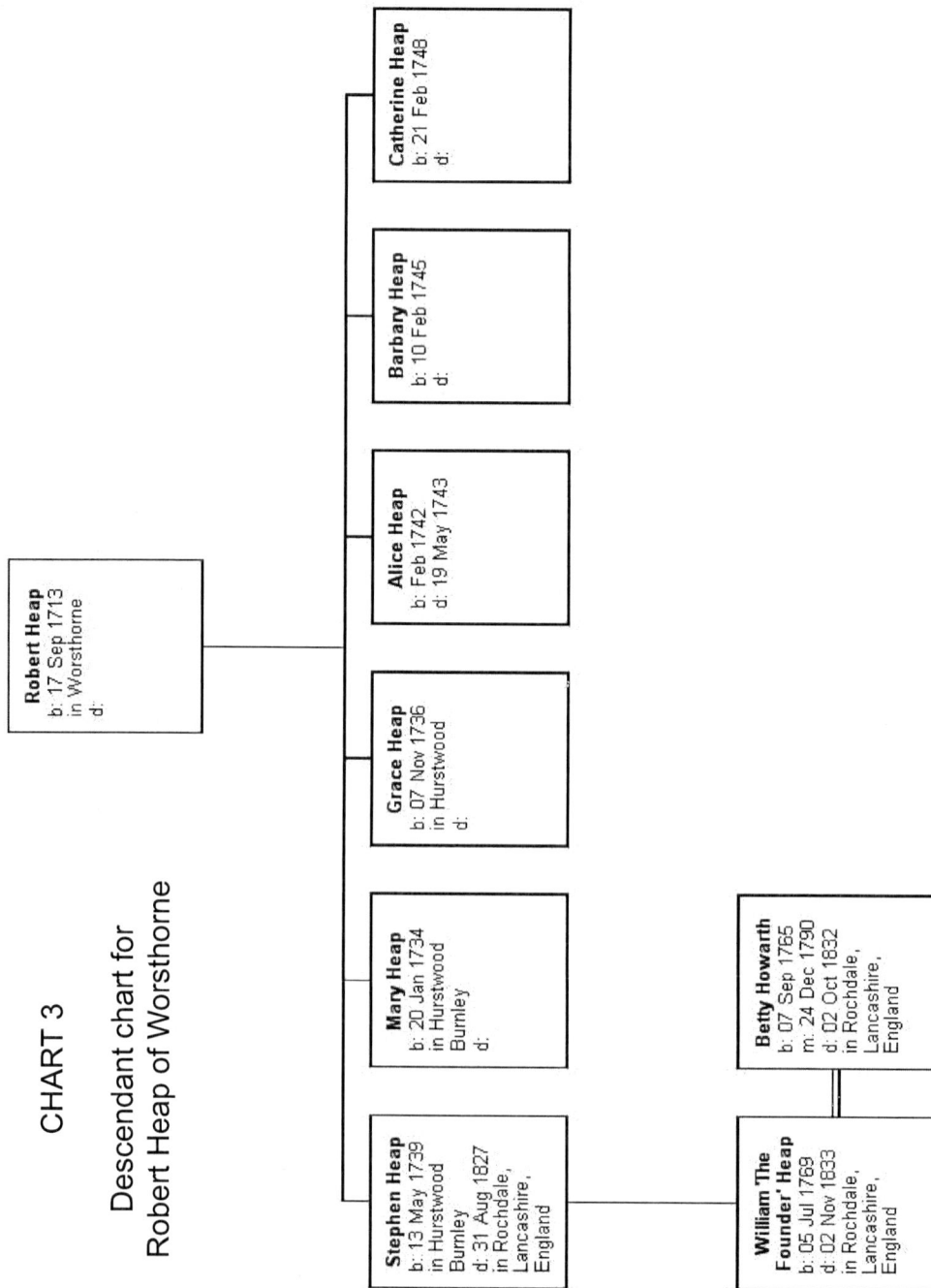

Robert Heap
b: 17 Sep 1713
in Worsthorne
d:

Mary Heap
b: 20 Jan 1734
in Hurstwood
Burnley
d:

Grace Heap
b: 07 Nov 1736
in Hurstwood
d:

Alice Heap
b: Feb 1742
d: 19 May 1743

Barbary Heap
b: 10 Feb 1745
d:

Catherine Heap
b: 21 Feb 1748
d:

Stephen Heap
b: 13 May 1739
in Hurstwood
Burnley
d: 31 Aug 1827
in Rochdale,
Lancashire,
England

William 'The Founder' Heap
b: 05 Jul 1769
in Rochdale,
Lancashire,
England
d: 02 Nov 1833

Betty Howarth
b: 07 Sep 1765
m: 24 Dec 1790
d: 02 Oct 1832
in Rochdale,
Lancashire,
England

wider area round Burnley and Colne. A recent Surname Profiler map based on the 1881[1] census showed this area had the highest density of the name HEAP in England. Far from being a help, this has confounded the issue as it has been almost impossible to arrange and fit these names together in families, although we have managed to establish that Robert had a further six children, siblings to Stephen, namely Mary b.20.01.1734, Grace b.07.11.1736, Alice b.Feb 1742 and died 19.05.1743, Barbary b.10.02.1745, Catherine b.21.02.1748 and possibly also Thomas b 05.02.1728 who died 08.11.1750.[2]

Robert of Worsthorne was born 17.09.1713 but we have been unable to trace the family further back as, where such records exist, they become even more difficult to understand or fit into the jigsaw. The parish records of Burnley, Nelson and Colne were searched, as were the records for all the parishes between Burnley and Bury. The Poor Law records (of which there are lamentably few) were also searched as were the Hearth Tax returns, all with negative result.

William was born on 5th July 1769 and his baptism is recorded in the family bible. We have been unable to find a record of William's birth in the parish registers although there is a record of a William Heap being baptised on 26th March 1769 at Burnley, if this were correct it would have William baptised before he was born later the same year! However by this time the family had become staunch Wesleyan Methodists, a belief which was to pervade their whole lives for many generations to come. Wesleyans, like other non-conformists, were permitted to be baptised in their own chapels but had to have their marriage solemnised in the Anglican Parish Church. A marriage certificate was an official document which might have to be shown or produced for a variety of legal reasons. Methodists, together with the other non-conformists denominations, were required to keep a record or register of all baptisms carried out in their chapels or other places of worship but many of the records are incomplete. There are some Methodist registers for both Bury and Burnley, they are far from complete, often difficult to read and in a poor state of repair. We have been unable to find a record of William's birth.

We have however a copy of the certificate issued of his marriage which took place at St Mary's Anglican Parish Church in Bury when he married Betty Howarth on 24th December 1789. His address is given as Bridge Hall which is a small hamlet just to the north west of Heap Bridge. William and Betty both 'made their mark' when they came to sign the register and were presumably illiterate. This says a great deal about the social structure of the more rural areas of Lancashire at the time, yet this illiterate man went on to purchase land, water mills and woollen mills not so many years later. He was to establish a thriving business that provided employment and a way of living for an increasing number of members of his family for generations to come.

Unfortunately we don't know exactly where William was working at this time. At some stage the family must have moved from Burnley to outside Bury and it seems likely he would have sought employment as a Fuller, probably at one of the woollen mills which were part of the Bridge Hall Estate. There he would have been employed to provide a fulling and finishing service for the yarn and cloth produced by the Bridge Hall mills. The fulling and finishing of the cloth was usually carried out by a different business separate from the spinning and weaving of the woollen cloth. The 1851 OS map shows three sets of tenting frames in the fields to the north of the river and in close proximity to Bridge Hall and Old Bridge Hall. Presumably these 'serviced' the Bridge Hall Woollen Mills downstream and south of the river.

The Bridge Hall mill complex at Heap Bridge is mainly associated with the manufacture of paper, a trade which continued well into the 20thC. Paper making on this site is well documented from 1716 and the whole site was redeveloped in 1810. The early development of the Bridge Hall Mills is obscured by the duplication of mill names within the Heap Bridge township. The oldest mill was at Old Bridge Hall. There was also a Broad Oak mill and a Bridge Hall Woollen mill. There had been a water driven corn mill on the Bridge Hall estate way back in 1651. Corn mills were often the precursor of fulling mills as the mechanism was much the same and one was easily converted into the other at little cost. In the early 18thC a Roger Holt was named as holding the Fulling Mill House and a William Crompton of Bridge Hall was described as a woollen clothier in 1716. In 1776 a Benjamin Pilkington of Bridge Hall, a fuller, is recorded as having assigned all his estates etc, etc. The Broad Oak estates returned to a separate tenancy in 1789 with a reference to the Broadoak Mill being a fulling mill.[3]

There is ample evidence of fulling having been carried out at Bridge Hall and it seems reasonable to assume that William continued to learn his trade whilst he set about planning his future and raising a family. It had been customary earlier in the century for the aspirant fuller to serve a seven year apprenticeship before he was allowed to set up on his own and practice his trade. But by the end of the 18thC this requirement had largely been dispensed with. Without doubt William would have learnt his trade from his father. The woollen trade was undergoing a rapid expansion to meet the demands of the home market and clothiers often had to travel many miles before they could find a fuller to process their cloth. It should be remembered that even at this late stage of the 18thC the spinning and weaving of woollen cloth was still very much a domestic 'industry' carried on in peoples homes with the clothier acting as the intermediary, putting out the cloth to be fulled and finished before taking back the finished cloth to be sold on in the open market.

The process known as fulling as a means of treating woollen cloth had been in use for over two thousand years. It was certainly known to the Ancient Greeks and one of the merchants caught up in the eruption of Vesuvius at Pompeii was a fuller. Before the advent of water driven hammers to 'full' the cloth, the cloth was 'walked' with the operatives or 'walkmen' required to stamp and tread the woven cloth in a water bath with various chemicals added to the mix, thus possibly giving us the derivation of the name 'Walker' which was borne by my maternal ancestors. The process of fulling is only applied to the cloth after the process of weaving is complete. The lengths of material are sewn together in a long strip and then folded concertina fashion. There may be a pre-soaking in water to wash off some of the impurities or the material may be placed directly into the fulling trough where it is pounded by the wooden hammers, the ends of which are so chamfered and arranged that they gradually turn the bundle of cloth as the hammers pound it in rotation.

After the cloth is placed in the trough it is first covered by a mixture of water and 'lant' which is allowed to soak into the material before the hammers are started into action. 'Lant' is stale urine which has been allowed to stand for ten days before use. The lant was collected by the 'lant man' in a lant cart who paid out 1d per household, the stench must have been appalling. The cloth was pounded in the fulling machine for ten to twelve hours. The lant extracted the lanolin and grease and other impurities out of the cloth which becomes thicker during the process and was reduced in width and length by approximately one third. Lant was still in use in the Rossendale valley as late as the 1960s when most other areas had replaced lant with soda or some other form of detergent, reducing the treatment time to four to six hours.[4]

After pounding the cloth is washed and then hung up to dry outside on 'tenterhooks' on the racks in the 'tenterfields' adjacent to the fulling mills. The racks are clearly delineated on the OS maps of the period which is an aid to identifying those mills where the fulling process had been carried out. The different racks were often given names appropriate to the period such as Wellington or Napoleon. The fulling was usually done on a commission basis with an agreed rate for the job. The fullers didn't have to buy or own the cloth. This considerably reduced the amount of capital which had to be invested in the business though some fullers preferred to buy the cloth and then resell after treatment.

The fulling mills were all water-powered until the advent of steam and as such they had to be located alongside a river or stream. Owning the water rights was essential, otherwise the owner of the water could soon put you out of business if he so desired. In addition to providing the power to drive the hammers, a vast amount of water was required to wash the cloth during the different stages of the process with all the effluent, including all the dirt and other impurities, being discharged into the stream to add to the ever increasing pollution. The mills were cheap and easy to run. The mechanism was very similar to the corn mill and there were plenty of these available for conversion the costs of which were low. So the fulling process provided a perfect starting point for the budding entrepreneur. The washed-out fibres and other debris left behind after the process was complete would be collected up and used as flock to fill eiderdowns or mattresses.

But there was more to the fulling process than just the hammering of the woollen cloth. The cloth required to be bleached and this was done either by leaving it out in the open air until the actions of the sun had done the trick (was there ever enough sun in Lancashire?); or later the bleaching was carried out in the Stoving shed where the cloth would be hung up on glass hooks, the sulphur candles would then be lit and the operatives rapidly retired from the building. Many of the fulling stocks were still in use well into the 19thC, after which they were replaced by rotary milling machines. In these the cloth is stitched at both ends to form an endless rope. This is then passed between weighted rollers and through a bath containing the lant or other chemicals used in the process. The milling machines greatly increased production and gave more control over the shrinkage process. William would have been using fulling stocks at Bridge Hall, but may well have installed the new rotary milling machines when he built his new mill at Caldershaw.

After the fulling, drying and bleaching was complete the nap of the cloth had to be raised in a Gig Mill which consisted of series of teasels fixed to a rotary drum. The cloth was fed onto the drum so that it opposed the direction of the ends of the teasels. Teasels were used for this process long into the 19thC. After the surface of the cloth had been raised it then needed to be sheared in the cutting machines so that all the ends were of the same length giving a smooth finish to the material. After shearing the cloth was finally ready to be dyed. Theoretically dyeing could take place at any stage of the process after the wool had been spun into yarn until the cloth had been finished and was ready to be sent out to the clothing manufacturer. In practice dyeing was nearly always the last process to which the finished cloth was subjected. All these processes were part of the finisher's art. We don't know whether William had access to all the necessary machinery at Bridge Hall, but he was certainly using Gig mills at Hamer. By the time he had established himself at Caldershaw he would have installed all the necessary machinery in his new mills.

The Fulling Millers had three big advantages over other trades and occupations involved in the woollen trade. Firstly, they were already working in mills designed to house the necessary machinery. The fulling stocks were so large that there was no way they could have been fitted into a workman's cottage. Secondly, they were already employing other workmen to help them run the business. These may well have been members of the family, but were nevertheless in paid employment. Thirdly, Fulling Millers had the space in their mill to house the new machinery, the gig mill raising machines and the new shearing machines, when they came into use in the middle of the 19thC. Lastly, they were masters of their own trade which was becoming increasingly complex and varied as new processes were invented and new finishes demanded by their clients.

Needless to say the introduction of all this new machinery was not without its problems and was bitterly opposed by the workmen who had previously carried out these tasks in their own homes. There were riots, machinery was destroyed or damaged and mills burnt down, but nothing could stop progress. The new mills and their machinery could produce ten times the amount of finished goods in a fraction of the time and at a fraction of the cost and every year there was an increase in demand for their product. Unfortunately we have no record of William's activities during this period. There is no record of his having been involved in any of the riots nor of any of his mills having been attacked.

We do know that William and his family had embraced the Wesleyan Methodist faith with a fervour which was to support them and guide their steps as they clawed their way up the social ladder. On the whole Methodists were recognised as being good employers who looked after their workforce and paid them a fair and reasonable wage. I would like to think that perhaps this was a factor in their escaping the worst of the industrial disruption that was a feature of labour relations in the textile industry at this time. William was clearly determined that all his children should be brought up as Wesleyans. All his elder children were baptised in the Union Street Wesleyan chapel in Bury, William in 1797, Rachel in 1802, John in 1805 and James in 1809.[6]

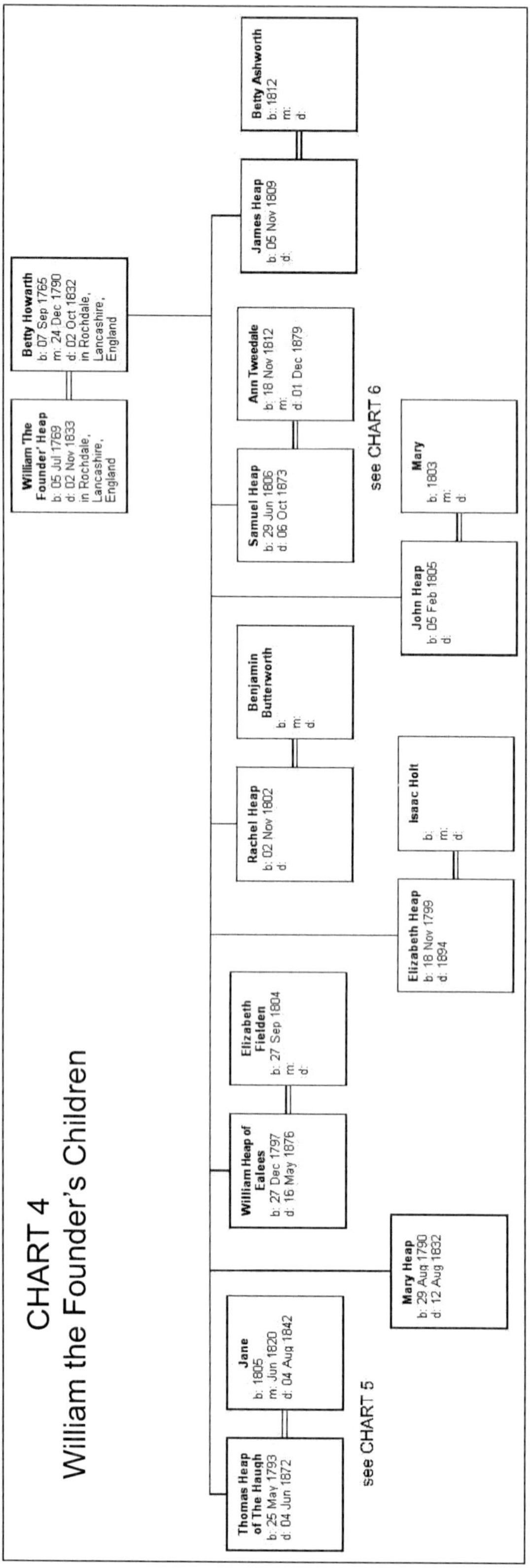

CHART 4
William the Founder's Children

William The Founder' Heap
b: 05 Jul 1769
d: 02 Nov 1833
in Rochdale,
Lancashire,
England

Betty Howarth
b: 07 Sep 1765
m: 24 Dec 1790
d: 02 Oct 1832
in Rochdale,
Lancashire,
England

Thomas Heap
of The Haugh
b: 25 May 1793
d: 04 Jun 1872

Jane
b: 1805
m: Jun 1820
d: 04 Aug 1842

see CHART 5

Mary Heap
b: 29 Aug 1790
d: 12 Aug 1832

William Heap of
Ealees
b: 27 Dec 1797
d: 16 May 1876

Elizabeth
Fielden
b: 27 Sep 1804
m:
d:

Elizabeth Heap
b: 18 Nov 1799
d: 1894

Isaac Holt
b:
m:
d:

Rachel Heap
b: 02 Nov 1802
d:

Benjamin
Butterworth
b:
m:
d:

John Heap
b: 05 Feb 1805
d:

Mary
b: 1803
m:
d:

Samuel Heap
b: 29 Jun 1806
d: 06 Oct 1873

Ann Tweedale
b: 18 Nov 1812
m:
d: 01 Dec 1879

see CHART 6

James Heap
b: 05 Nov 1809
d:

Betty Ashworth
b: 1812
m:
d:

We do not know exactly when William moved to Rochdale from Bridge Hall but he is listed as one of the twelve Fullers in Rochdale in the Commercial Directory for 1814-15 and thereafter there is a similar entry for 1816-17. In the *Pigot and Deane Directory for Manchester* of 1824-25 they are listed as Dyers at the Hamer Mill in 1814. We don't know whether William bought the Hamer Mill or just rented space there to carry on his trade. It was by no means unusual for a mill to be used by a number of different firms at the same time and the Hamer Mills were obviously quite extensive – 'there were two fulling mills each of three stocks and a perching mill besides, all standing on the river Roche'.[7] There seems to be no clear description of a Perching Mill but it is thought the operatives sat perched up on stools from which they could lean across the woven cloth and trim off the loose ends and repair the damaged threads. William would have had the opportunity to see and experience another element of the finishing process whilst he was at Hamer, knowledge he would store up for future use when he owned his own mills. This was not so very far away: by 1825 he had purchased his first mill at Caldershaw including the water rights of the nearby River Spodden, the power source to run his machinery.

At last he was on his way, and the seed which was to grow and flourish as the Dying and Finishing firm of Samuel Heap and Son was born, bringing with it William's passport into the rapidly emerging middle class. England was changing from a predominantly agricultural nation whose affairs were still largely controlled by the Tory Squirearchy into a burgeoning industrial nation which was to lead the world, a world in which William's grandsons were to play their part as Mayors of Rochdale. The old order was coming to an end and a bright and rich future lay ahead for those who had the vision to see and grasp the opportunity and make their fortunes in the process.

Notes and references

1 Surname Profiler. CASA. UCL (London) 1999
2 Parish Registers St Peter's Church, Burnley
3 Tillmanns, Martin: *Bridge Hall mills, three centuries of paper manufacture*. Compton Press 1978
4 Aspin, Chris: *The Woollen Industry*. Shire Publications, and personal communication Tony Walker, Helmshore Cotton Museum, Rossendale
5 Taylor, Rebe. *Rochdale Retrospect*. Rochdale Corporation 1956. pp. 90-95
6 Wesleyan Methodist parish registers. Union Street chapel, Bury
7 *Rochdale Observer*. Samuel Hamer Estate sale. The Hamer Mill

4

WOOL

When people spoke of Lancashire eighty or more years ago they would conjure up a picture of dark satanic mills belching out smoke and polluting the atmosphere, tall mill chimneys pointing up to the leaden skies in serried ranks, built of anonymous red brick with the name of the manufacturer inscribed on the side in large white lettering picked out in tiling since painted inscription would soon be obscured by the grime. There were clear days and blue skies, but they were a rarity. I can remember returning to Rochdale after staying with my maternal grandparents in Ilkley, coming over the top of Blackstone Edge following in the footsteps of the Romans, seeing a sea of smog penetrated only by the tops of the mill chimneys. This was Lowry country. Lowry was brought up in Manchester and I know of no other who could so vividly portray the lives of the textile workers condemned to work in this industrial hell. Such would have been the view of the southerner if he ever had cause to give the matter even a moment's thought. But by the early 20thC the textile worker was well paid, adequately housed and more than content with his way of life.

To most people Lancashire was synonymous with cotton and it came as a surprise to learn that Rochdale was also the centre of the wool trade, a trade much older than cotton and which dated back to the middle ages. Southerners would not have been alone in their misconception. I too had always considered Rochdale a cotton town. The family fortunes had depended on the textile trade and in my ignorance I had automatically assumed their investment lay in cotton. The family did have an involvement in some of the cotton mills in the town, but wool was the basis of our fortunes such as they were. Samuel Heap and Son were dyers and finishers of woollen goods almost to the exclusion of cotton until well into the 20thC. This misconception was perhaps understandable. My Father would have nothing to do with the family firm which he saw, with some justification, as the source of the increasing financial problems facing some members of the family due to the fall in the value of their investment. He had few kind words to say about the way the business was managed.

As early as 1558 flannel was the staple trade of Rochdale and in the reign of Elizabeth I. Her Majesty's Alnager[1] had to appoint a deputy in Rochdale to put the official stamp on the woollen cloths so great was the trade. Rochdale was one of the first towns in Lancashire to obtain a market charter and clothiers and merchants would come from miles around to buy and sell the raw wool and purchase the finished cloth. There was nothing unusual in this, the farming of sheep and the buying and selling of wool were almost universal throughout the country. As one writer put it in 1683 'there are more people employed and more profit made and money imported by the making of cloth than all the other manufactories of England put together'. Forty years later Daniel Defoe described English woollen goods '...as the richest and most valuable manufacture in the world'.

Much of the wool was exported to the continent and further afield in its raw state. In 1777 Rochdale was described as 'a town remarkable for its many wealthy merchants and has a large woollen market. The neighbourhood abounds in clothiers, every house is a manufacturary and is supplied with a rivulet'. A Thomas Smith held a large area of land behind what is now the Wellington Hotel connected by means of a weir to his new fulling mills – soon to become a competitor for William Heap.

The woollen trade was essentially a cottage based industry at this time, the wool being spun and woven in peoples houses. In the 15th and 16thC many cottagers would combine the rearing of sheep with standard agricultural work during the summer months and then take up the spinning and weaving during the winter. Agriculture and woollen production marched hand in hand for decades. For hundreds of years the spinning wheel and the hand loom were to be found in nearly every cottage, fulling mills were as common as corn mills. It was impossible to travel far without passing fields full of tenterframes on which the cloth was stretched and dried. Although fine British cloths were exported to Europe throughout the 12th and 13thC, the trade in the raw unprocessed wool remained much more important than its manufacture. By the 14thC England exported 5,000 pieces of cloth annually, a trade that was to increase year by year.

Most of the cottages would have been able to accommodate only one loom and perhaps two spindles. Some of the individual weavers thrived and later some houses, particularly in the towns where they were built of stone or brick, would be constructed on three floors with six or more lights on the upper floors which could house a larger number of looms and make use of Crompton's Mule. In 1779 Samuel Crompton, son of a Bolton farmer, invented a machine which wedded Arkwright's rollers and Hargreaves' spinning jenny and which was known as a spinning mule.

Hand loom weavers at the beginning of 19thC earned 10 shillings a week with spinners at six to seven shillings a week. Cottage rents were £4 per year. Beds were stored under the looms during the day. Children worked at winding the bobbins. Hand loom workers were either self employed or worked to a wealthy clothier who was often one of the local 'gentry', such as Clement Royds up at Falinge. The new mules allowed the number of spindles to be increased to 120 but at this level they were increasingly difficult to turn by hand. This increase in the number of spindles was essential since at least four of the older type of spinning wheels were needed to keep one weaving loom supplied with yarn.

The staple manufacture of wool remained the main industry in Rochdale long after the surrounding towns had surrendered to cotton. It consisted chiefly of the manufacture of baizes, flannels, kerseys, coatings and cloths[2] – the last two being generic terms for the light weight material used for the outer garments for both men and women. Flannel was a light weight cloth with a napped surface introduced in the mid-18thC. Rochdale soon became known as the flannel capital of Lancashire and so it remained until well into the 20thC. By the end of the 19thC Samuel Heap and Son was using the old mill at Caldershaw solely for the finishing of flannel while the more modern processes and the finishing of cloths other than flannel were carried out at their other mills at Spotland Bridge and up at Healey. By this time all of William's sons, other than Samuel who remained at Caldershaw, had set up their own businesses. Thomas was manufacturing flannels at Milnrow and Newhey and William at Ealees down in Littleborough.

1782 saw the first cotton mill in Rochdale and by 1799 the Caldershaw cotton mill had two new spinning frames each of 252 spindles. It must have been this mill which was purchased by William as part of his initial investment. Thereafter the cotton industry grew by leaps and bounds while the wool industry remained at its then level. It not until 1850 that cotton overtook wool. In 1835 there were two thousand wool workers in the town forming nearly half the hands in all the Lancashire woollen mills but there were already 7,500 employed in cotton. In 1818 there had been 128 wool manufacturers in the town. Six years later there were 205. By 1856 there were still 108 mill owners in wool but the numbers were falling year by year.[3]

The social background of manufacturing was changing from the old merchant families like the Royds family of Falinge who were descended from the wealthy clothiers, to self-made entrepreneurs such as Hugh Kelsall. He began by installing six pairs of hand looms and four spinning jennies in a house in Packer street, an area of the town just off the town centre notorious for the poor working conditions and the almost total absence of any form of sanitation. Just as Packer Street provided an opening for one entrepreneur, so did Caldershaw provide the perfect starting point for another in a different section of the industry – William Heap, Fuller and Dyer and Finisher.

While the new cotton mills were powered by steam, the wool industry lagged behind. Some of the hand loom weavers were still eking out an increasingly precarious existence in 1880. There were more technical problems to be overcome in the mechanisation of the woollen industry which delayed the transition. There really could be no competition. Power loom weavers were paid at a higher rate than the home based hand loom weavers, the quality of the finished product was much improved and the production rate was doubled if not trebled. That is not to say that steam power was not in use in other sections of the woollen industry. The fulling machines were easily converted to steam – Samuel Heap and Son introduced their first steam powered engines in 1825. Power driven carding machines and the slubbing billies (for twisting wool slivers before spinning) had been in use since 1780. The first process to be mechanised was carding, and the first steam driven carding machine was brought into operation in 1833. At that time only two mills in Rochdale were using steam to drive the spinning jennies and the looms. In 1825 George Ashworth of Sunny Bank had installed the first steam-powered wool loom, three years before the firm of Kelsall and Kemps was established.

Thereafter progress was rapid. By 1841 most fully mechanised woollen mills in the Rochdale area employed steam power. Of the 49 mills working full time only seven relied exclusively on water power. But there were still many hundreds of handloom weavers scattered throughout the parish, employed either directly or on contract to local employers. Their circumstances deteriorated as the century progressed. John Cole paints a vivid picture in his *Rochdale Revisited* of the rise and fall of the Milkstone Weavers who lived in abject poverty, quoting one Thomas Blomley, the head of a family of six, with a weekly income of two shillings paying one shilling a week in rent. The house contained but one bed, one cover lid and two sheets, out of work for ten weeks he and his family nearly starved to death[4] … and this is what they called progress! But there was a brighter future ahead for Milkstone Road which was to become the birthplace of Gracie Fields: 'Our Gracie', who sang her way out of poverty to world-wide fame and riches.

The dramatic changes in peoples lives brought about by the rapid expansion of the textile industry and the introduction of factory life – which we now so easily describe and accept as the Industrial Revolution – was resisted tooth and nail by many of the workers and brought about a change in the relationship between the master and the men. The yeomen hand loom weavers were accustomed to freedom, with their own small holdings, their own sheep, and the open moors on their doorstep. They could follow at will their delight in 'chasing hares and enjoy the song of the larks'.[5] They worked in their own time depending on the day and the weather. Provided they completed their given work within the agreed time-span and the quality of the finished article was acceptable to the clothier, they were free men. Loss of individual freedom, long working hours and confinement within a barracks like mill seemed more like a prison. There was little room for manoeuvre. It was not long since the new entrepreneurial mill owners had been yeomen weavers themselves and they had little sympathy for their employees. If the men wouldn't work, their wives would, as would their children, and employing women and children was a much cheaper option. Furthermore, the children could be bound and disciplined as apprentices.

Inevitably this led to disputes between the employer and his work force, usually over pay. The Combination Acts of 1799 forbade workmen from combining together in pursuit of higher wages and shorter hours. This left them with only one option – riot, wreck the machinery and burn down the mills. Add to this the ever rising price of bread due to the Corn laws and the constant under-swell of opinion demanding a greater say in the way they were governed – the Chartist Movement and demands for reform and the right to be represented in Parliament.

Meanwhile the country was involved in a bitter and long drawn out war with France – the Napoleonic wars which resulted in ever rising taxes and an increasing stranglehold on trade as France sought to impose her Continental System designed to prevent trade with Britain. Britain retaliated with her Orders in Council effectively imposed a blockade on French ports. However the war did result in increasing demand for cloth for uniforms and blankets and suchlike. It was a sign of British textile supremacy that Napoleon's soldiers were wearing British greatcoats and sleeping wrapped in British blankets when

they defeated the Russians in 1807. Benjamin Gott of Leeds was said to
be manufacturing clothing and blankets for the armies of England, Russia,
Prussia and Sweden.[6] British manufacturers had no conception of the need for
economic warfare. Fighting wars was a job for soldiers, it was the manufacturer's
job to make money and devil take any regulations which put barriers and
difficulties in their path.

Disputes between the hand loom weavers and their employers over pay in
1808 resulted in the employers gathering in the shuttles to prevent work. The
mob rioted and broke every window in Yorkshire Street and burnt down the
prison. The magistrates had to call in the Halifax Volunteers before order was
restored – the Rochdale Volunteers had been disbanded and all the regulars
were away fighting the Peninsular war.[7] The end of the war in 1815 only
made matters worse with a depression in trade and increasing demand for
reform which culminated in a mass meeting at St Peter's Fields, Manchester,
in 1819, demanding the repeal of the corn laws and other measures. Matters
got out of hand and the magistrates, expecting further trouble, called in the
local Yeomanry. They were unable to restrain the crowds, so the magistrate
called in the regular cavalry to disperse the crowd. A savage struggle followed,
eleven people were killed and over four hundred wounded. Within a few
days the damning term 'Peterloo' had been coined, a word still remembered
with horror and much bitter feeling in Lancashire even today. It was said that
a thousand people from Rochdale attended the meeting although it is not
recorded whether any of them were killed or injured. It is unlikely that any
members of the family were present as they would have numbered themselves
amongst the employers. I wonder whether any of William's workers were
there and what would have been William's attitude had he known. As a true
Wesleyan Methodist I would like to think he would have been in sympathy
with many of their demands – providing they didn't bring their revolutionary
ideas inside his factory gates!

There was some slight relief with the three labour acts of 1824 which
repealed the act which gave the Justices of the Peace the right to fix wages,
repealed the Combination Acts, and the act which prevented the unemployed
travelling out of their own district to seek work.

However disputes between the employers and the work force continued,
with the employers being forced to agree a new scale of wages and payments
– only to have one of them renege on the agreement. In 1827 there was a
dispute at Kelsalls (forerunner of Kelsall and Kemps) as Kelsall refused to pay
according to the list. Two years later there were more riots and strikes when

the employers attempted to reduce the wages because they had accepted a Government contract at a low price. Twenty people were arrested, the mob attacked the Rope Street prison, the troops were called in and six of the workers were shot and killed. The ring leader was transported and the remainder given very light sentences, as if the Justices recognised the injustice of the system and the failure of the authorities to prevent further reasons for violence.

In 1831 the first power loom shed was erected leading to further riots as the home weavers saw yet more of their work being lost. The Plug Drawing riots followed (the removal of the plugs to the boilers prevented the operation of the new machines) though this was as much in support of the Chartists and their demands for reform as opposition to the introduction of the new machinery.

Then at last the great Reform Act of 1832 was passed and Rochdale was made a Parliamentary Borough entitled to be represented by a Member of Parliament. A limited suffrage allowed any householder paying a rental of £10 or more to vote... Change was on the way at last, changes which would allow William Tweedale Heap and his brother Charles to play their parts in shaping the Rochdale of the future.

The replacement of water power with steam had other consequences. Factories could be built anywhere as they were no longer dependant on proximity to a nearby stream. The steam engine could drive any number of looms and for it to be economically viable the looms and other machinery, together with the workmen needed to operate the machinery, had to be housed in a factory built for the purpose. There was an ample supply of coal in south east Lancashire, most of which could easily be extracted by open cast or shallow mines; and the numerous streams and rivulets running off the moors could be diverted to fill the mill lodges which provided a reservoir of water to be turned into steam. All that was now required was a cooperative workforce which had to report for work on time. Once the engines started to turn they would run continuously until the end of the working day. Each morning at about 4am the 'Knockers-Up' began their rounds, rattling their bunch of umbrella wires strapped to the end of their pole, beating their unearthly tattoo against the bedroom window pane until the workman showed some response to indicate that he had heard. The factory siren would sound at 6am or earlier and woe betide anyone who wasn't through the factory gates by the time it had finished sounding. The gates were locked and those who had not made it would lose that day's pay or, if they were unlucky and they were a repeated offender, they might even lose their job. Factory life was harsh and unforgiving.

A woollen industry does still exist today, although it is operating at a far lower level than in the early 20thC. Competition from abroad has largely killed off the local industry. Not only can woollen goods be produced far more economically abroad with much lower labour costs, but countries which had previously imported our woollen goods now manufacture their own. With added competition from the use of artificial fibres which are harder wearing and more adaptable, our woollen industry has largely disappeared.

Notes

For those who are not familiar with the woollen industry these brief notes may help them understand the process by which a fleece is turned into the finished garment. There are many different processes involved and Baines in his classical work lists 34 quite separate processes that make up woollen cloth manufacture. The raw fleece is first sorted and scoured which removes dirt, natural grease and all other impurities that can account for half the weight of the wool. Scouring used to be part of the fulling process (see chapter 3) but the use of lant has been replaced with a series of detergent and/or chemical washes. The wool is then blended with different wools of varying texture and colour depending on the requirement of the final product. The wool is then passed through the carding machines when the wool is teased out into a fine web of intermingled fibres. The web is then condensed and divided into loose threads known as slivers. These are drawn out, twisted, doubled until they form a fine thread which can be wound onto the spindles or onto a beam forming the 'warp and the weft'. The woven cloth is then inspected for loose threads and defects before being sheared. It was at this stage that the woven cloth was 'fulled'. The cloth is then subjected to a series of wet and dry processes dependant on the finish required. The cloth was then bleached and dyed. The finishing process could be a complicated affair requiring the support of a fully equipped laboratory and it was in this area that Samuel Heap and Son excelled, always able to keep one step ahead of the competition.

References
1 Taylor, Rebe. *Rochdale Retrospect*. Corporation Rochdale, 1956. p.37
2 ibid p. 91
3 ibid p. 91
4 Cole, John: *Rochdale Revisited*. p. 6
5 Taylor, Rebe (as above) p. 93
6 Briggs, Asa: *The Age of Improvement 1783-1867*. Longman. Second Edition 2000, p. 142
7 Taylor, Rebe (as above) p. 95

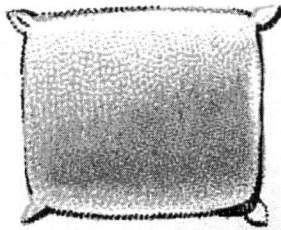

5

THOMAS HEAP AND THE POOR LAW

Thomas was born on 25th May 1793 at Bridgehall and baptised into the Wesleyan Methodist faith at the Union Street Chapel in Bury. He was the eldest son of William The Founder. He left the family home at Caldershaw when he was still a young man and moved to Newhey in 1819. He married Jane the following year and set up his own fulling business at the Ogden Mill. When his father died in 1833, Thomas inherited a seventh share in the family firm along with his siblings. But he was fully occupied running his own business at Newhey and was happy to leave the running of Caldershaw in the hands of his brothers. Along with his siblings, he was content to sell his share to Samuel in 1859.

Thomas was soon to expand his business vertically and by 1844, instead of just finishing the cloth which had been spun and woven by other manufacturers, he had set up his own spinning and weaving sheds and was to describe himself as a flannel manufacturer. The 1851 census records him as such and as a fuller employing 70 men, 28 women, 28 boys and 25 girls – quite a sizeable workforce for those days.

The business thrived at Newhey and at the time of his death he was Chairman of the New Ladyhouse mill, the old mill at The Haugh and the Newhey Spinning Company.

Thomas could reasonably have expected to found a dynasty. Certainly he was more than able to demonstrate the family's fecundity, fathering six sons and five daughters. Many of his daughters married into the textile trade, thus furthering their control over the woollen industry in Newhey and Milnrow. When his son James married Mary Berry, whose father owned the other large mills in Newhey, they must have seemed set for life and the next three or more generations.

Alas, it was not to be so. John, his fourth son drank himself to death –

perhaps he couldn't compete with his more successful brothers. Benjamin, the youngest, took himself off to Weston Super Mare after playing the organ at the opening of the new Sunday school in Milnrow endowed by the family. The church school still flourishes and stands next to the parish church of St James the Apostle. Unfortunately this is not the original church which was demolished during the early years of the 20thC. The engraved stone slab graves of Thomas and his son and grandson can still be found hiding under the grass in a corner of the churchyard and can easily be read. Thomas, his eldest son, died at the early age of 26, but not before he has fathered one son and three daughters. His grandson, also called Thomas, died at the tender age of six years.

Thomas and his family were described as of The Haugh but they were to build for themselves a stark but imposing mansion, Cliffe House, on a hill to the west of the village, a residence befitting the status of the leading industrialist in the village. This was demolished in more recent times and the war memorial now stands in its place.

Anyone who studies these early Victorian families will be struck by the large number of children. It is nothing to find families with ten or more children, the poor wives must have spent their time being pregnant. Many of the children died shortly after birth or in infancy and their names lie forgotten. Further confusion is caused by the re-use of the given name of a dead child. When their births are recorded there are often two or more sons with the same given name. Certain names recur constantly. Samuel, James and William appear to be the favourites within the family. This can be the cause of further confusion for the family historian faced with the task of trying to arraign them in their correct order and proper place.

Thomas possessed talents other than those of a flannel manufacturer. He was a member of the Commission of The Peace for the County and he sat on the Board of Guardians of which he was Chairman from 1846-1870. It is perhaps in this capacity that we should remember him as his record of service to the community is something of which we can be justifiably proud even today. Compare this with the wretched Joshua Heap, a contemporary of Thomas' sons, whom we shall meet in another chapter

Who were these Guardians of The Poor and what was their function? If we are to understand the predicament in which Thomas found himself when he became Chairman of The Board in 1846, we must first turn the clock back to 1601 when a number of Acts of Parliament were consolidated into what has become known as the Elizabethan Poor Law. The Act established the parish as

CHART 5

Descendant chart for Thomas Heap
of The Haugh

Thomas Heap of The Haugh	Jane
b: 25 May 1793	b: 1805
d: 04 Jun 1872	m: Jun 1820
	d: 04 Aug 1842

Thomas Heap	Lucy
b: 20 Mar 1821	b: 08 Nov 1820
d: 06 Feb 1849	m:
	d: 05 May 1908

Ann Heap	Mr Butterworth
b: 1826 in Newhey	b:
d:	m:
	d:

Elizabeth Heap	Mr Mills
b: 1829	b:
d:	m:
	d:

Thomas Heap	Jane Kershaw Heap	Mr Howard	Rachel A Heap	wealthy irishman	Jemina Heap	Gibbon	Elizabeth H Butterworth	Mr Baron	Jane Mills	Rev Edgar A Fewtrell
b: 23 Sep 1848	b: 1843	b:	b: 1845	b:	b: 1847	b:	b:	b:	b:	b:
d: 11 Nov 1853	d:	m:	d:	m:	d:	m:	d:	m:	d:	m:
		d:		d:		d:		d:		d:

Edgar A Fewtrell
b: 17 Jul 1893
d: 20 Jul 1893

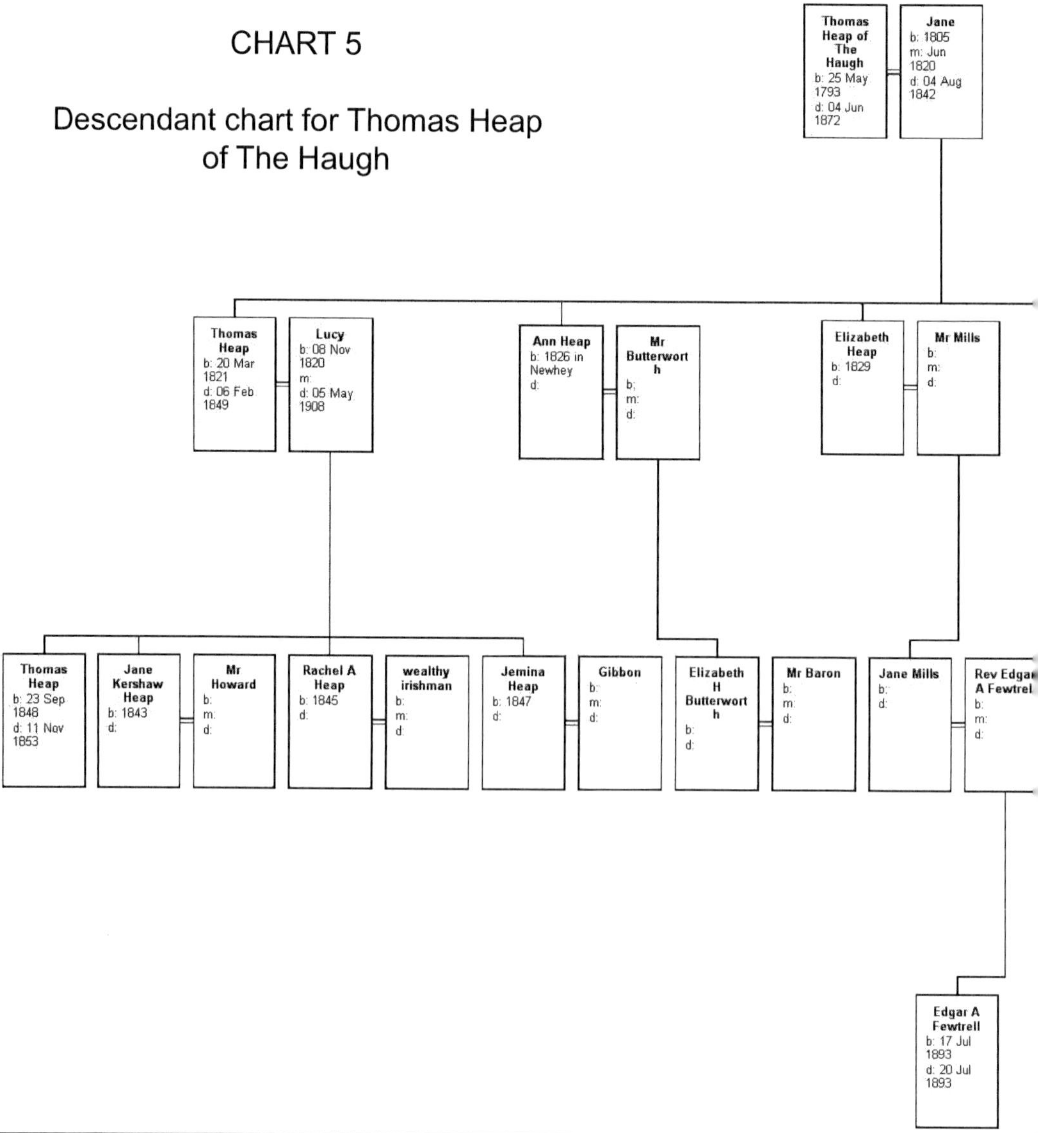

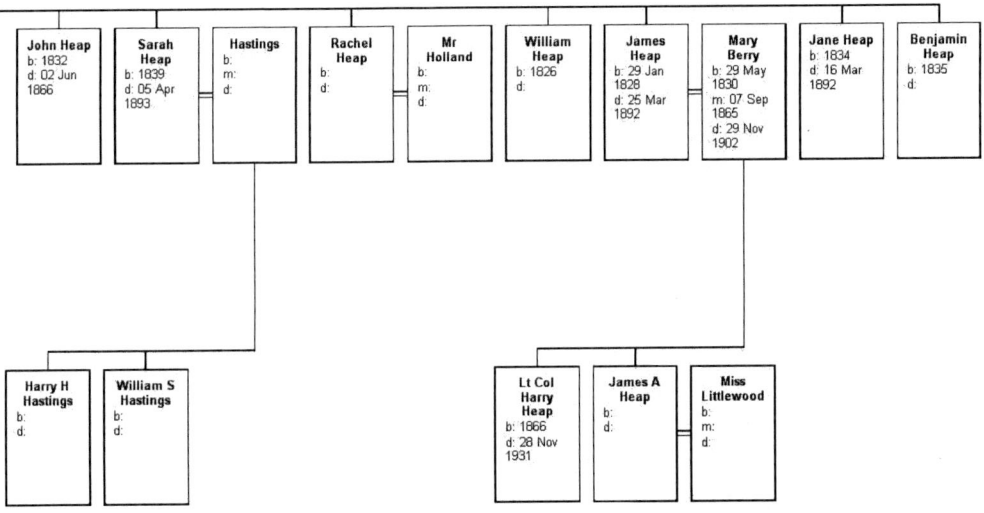

John Heap
b: 1832
d: 02 Jun 1866

Sarah Heap
b: 1839
d: 05 Apr 1893

Hastings
b:
m:
d:

Rachel Heap
b:
d:

Mr Holland
b:
m:
d:

William Heap
b: 1826
d:

James Heap
b: 29 Jan 1828
d: 25 Mar 1892

Mary Berry
b: 29 May 1830
m: 07 Sep 1865
d: 29 Nov 1902

Jane Heap
b: 1834
d: 16 Mar 1892

Benjamin Heap
b: 1835
d:

Harry H Hastings
b:
d:

William S Hastings
b:
d:

Lt Col Harry Heap
b: 1866
d: 28 Nov 1931

James A Heap
b:
d:

Miss Littlewood
b:
m:
d:

the unit of administration for the relief of the poor. Overseers were nominated in each area to act with the Justices of the Peace and the Churchwardens in levying a Poor Rate from householders and landowners. Monies accrued from this source would be used for the maintenance of the poor and the principle of voluntary charitable donations was abandoned. Needless to say it was unpopular, but it did work. Those unable to work were provided for financially while employment was found for the able bodied poor. Those who refused to work became vagrants and were hounded from parish to parish.

The Act was amended in 1722 permitting parishes to tackle the problem by erecting workhouses. Those who refused to enter these 'poor houses' were denied relief. A further Act in 1782 encouraged parishes to join together into Unions but few took advantage of this. The newly appointed 'Guardians' were made responsible for finding work for the able bodied unemployed. Only by working would they qualify for 'outdoor relief'. 'Indoor relief' (in the workhouse) was to be provided for the 'impotent' poor alone.

In these days of the welfare state which supposedly provides for our every need from the cradle to the grave, it is easy to forget there was this long established and often quite workable scheme which operated from the Elizabethan era through until 1834 (and much longer in some areas of which Rochdale was one).

With increasing unemployment in the early part of the 19thC, the old Poor Law scheme became unworkable, particularly in the south of England where parishes complained of what they considered an unfair burden placed on the rates. So the Government of the day decided to change the system and introduced the Poor Law Amendment Act of 1834.

This new Act worked on the principle of 'less eligibility', meaning the conditions under which relief was given to the poor should be less bearable than those 'enjoyed' by the lowest paid artisans. All outdoor relief was stopped except for the aged and the infirm. The 'new workhouses' were to be the fate of the able bodied poor and should be made unattractive enough to ensure that no malingers sought pauperism as a 'bounty on indolence and vice'. The old poor houses were to be abolished. Parishes were to be combined into Unions with one Union Workhouse. Control was to rest with central government, overseen by a central board of three Poor Law Commissioners who required the appointment of Boards of Guardians in each Union to oversee the proper working of the new system.

The result was the Victorian workhouse with all its concomitant evils. Institutions which had previously been regarded as almshouses for the aged and the infirm were transformed quite deliberately into houses of correction for those unfortunate enough to be without work.

There was widespread opposition to the new act, particularly in the north of England where the social and economic circumstances of the population differed greatly from those in the south. The northerners resented the imposition of central government control and what they saw as unwarranted interference into matters which they considered to be their own concern. Many towns and parishes, particularly those in the cotton and woollen towns of southeast Lancashire, refused point-blank to implement the new system and continued to operate the old Poor Law which they considered met their needs far better than the provisions of the new Act. The old Poor Law was economic and humane and had been administered with compassion and understanding, an attitude strengthened not weakened as the evils of the new workhouses became all too apparent.

Opposition to the new Poor Law continued unabated. New Guardians were elected but nearly all declined to operate the new law and the relief of the poor in Rochdale, and its constituent parishes, continued under the old regime. The battle against the implementation of the Act was led by Thomas Livsey and eventually ended up in the High Court in 1844 with Livsey and his fellow Guardians being prosecuted by the Government for failing to implement the act, but they escaped on a technicality. But enough was enough, the government reacted by requiring the Justices of The Peace, many of whom were also appointed Guardians, to apply the Law. Livsey was to resign shortly afterwards and died three months later. Thomas found himself appointed Chairman of the Guardians, a post he was to hold for the next 24 years, during which he succeeded in continuing to delay the implementation of the Act in full while skilfully dancing around the edges. A site for the new Union Workhouse was chosen at Dearnley and it was finally built in 1877. Birch Hill Hospital now stands on the workhouse site at Dearnley and the old Victorian workhouse buildings are still in use as the administrative office block. So perhaps after all some good did come out of the Union workhouse.

The *Rochdale Observer* reported in Thomas' obituary:

'[he]...was distinguished by the amiability of his character, evincing on all occasions a desire to relieve the poor liberally where the necessities of the case required it. On the other hand, to the idle dissolute he was justly severe. Brought so much in contact with deserving poverty, Mr Heap was ever ready to render assistance. He also took a warm interest in the management of the Lunatic Asylums to which the paupers were sent, making the most minute personal enquiries into the condition of the affected. The pauper children also came in for a share of his sympathies, particularly those who were put out to service by the Guardians. He was frequent in his visits to the houses where they resided making the strictest of enquiries into their domiciles, the food supplied, the health and comfort of the children, and it was said that he never closed any of these visits without leaving a small sum of money behind to be expended for the benefit of the orphans.'

With Thomas dead, it remained for Thomas' sons, William and James, to carry on the business and carry on the name. The business of Thomas Heap and Sons, carders, spinners, and flannel manufacturers of the Haugh and Ogden mills, flourished. Some of these mills were quite extensive properties. The Haugh Mill was described as being three stories high, 20 yards long and 12 yards wide, with waterfall, wheels, drums, shafts, reservoirs and appurtenances, and a 'close' of land called The Long Haugh. There were also five cottages, a barn and a 'shippon'. The buildings very prone to fire and the mill was damaged in 1861 and again in 1872 and 1884. The Two Bridges Mill was totally destroyed by fire. The fire engines had to come all the way from Rochdale and there were often delays while they found the necessary number of horses to pull the engines. Thomas Heap and Sons were the largest employer of labour in the village and at the time of closure in 1907 they employed over 250 workers, many of whom had spent their whole working life in service with the firm.

As befitting their status within the community the family changed their political affiliations. James was a Conservative through and through, President of the Newhey Conservative Association, he was a founder member of the Milnrow Local Board (fore-runner of the Local Authority responsible for local government) and Chairman of The Board from 1870 to 1873.

James was a considerate, caring and generous employer, funding the pensions of long serving workers out of his own pocket and never to be found wanting when funds were required to enhance the facilities in the village. His obituary says of the Heap Family 'by their enterprise and industry they have been the making of the flourishing village of Newhey'. But it was not all a bed of roses. In 1878 they reduced wages by one penny in the shilling on weavers earnings and all other employees by 10% and in 1880 the workers came out on strike for an advance in their wages. They returned to work in March following an amicable settlement.

James had two sons, Harry Heap and James Arthur Berry Heap. We know very little about these two young men except that one of Harry's main interests lay with the military. He was commissioned into the Lancashire Militia Volunteers at an early age and eventually rose to the rank of Lt Col commanding the 6th (Rochdale) Territorial Battalion of the Lancashire Fusiliers. When he attained his majority in 1887 the bells of St Thomas church rang out from early morning until late at night, flags were flown at the mills and the Conservative Club, firework displays were held that evening at Cliffe House. Harry's twenty-first birthday had been celebrated with a day's outing for all the workers to Blackpool, travelling on a special train. When his younger brother Arthur came of age in 1888 the workforce was taken on an outing to Belle Vue in Manchester with a knife and fork tea and fireworks as soon as it was dark.

James was to suffer an early death at the age of 64 in 1892. Cliffe House was sold in 1907 to a Mr Edmund Clegg, flannel manufacturer. The mills were sold later the same year, presumably because the two sons had little interest in carrying on the business although Harry remained a Director of the Newhey, Haugh and New Ladyhouse Ring Spinning Companies until his death in 1931. He was 65 years of age when he died. He had married Lillian T. Robinson and they had three sons. James Arthur Berry Heap married the eldest daughter of J S Littlewood of Rochdale.

We don't have a record of Thomas' religious affiliation other than that he was baptised into the Wesleyan Methodist faith. After his death his two sons, James and William, donated the money for the construction of a new parish church at Newhey in memory of their father. The parish church of St Thomas was an Anglican Church of England foundation and it is inconceivable that they would have done this had their Father remained a Wesleyan Methodist; after all, Wesleyan Methodist chapels were two a penny and going up all over the place. The new gentry had arrived and this reversion to the Church of England was characteristic of many of the new rich. Status in the community demanded that you be seen in church every Sunday. What better way to achieve this and underline your success than to build your own church and have your own pew!

William died just before the church was finished in 1876. It was modelled, for reasons which are not clear, on The Holy Trinity church at Weston Super Mare. It stills stands today perched on top of a hill in the centre of Newhey with a thriving Christian community. James and his wife Mary Berry lie buried just outside the main doorway in a plain but massive marble tomb. Close by is the simpler tomb of Thomas' granddaughter, Jane Mills, who was married to the Rev Fewtrell, one of the last curates to serve at the church.

Inside there is a memorial tablet erected in memory of James by his workforce and two memorial windows, the first to the memory of Thomas and Lucy his wife and their son Thomas who died aged six, commissioned by three of William's granddaughters. The second window is in memory of Sarah Hastings, one of Thomas's daughters, and her two sons Harry Heap Hastings and William Smith Hastings.

There was also a large double pew solely for the use of members of the family and a collection of silver communion vessels donated by the family, and the church bell dedicated to the memory of the two founders which summons the congregation to worship every Sunday. Unfortunately the south east corner of the church was destroyed by fire in 2007. Happily most of the Heap memorabilia were undamaged although it was decided to remove the Heap pew as part of the reorganisation of the pews.

6

WESLEYAN METHODISTS
AND THE FAMILY

The Hamer Mill, 14th June 1817

'Dear Cousin,

... you say you are in a land which flows with milk and honey and that
you have fulfilled your talent ... but whether you mean in respect of
your earthly or your heavenly sovereign I am not able to construe ... I
often think of the hymn which says "while all my old companions dear
with whom I once did live, joyful at God's right hand appear, a blessing
to receive, shall I amidst a ghastly band dragged to the judgement seat,
far on the left with horror stand, my fearful doom to meet". Thank
God that this need not be the case for the same Lord all over all is rich
unto all that call upon him and he offers us both his pardon. We both
may meet on his right hand to praise him that he hath redeemed us for
ever and ever. Oh! then my dear Richard, if you have not yet overcome
the wicked one, if you have not begun to seek the Lord in earnest, begin
now for you cannot tell what a day may bring forth, for death may come
suddenly and call you to the bar of God.

If there are any Methodists near you go and become a member of
their society for it will be a great help to your soul and whatever becomes
of your body provide for the welfare of your immortal soul...'

So wrote Thomas Heap, the eldest son of William The Founder, to his
cousin Richard Howarth at Ten Mile Creek in the Township of Grantham in
the Niagara District in Upper Canada in 1817. Richard was his nephew, son
of one of Betty Heap's brothers. Betty, born Betty Howarth, was the wife of

William The Founder. The Howarths were not just relatives, they had a close working relationship with the family as they participated in some of the loans made to William Heap enabling him to purchase the land and water rights at Caldershaw. It was here that William was to construct his fulling mills that were to become the dyeing and finishing business of Samuel Heap and Son on which the family fortunes were based.

There are eight surviving letters written either by Thomas or his brother William between 1817 and 1851.[1] There were a further three letters but these are now missing. Richard Howarth was born in Bury and had served in the army from 1807 as a driver with the Royal Artillery until he took his discharge in North America. He remained in Canada for the rest of his life until his death in 1871 and as far as we know he never returned to the United Kingdom.

Unfortunately we only have copies of the letters from Thomas and William to their cousin, we have no idea what he said in return.[2] No reason is given why the letters suddenly ceased in 1851, perhaps the correspondence just faded away

The letters tell us many things: first – the ease and rapidity of communication with the Americas, second – they were written by two intelligent and literate men fully *au fait* with the current social and political problems that affected the country as a whole – and this from the sons of a Father who had to sign his name with a cross on his marriage certificate only twenty years earlier, and third – they afford us a fascinating glimpse into the lives of our late Georgian and early Victorian ancestors: the price of corn and the cost of a loaf of bread; the difficulties with trade so far as it affected their business of finishing and flannel manufacture; the agitation for reform and the rise of the Chartists, all this interspersed with exhortation to worship God and follow the dictates of the Methodist faith and beliefs.

We are not concerned here so much with the historical happenings in Rochdale and in the country as a whole, but with the religious fervour that comes across in almost every line, a passion repeated in all the earlier letters but which seems to have lessened somewhat by the time we get to the 1850s. This declaration of faith and Christian beliefs was clearly an everyday part of the lives of our ancestors at this time, and they carried this through and put their beliefs into practice in their family life and in the way they ran their businesses.

This religious belief was no mere flash in the pan restricted to two brothers in what was clearly a deeply religious family. It persisted through the next three or more generations. Their nephew, Charles Heap, was a Sunday school teacher and had been accepted for training in to the Ministry. His brother, William Tweedale, followed in his footsteps. The family was deeply involved in the establishment and running of the Lanehead Wesleyan Chapel[3] in the second half of the 19thC. My grandfather Walter Heap married a Wesleyan Minister's daughter and worshipped as a Wesleyan until he suffered a change of direction and became a Free Mason. My cousin Richard, who holds high office in the Masonic Order, maintains there is no conflict between the two.

Some of the correspondence which survives in the archives of Samuel Heap and Son is full of letters from disgruntled employees appealing to what they saw as the better side of their employer's nature resulting from their Wesleyan faith, in order to achieve their own aims which were usually a demand for money ... and in some cases they were successful.[4]

Walter and the other directors clearly felt under an obligation to find employment for the less fortunate members of the family all of whom were Wesleyans, and to keep them in that employment throughout their working life – even if it was not always in the best interests of the firm as there would have been others who were better qualified to fill the post. The family tree is littered with non-conformist Ministers, all of whom seem to have had a predilection for nubile Heap spinsters. I myself was christened into the Wesleyan faith in a private house ceremony at my maternal Grandparents' house in Ilkley, my parents marriage having been solemnised in a Presbyterian church. It was not until the late thirties or early forties that my mother took us back into the Church of England fold and we attended the Parish Church of St Chad, though my Mother's motives were governed not by her religious beliefs but by her social aspirations.

What caused our ancestors to desert the established church which had baptised, married and buried them for countless previous generations? What caused this explosion of non-conformity throughout many parts of the country, particularly in south east Lancashire and Cornwall? What was there behind this new faith which so captured the minds and hearts of their followers that many of them were willing to devote their lives and much of their money to following the dictates of their new faith? Was it the rebellious nature of a newly emerging middle class who demanded change for change's sake – non-conformity on Sunday, Chartism on Tuesday, Reformism on Wednesday?

There is no simple answer. This was not just a matter of religion and belief. There are much wider social and political connotations which are just as important, if not more so, as merely a new way of approaching one's God.

Perhaps we should begin with John Wesley and his brother Charles, as without these two men there would have been no Wesleyan Methodists as we know them today although perhaps if it had not been John Wesley it would have been someone else in his place. During the latter half of the 18thC and through into the 19thC countless different sects and religious organisations were to emerge in opposition to the established church though this was nothing new. Baptists, Anabaptists, Quakers and Presbyterians had long since opted out and operated outside the established church. With John Wesley they were to experience something rather different. This time their defection was seen as a direct attack on the Established Church. Nearly all the recruits to Methodism were people who had previously worshipped at the Parish Church, if they had worshipped at all. Dissatisfaction with the Anglican church had been growing apace and attendance at Parish Churches had been falling for some years, particularly in the new towns associated with the rise of industrial power and the emergence of the middle classes.

John Wesley was born in 1703, the son of a Church of England Vicar in the small rural community of Epworth, but with both his parents coming from a Dissenting background. The family was constantly in debt and relations between his parents verged on the tempestuous. Nevertheless they were able to provide John with an education at Charterhouse where he won an Exhibition to Christ Church, Oxford, and graduated BA in 1724. He obtained a Fellowship at Lincoln College and he seemed set for an academic career. He was ordained priest into the Church of England in 1728 and became the natural leader of a band of four students at Oxford known as 'The Holy Club' who adopted a somewhat evangelical approach to their religious beliefs and practice. They soon extended their activities into the field of pastoral care, where they were became known as the Oxford Methodists thanks to their methodical approach to their religion and beliefs.

In 1738, following a period of depression when he felt that he was succeeding in nothing either in his work or private life, John Wesley underwent some form of conversion which marked his move from the High Anglicanism to the Evangelical Church. Wesley the ritualist was transformed into Wesley the Preacher and thereafter nothing was to stand in the way of the development of Wesleyan Methodism as we remember it today, apart, that is, from the increasing opposition from the established church often leading to open violence. To his dying day John Wesley still saw himself as a member of the Church of England. He saw no reason why his brand of Methodism should not be practiced within the established church. Communion was still to occupy a central place in his services and he retained his preference for formal prayers over extempore prayer. Preaching the word of God, as he saw it, in relation to every day life was to occupy a central place in his teaching.[5,6]

His services consisted primarily of prayers, hymns and the sermon, and it was in his sermons that Wesley presented his new ideas. The message was simple: repentance, a new birth, justification, the joy of salvation and the pursuit of sanctification, all derived from the meaning of scripture and the use of reason. Wesley propounded a set of rules for his followers: do no harm to others, do not go to law against your brother, no fighting among yourselves, no buying or selling of spirits, do good for the whole community, help each other in business, feed and clothe the poor and take your religious observance seriously.

He was a gifted and charismatic preacher able to control the huge crowds that attended his services. He had the ability and authority to deal with often violent opposition without loosing his temper, and was able to turn round even his most antagonistic opponents. Often physical violence was used not only against the Preacher but against the congregation as well, mobs of ruffians having been organised for this specific purpose. On occasion the Magistrate was even persuaded to turn out the Dragoons to disperse one of their meetings.[9]

The Established Anglican Church rose up in opposition and forbade him the right to preach in their churches, so he made increasing use of peoples houses. There is one occasion in 1749 where Wesley was preaching in a house in Rochdale and the crowds were so great that they gathered outside and Wesley had to preach to them through the open window. From this it was but a short step to preaching out in the open. Vast congregations numbered in their thousands were not uncommon in those parts of the country where Methodism had gathered a strong following, such as south east Lancashire and around the tin mines of Cornwall.

We do not know precisely when our ancestors joined the movement but all William's children were baptised into the Wesleyan church, the eldest child, Thomas, being baptised in 1793. We know that his father, William, was born in 1769 but we have no record of his baptism. The early Methodist baptismal records were abysmal, incomplete, poorly recorded and difficult to read. William's father, Stephen, was born too early to have been baptised a Methodist.

There was no new religious awakening, a Billy Graham type of Crusade, causing this rise in Methodism. It was more an expression of an increasing dissatisfaction with the Established Anglican church. The Vicar or Incumbent of the Parish had for too long been the only source of authority in the townships and much of the power which he exercised was over secular matters. The Established Church was dominated by the Tory gentry and one can see the newly emerging middle class being banished to the back of the church, along with the agricultural labouring class. It is easy to see how this would have been unacceptable to the middle class entrepreneur starting to run his own business, employing labour, and setting about establishing a place for himself in the community. But he was still a God fearing man who needed the support and leadership of a church to interpret the gospel and to intercede with God on his behalf. Methodism might have been tailor-made for his needs and it should really be no surprise that it took off as it did in those parts of the country that were beginning to grapple with the Industrial Revolution and all the social ills resulting there from.

Deprived of a church in which to worship, the Methodists started to provide their own chapels. These began as humble meeting houses, a place where they could gather together on a Sunday and listen to the words of the circuit teacher and where they could build-on a Sunday school that would teach their children to read and write and bring them up in the new faith. A place moreover where they could meet their friends and conduct their amorous liaisons. My Aunt Kathleen would tell of notes and *billets-doux* tucked inside prayer books and passed along the gallery until it reached their intended, fixing an assignation after the service was finished. All this under the eyes of the Minister!

After the death of John Wesley, the Methodists began to argue amongst themselves and various splinter groups formed, such as the Primitive Methodists and those who followed the Countess of Huntingdon. Rochdale was no exception and as the Rev Eagles said in his article on the Early History of Methodism in Rochdale, 'we certainly see in its Methodist history that curious characteristic of Rochdale people which must again and again become prominent in the history of the town. These good folk, most honourable and strictly religious men, opposed vigorously the imposition of authority whenever it seemed unjust or even exaggerated in character'. They found themselves in constant opposition to some of the decisions of Conference.

But other changes were taking place. Methodism had been adopted, not only by the emerging middle classes, but also by the working class and their views were not always in agreement; after all they had different social aspirations and standards. Two groups emerged, the radical, increasingly left wing dissenting nonconformists centred on the Union Street chapel, and the middle class reformist nonconformists who attended the Baillie Street chapel.

Although initially nearly all the successful 'clothiers' were nonconformists, with increasing wealth and property their dissenting ideas became blunted and their sons passed without difficulty into The Commission of Peace and the Anglican community. The wheel had come full circle and they emerged with all the prejudices of the country gentleman and voted Tory.

Those of the manufacturing middle classes who retained their allegiance to the dissenting chapels were in fact more thrusting, energetic and ambitious than their Tory/Anglican counterparts and textile based nonconformists were in the vanguard of all the reformist movements of the 19th century.[10]

What of our family in all of this? Although there are records of some of them attending the Baillie Street chapel, by 1857 we find them attending instead the Lanehead chapel that lies high up above Caldershaw, on the very edge of Rooleymoor. Rochdale was initially part of the Nelson/Colne circuit and the itinerant Preachers made their way south from Bacup, climbing up onto the desolate waste of Rooleymoor before descending into Caldershaw which lay just below the southern edge of the moor. Lanehead was well situated as a stopping off point.

Another approach was from the east and there is a delightful description of a John Butterworth travelling across Blackstone Edge from Ripponden who discovered God when he was half way across:

'I was alone and several times I stopped and knelt down upon the moor in prayer. Once I felt such a power in wrestling as I have never experienced since and I did shout with all my might on the open moor "Glory be to God, I will praise thee. Though thou was angry with me thine anger is turned away and now thou has comforted me." At that time I was engaged in some business which was not very pleasant and kept me away from home, I think the blessing which I received whilst crossing the moor strengthened me..." '[8]

The records of the Lanehead chapel[7] are scanty but it appears to have been built in 1850 and remained in operation until 1957 when it was closed. It was demolished in the 1960s, and now all that remains is a pile of stone although it is still fondly remembered by some of the older inhabitants of the village. We have no specific records of the benefactors who contributed to the building of the chapel but we have a great deal of evidence of Samuel, Charles and William Tweedale's involvement with the Sunday School which was built around about the same time. It is inconceivable that they did not make a major contribution to the costs of the chapel. Lanehead today is a delightful and attractive village of stone houses that would have been weavers' cottages lining the road which runs up onto the moor. You can still see the old mill lodge across the road from the remains of the chapel. There are still two working farms.

The population of Lanehead and Smallshaw consisted of miners, quarrymen and factory operatives employed principally at a new mill built at the latter place by John Tweedale and Sons for the manufacture of cotton and the mills of Samuel Heap and Son down at Caldershaw. At the time there were two coal mines in operation, one behind The Black Dog and the other up on the moor. As the summer of 1845 drew to a close it became apparent to some of the more prominent men in the community that something must be done to lay hold of the young men who were running wild at the weekend, spending their Sunday mornings in pigeon flying, wrestling matches and cock fighting. Few of them could read or write and many scarcely knew their own Christian names as a large number went by nicknames. As for the education of the children, it was almost non existent. A room was found above an old mill at Fernhill and in no time they had an attendance of over one hundred persons … with the school came the Wesleyan Methodists with their prayer meetings and hymn singing. The Wesleyan Lanehead community was born and went from strength to strength. A new school was built and opened in 1857 with its own Band of Hope dressed in white knickers and scarlet jumpers. There was an annual Good Friday tea party and a summer picnic held at Lower Dunnisbooth farm up on the side of the moor. The minutes record the number of loaves and pounds of butter which had to be provided and the gallons of tea which were consumed. Over a hundred members attended the Whitsuntide tea party which required the provision of 12 x 2lb loaves, 6 brown loaves, 12 sweet loaves, 80 plain tea-cakes, 50 current tea-cakes, 5½lbs of butter, 5lb of loaf sugar, 1lb of tea, 6 quarts of milk.[7]

William Tweedale Heap and his brother Charles were to play a leading role in these activities, William Tweedale holding the post of secretary and then superintendent from 1854 until 1883 and possibly longer.

So ends the story of the family's commitment to the Wesleyan Methodist faith which was to continue well into the early years of the 20th century. It undoubtedly played a significant part in both their personal and private family lives as well as in the way they conducted their businesses for the greater benefit of their work force and others with whom they came into contact. Perhaps it should be a lesson to us. If we were to conduct our own lives today in a similar manner, we might have less youth crime and less corruption in high places.

References

1   appendix IV: The letters of Thomas and James Heap
2   appendix V: The Lye-Stamm papers
3   Handley, John: *History of Lanehead Sunday School.* Reprinted from *Light and Love*
4   Samuel Heap and Son. Archives held by Touchstones Rochdale Local Studies
5   John Wesley – Wikipedia
6   Waller, Ralph. *John Wesley: a personal portrait.* SPCK, 2003
7   Lanehead chapel Wesleyan Sunday school minute book. January 1920-March 1936
8   Moore, B.: *History of Wesleyan Methodism in Burnley and East Lancashire.* Gazette, Burnley, 1899
9   Hall G.D.: 'Congregationalists, Methodist and Lancs Nonconformists, 1790-1907'. Unpublished thesis
10 Cole, John: *Textiles, Nonconformity and social control.* May 1988

7

SAMUEL HEAP AND SON
A SHORT HISTORY

The history of the family after 1800 is centred around one man, William Heap, and the fulling, dyeing and finishing firm at Caldershaw that came to be known as Samuel Heap and Son, named after one of William's sons and grandson. The firm prospered until well into the twentieth century, but had increasing difficulty in coping with the economic climate after the second world war. Like much of the cotton and wool industry in south east Lancashire it could no longer compete in the global market and it was taken over by Courtaulds in 1964.

Courtaulds had at least one redeeming feature in that they tended to commission someone to write a history of the firms they were taking over, so all would be recorded for posterity. Such was the case for Samuel Heap and Son, and a young historian by the name of Negley Harte was commissioned to carry out this work. Negley was a young history graduate who had already shown an interest in the textile industry and was later destined to become Senior Lecturer at University College London. Negley had other qualifications which ideally fitted him for the task. He had been born, educated and brought up in Rochdale, so he was familiar with the area and with the problems he would have to face.

Negley was given free and open access to all the papers held by the firm and was guided in his task by Arthur Wingfield, the out-going Secretary to the Board. Alas, the product of his labours was never published, but the draft still exists and has proved of immense value in writing this chapter.

Realising that the history of Samuel Heap and Son would be central to any account of the history of the family, I approached the firm way back in 1954 when I was still a brash young student at medical school in London but met with little success. I was shown a copy of William's last Will and Testament which conveniently lists the names of all his children and their spouses, and copies of two indentures recording the sale of the land and water rights at Caldershaw to William in 1823 and then from William's children to William Tweedale Heap in 1859. But clearly there had been more, much more, all of which was made available to Negley Harte in 1964. So far as we know all these documents, and other papers relating to the firm, are still held in the Courtaulds archives, but we have been unable to gain access

Samuel Heap and Son has, over the years, provided employment for many members of the family in one capacity or another, from Chairman of the Board to much more lowly offices. It has been hinted on occasion that perhaps some did not always pull their weight and did not deserve their place and would, perhaps, not have been employed were it not for their family connections. Nevertheless, employed they were and gave many years of service. It could be argued that the Wesleyan Methodist ethic demanded that the more fortunate members of the family cared for the less qualified and in the long run both benefited. The same can be said for the rather curious financial arrangements referred to in an earlier chapter, sooner or later everyone stood to benefit.

The earlier members of the family were a fecund lot and by 1970 there were some 500 members of the family who could trace their ancestry directly back to William. Many of them had, at one stage or another, directly or indirectly, benefited from their connection with the family firm. Such arrangements are not uncommon in family businesses and, it has to be said, not infrequently contribute to their downfall. Although this may have played a part in the final demise of Samuel Heap and Son, it was, I think, only a minor factor. The writing had long been on the wall for the cotton and wool industries in south east Lancashire and in the absence of a brilliant entrepreneur who could have turned the company around, the ultimate fall was inevitable

We have followed William's progress as a Fulling Miller in an earlier chapter. He was last seen at the Hamer Mill in Rochdale as early as 1814, when he appears to have rented part of the premises which also operated as a perching mill. But William had his sights on something much bigger and better. The Industrial Revolution was well into its stride and William thought he knew exactly where it was heading and was determined to have his share. The spinning and weaving elements of the wool industry were still largely cottage based, only carding and fulling were factory based, primarily because they required a water power source in order to function and proper housing for their large machinery. Any attempt at horizontal integration within the industry was still years away, the fulling and finishing processes associated with it were still provided as a separate operation. They had the added advantage that the 'finisher' didn't have to buy or own the cloth that he was finishing. He merely provided the service for the owner of the cloth and was paid for it. As new processes were invented, finishing became more specialised and an art all of its own. Once he had purchased and installed his machinery, the fuller–finisher's overheads were low as he didn't have to carry the stock that didn't belong to him.

Rochdale was already the centre of the flannel industry and, together with the West Riding towns of Halifax and Huddersfield, it was the centre for the production of the coarser types of woollens, including baize and bockings. The demand for fulling in the 1820s was buoyant. It is estimated that some 8,000 pieces of flannel were manufactured every week in the Rochdale area and nearly all of these would require fulling, bleaching and dying.

On 13th June 1823 William bought the lease of a old carding mill situated in the township of Spotland on the edge of Rooleymoor. The mill had been built by Richard Bamford and James Holt in 1782. It was situated on the Caldershaw Brook which drained into the River Spodden which joined the River Roche as it made its way towards the centre of nearby Rochdale. Holt and Bamford had taken up the lease on the two fields of higher and lower Caldershaw. The water from the brook had been augmented after 1807 by water brought up by the fire engine from the nearby collieries at Ellenrod. William paid £575 for the mill and the unexpired part of the lease and is thought to have spent a further £900 on tearing down the old mill and building a new one to house his fulling stocks. William borrowed £1,500 from John Elliott, a local solicitor, to finance his operations, putting up the mill and its contents as security for the loan. The debt to John Elliott was paid off in 1833 just before William's death, from which we can assume that the venture had prospered.

When William The Founder died in 1833 his children inherited the business that was carried on under the name of William Heap and Bros. The Will was proved at the Bishop's court in Chester on 9 December 1833, the estate having a sworn value of less than £3,000. The Will required the proceeds be divided equally between his seven surviving children, Thomas, William, Elizabeth, Rachel (wife of Benjamin Butterworth), John, Samuel and James. There is no mention of his wife Betty who had predeceased him. There was a further clause in the Will which required that any child who wished to dispose of his or her share could only sell out to a member of the family – William had established a family business and was determined to see that it remained within the family.

Three of the sons had already set up their own businesses elsewhere and the Caldershaw mill was left in the hands of Samuel and James, initially assisted by another cousin, also confusingly named William, who was probably the same William recorded by the census as living at Bridgehall.

The business was flourishing as William (the second son) was writing to his cousin in Canada in 1838... 'we are partners in the fulling business and are finishing about 400 flannels a week. We employ 25 men and boys and have a pretty good run of business since we commenced on our own account'. This would appear to be in direct contrast to the general discontent which affected many people in the town with a rising poor rate relief, heavy taxation following the end of the Napoleonic wars and a rising price for corn.

In 1837 the family took out a long lease on a plot of land adjoining Caldershaw known as Gooseholes, and later that year purchased more land known as the Tops of Spotland Estate for £1,155. This was the same year in which they bought the Shepherd Mill in Norden for John. In the 1840s and 50s there was a reassignment of these lands between various members of the family and a rather shadowy figure called James Booth, a druggist. In 1847 they took out a lease on Catley Lane farm from the Trustees of Bury Grammar School, this included the water-rights which enabled them to power the adjoining fulling mill. In 1848 Samuel and James built a three-storey steam powered cotton mill (known as Caldershaw New Mill or Rake Bridge Mill) which was let to Samuel Brierley for 14 years at £260 per year. Samuel bought up his brothers share in the mill for £2,000 in 1855.

In 1859 Samuel bought up the shares belonging to his six brothers and sisters and the interest of the shadowy Booth, the mill and the land being transferred for £3,600 to William Tweedale Heap, Samuel's eldest son. It was from this date that the business became known as Samuel Heap and Son, a title which it held until the concern was finally taken over by Courtaulds in 1964. William Tweedale Heap (my great grandfather) first started work at the mill aged fifteen when he was paid 5/2d for six days work! William Tweedale slowly worked his way up the firm until he ended up in partnership with his father, Samuel. In 1867 William Tweedale left the mill to join the local firm of William Tatham and Co, engineers and machinists engaged in the construction and manufacture of textile machinery. The reasons for this sudden departure are not known. Perhaps he disagreed with the way his father was running the business. Undeterred by this potential setback, Samuel took one of his younger sons, Charles, into partnership and it was Charles who took sole control of

CHART 6

Children of Samuel Heap and Ann Tweedale

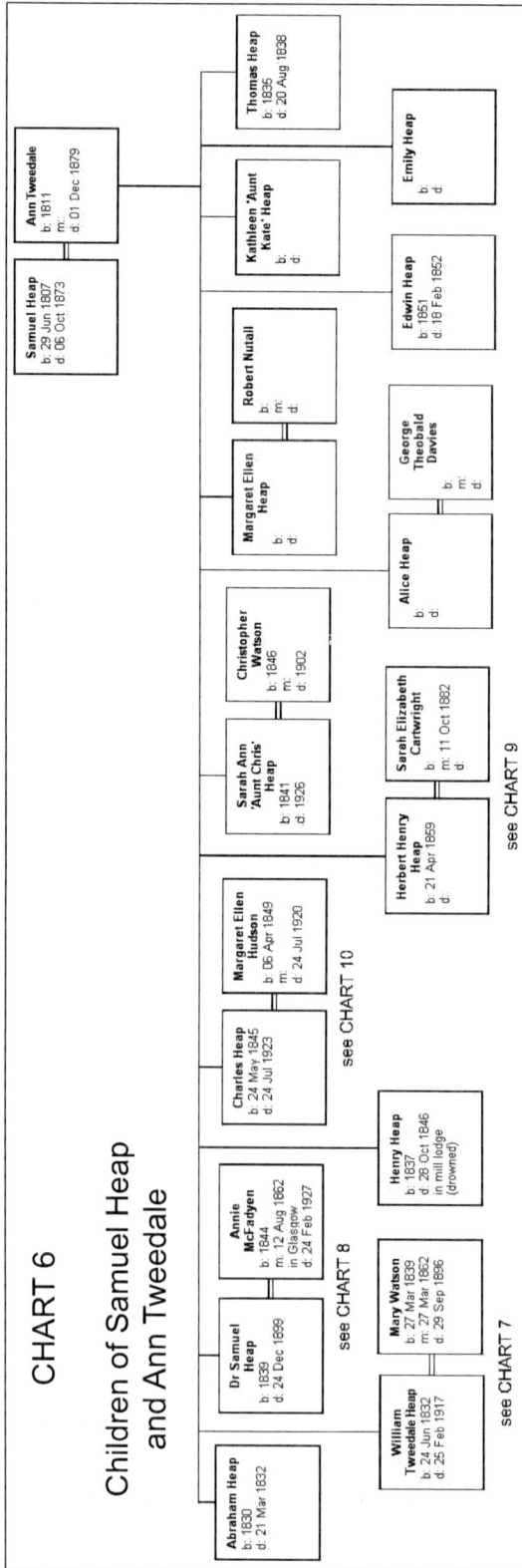

Samuel Heap
b: 29 Jun 1807
d: 06 Oct 1873

Ann Tweedale
b: 1811
m:
d: 01 Dec 1879

Abraham Heap
b: 1830
d: 21 Mar 1832

William Tweedale Heap
b: 24 Jun 1832
d: 25 Feb 1917

Mary Watson
b: 27 Mar 1839
m: 27 Mar 1862
d: 29 Sep 1896

see CHART 7

Dr Samuel Heap
b: 1839
d: 24 Dec 1899

Annie McFadyen
b: 1844
m: 12 Aug 1862
in Glasgow
d: 24 Feb 1927

see CHART 8

Henry Heap
b: 1837
d: 26 Oct 1846
in mill lodge
(drowned)

Charles Heap
b: 24 May 1845
d: 24 Jul 1923

Margaret Ellen Hudson
b: 06 Apr 1849
m:
d: 24 Jul 1920

see CHART 10

Sarah Ann 'Aunt Chris' Heap
b: 1841
d: 1926

Christopher Watson
b: 1846
m:
d: 1902

Herbert Henry Heap
b: 21 Apr 1859
d:

Sarah Elizabeth Cartwright
b:
m: 11 Oct 1882

see CHART 9

Margaret Ellen Heap
b:
d:

Robert Nutall
b:
m:
d:

Alice Heap
b:
d:

George Theobald Davies
b:
m:
d:

Kathleen 'Aunt Kate' Heap
b:
d:

Edwin Heap
b: 1851
d: 18 Feb 1852

Thomas Heap
b: 1835
d: 20 Aug 1838

Emily Heap
b:
d:

72

the business when Samuel died six years later. Charles' dynamic leadership was responsible for the growth of the firm over the next fifty years and for its success.

Charles was only 22 when he joined his father in the business. He was a staunch Wesleyan Methodist, as were all the other members of the family. Charles had been destined for the ministry and was already preaching on one of the circuits when his father died. He gave up his vocation and returned to the family business to which he brought an evangelical fervour that was to characterise his life thereafter.

As far as we know, when Charles took over the business the mill was still fulling the woollen cloth in the traditional manner, though by now the machinery was driven by steam. In addition to fulling, the cloth was bleached and dyed which was part of the same process. The business only handled woollen goods. Charles began to experiment with the finishing of cotton cloths then being introduced from the continent as Dutch Dometts. The cotton industry was expanding rapidly in Rochdale and cotton cloth was cheaper than wool, lighter and easier to wash, and more versatile. Charles' experiments proved successful and this part of the business began to expand rapidly.

In the 1880s he introduced the raising machine into Britain, creating the type of raised cotton cloth known as 'flannelette'. Previously cloth had to be raised using natural teasels fitted into a wooden frame on a revolving machine. The new machinery had been invented by Charles Edward Moser, a German engineer who had settled in Leeds. The machine had independently controlled teasling rollers made of metal which raised the nap of the cloth giving it a fur like surface. The later machines had a double-action allowing greater control over the height of the nap and producing a more uniform product. Charles entered into an agreement with Moser which allowed him to export the machines to America, with disastrous financial consequences for the firm (see chapter on Transatlantic Connections). Unfortunately Charles became involved in a dispute over patent rights between Moser and a French company which also claimed the invention. This dispute was to drag on over the next ten years.

Charles wasn't greatly concerned, the flannelette business was flourishing, it felt and looked like flannel but was much cheaper. During the last fifteen years of the century the business expanded rapidly, new machinery was installed in the two existing mills, and four new mills were bought to allow the firm to cope with increased demand. The nearby Brookside Mill, an old cotton spinning mill built in 1835, was purchased for £2250 in 1887; the Bentfield

Mill in Saddleworth was taken over as a going concern a year later; the Healey Hall mill was acquired for £3,750 in 1899 and the Spotland Bridge mill for £2,700 in 1893. The Smallshaw mill at Lanehead was purchased for £100 to enable Charles to secure the water-rights and the demolished stone with which he reconstructed the Healey mill.

William Tweedale had re-joined his brother in 1889 and in 1893 they set up a Limited Company with Charles owning £33,700 of shares and William Tweedale £27,250. The total share capital amounted to £66,200, the remaining capital being owned by other members of the family and one outsider.

The acquisition of the Bentfield and Healey Hall mills was not an entirely successful venture. There were continual minor disputes with the Robinson family who had owned the mills and who continued to manage them for the main Board. The Robinsons were continually asking for an additional share of the profits, which was always denied them. In many years the mills failed to make a profit. They specialised in 'mercerising' the cotton, a process imparting a glossy silk like finish to the cloth. In 1912 the mills were let to the Robinson brothers for ten years at £450 a year and finally sold back to them in 1912. Thereafter they set themselves up in competition with Samuel Heap and Son!

The period 1894-1914 saw steady but unspectacular growth. In 1895 a new warehouse was built at Spotland Bridge to which a third storey was added in 1908 and a fourth in 1912. Another large warehouse was built at Rake Bridge in 1896 and a third over the lodge at Brookside in 1902. All these new mills and facilities were involved in the production and treating of flannelette, the processing of woollen goods being restricted to the old mill. The concern was clearly flourishing since there were reports of industrial espionage with competitors attempting to obtain information from the workforce late at night.

New filters and tanks were fitted in 1894 and new steam engines installed. In 1900 a new process was bought which rendered the cloth unshrinkable. A licence to use a new French process for bleaching was acquired and in 1893 William Marshall was engaged as a research chemist to manage the laboratory which came to play an increasingly important part of the business. Between 1900 and 1907 three more farms were purchased and a new office block built across the road from the Rake Bridge mill. In 1913 the firm purchased their first motor lorries to replace the horse drawn vans that had previously handled their traffic in and around Rochdale and through into Manchester.

The additional demand created by the first World War was responsible for the boom in output in the years 1914 to 1918 when good use was made of the new buildings and mills bought and erected since 1896. The old mill was further extended and a mechanics workshop built. The mills were working day and night to full capacity thanks to the demand for blankets as a result of the war. By 1918 the mills employed 262 men and 153 women. The company's share value was doubled by the creation of 7,000 new shares, most of them going as a free bonus issue to existing share holders. Business was booming and the family must have revelled in their new found wealth.

The firm continued to prosper in the years following the war – unlike the rest of the cotton industry which suffered a disastrous slump from which it never fully recovered. Under Charles Heap's guidance the firm had diversified, handling both wool and cotton and doing business with a large number of small spinning and weaving concerns over a wide area so that the loss or failure of one company had only a minimal effect. The firm had also been involved in the early experiments in the dyeing of rayon, or artificial silk as it was known. Once Courtaulds, the main proponent of the art, went into full production, Samuel Heap and Son was ready and waiting to provide the dyeing and finishing of the new product with a new process devised by Marshall, the firm's chemist. The firm also moved into the dyeing and finishing of woollen knitted goods by a new process pioneered and invented by John Hudson Heap, one of Charles' three sons, all destined to become directors. The woollen knitted goods were manufactured in Leicester and Nottingham. Further mills were purchased together with three farms, Ellenrod, Whitefield and Kit Booth – all up on Rooley Moor. The farms were let to tenants, Samuel Heap and Son were only interested in the water rights. Dyeing, finishing and bleaching necessitated the use of vast quantities of water. In 1924 they bought the Boarshaw Spinning Co in Middleton as a going concern, operating as the Boarshaw Raising and Finishing Co Ltd, a wholly owned subsidiary. This must have been their most successful investment as long after the other parts of the business were making a loss, the Boarshaw business continued to make a profit.

Then in 1923, Charles Heap, the architect and innovator of their success, who had guided and directed their actions since 1873, died at the advanced age of 78 after being confined to his bed for the last two years of his life. His elder brother and partner, William Tweedale Heap, had predeceased him in 1917, aged 74. The business was now left in the hands of Walter Heap, son of William Tweedale and my grandfather. Walter did not have long to enjoy his Chairmanship as he collapsed and died in 1930 when only 54 after returning home from a grand Masonic Dinner in Manchester. Walter had had to endure a number of lawsuits on patent rights, including a long drawn-out case with the Bradford Dyers Association which the firm lost at great cost in 1929, together with various disputes over trademarks. Profits were falling and the firm suffered a net loss in 1929, for only the second time since its incorporation in 1893. All this no doubt contributed to his early death. Walter was succeeded by Fred Heap, eldest son of Charles Heap, who died in 1937. Charles' next son, John Hudson (Jack) Heap had died in 1933, so Fred was succeeded as Chairman by their younger brother, Samuel Heap, who remained in the chair until 1951.

When Ernest Muehleck left the company after his reorganisation in 1936 he recommended that his assistant, Fred Howard, be appointed to the Board. The first non-member of the family to be appointed a Director, he was to continue as general manager. Fred had been with the firm since he joined as a junior clerk in 1909. He was a blunt and forthright Lancastrian and he continued to carry out his duties with much vigour until his retirement in 1955. When Sam Heap died in 1951, Fred Howard suggested a much younger man should take the chair and George Hudson Heap, grandson of Charles Heap, was elected to the post which he held until the take-over by Courtaulds in 1964. But the foot was now in the door, the long period when the family alone controlled the firm and made all the decisions was rapidly coming to an end. A J Wingfield, the company secretary, joined the board in 1934, to be followed by R R Rudman, the Chief Engineer, E Mattinson of the Sales Staff, and Raymond Howard – one of Fred Howard's sons.

Despite these rearrangements the years from 1929 to 1939 were to prove disastrous. The company made a loss in 1929 and continued to do so every year, except 1930, until the outbreak of war in 1939. The firm was constantly on the edge of bankruptcy and liquidation. Working capacity had fallen to less than three quarters of the output in the years prior to 1930. The causes were not far to seek. The whole textile industry was suffering from excess production and increased competition from abroad. The situation was made worse by price cutting within the trade. The dividend continued to fall and in 1932 no dividend could be paid at all. Desperate affairs call for desperate measures and in 1934 an outsider, Ernest Muehleck, was brought in as Director and Manager and given carte blanche to put the firm on a new footing. Muehleck was an American and part of the Bedaux organisation which had previously prepared a report on the firm. He was quite ruthless. The business underwent a complete reorganisation. All outstanding loans were called in and a number of Directors perks were eliminated. 'We are running a business and not a philanthropic organisation', he is reported to have said. The Spotland Bridge mill was sold and the finishing of flannelette goods transferred to the Brookside mill. The Healey mill was closed down, 'it is one of the most inefficiently run mills that I have ever seen' said Muehleck. The services of over two hundred employees were dispensed with. The total loss in 1934 was more than £24,000. Concerned over the calibre and quality of the sales staff, Muehleck said 'selling must be done through principals rather than pedlars'. Many of the sales staff were either moved or lost their jobs. The research and development side was strengthened by the appointment in 1934 of a Swiss chemist, Josef Wehrmuller, who was to look into the dyeing of artificial silk crepes. The trade in knitted fabrics was ended as it was no longer economic to transport the goods to and from the Midlands. In 1935 the finishing of woollen cloths, which had formed the heart of the business at its inception, was also brought to an end. The firm's efforts were now concentrated on the dyeing, raising and finishing of cotton and rayon cloths.

In 1936 the firm obtained a licence to use a patented crease resistant process under the trade mark of 'Creesrist'. But muddle, faulty machinery, and lack of expertise resulted in large losses. The difficulties were not fully overcome until 1948 when the new process accounted for half the output of the firm. By concentrating on higher quality lines with wider profit margins, the firm at last went back into profit in 1940 when the increased demands due to the War had again begun to benefit the firm.

The years following the war were on the whole a time of increasing prosperity with the dividend rising again to 10%. The Spotland Bridge mill had been sold in 1934 and in 1942 the empty Healey mill was sold to the Ministry of Supply. But by 1948 there was increasing demand for cotton blanket raising and the firm purchased the Silk Street Raising and Finishing Co in Newton Heath for £10,000, running it as a wholly owned subsidiary. The firm was now finishing not just goods manufactured in Lancashire, but also cloth imported from British customers in Europe and Asia.

The firm continued to make a profit but Samuel Heap and Son was still only a medium sized business in the changing economy of the 1950s and 60s. This demanded vertical integration on a much larger scale such as had taken place with the Calico Printers Association and the Bradford Dyers Association – both of which operated in competition with Samuel Heap and Son. The firm also faced other difficulties in the early sixties: the Rake Bridge mill was destroyed by fire and had to be rebuilt, and again substantial losses were being made. By 1964 the Board had had enough and unanimously agreed to

Courtaulds buying the total issued share capital of the firm after nearly 140 years of independent activity in the Textile Industry. None of the Directors were retained in post and from thereon the family had no further connection with the business.

Courtaulds invested large sums of money in re-equipping the mills with more up to date machinery, rebuilding and extending many of the existing buildings. But the writing had been on the wall for the textile industry for some time. It could no longer compete with Asian producers whose overheads and wages were a fraction of those operating in the United Kingdom. The end was in sight. In 1987 Courtaulds closed down the whole site and sold out to Quorum Estates, who demolished most of the mills and divided the rest into small industrial units

Notes
Chairmen of the board of Samuel Heap and Son

Charles Heap – the first Chairman of the Board following the formation of a limited company in 1893. He was to hold office until his death in 1923

Walter Heap – nephew of Charles Heap and the head of the other side of the family. His father being William Tweedale Heap. Walter held office from 1923 until his sudden and unexpected death in 1930

Frederick (Fred) Charles Heap – son of Charles Heap the first Chairman. He held office from 1930 to 1937

Samuel Heap – married to Mary 'Tottie' Leathley, son of Charles Heap the first Chairman. He held office from 1937 until his death in 1951

George Hudson Heap – grandson of Charles Heap the first Chairman. He held office from 1951 until the take-over by Courtaulds

1 The earliest known engraving of the Bridge Hall mills – 18thC

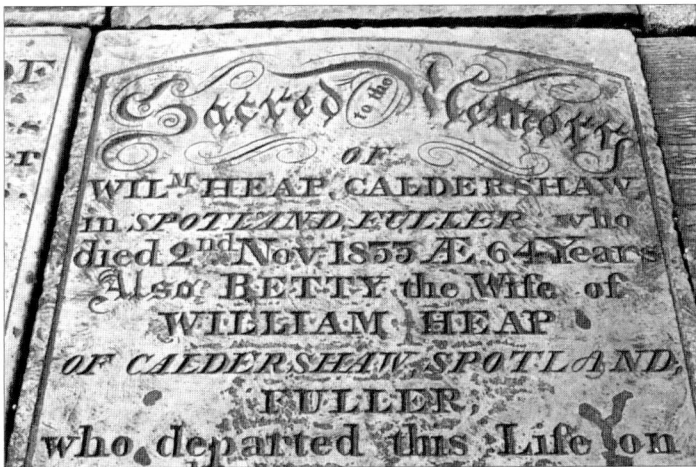

2 Gravestone of William Heap the Founder, 1769-1833 – St Chad's old burial ground, Rochdale

3 Gravestone of Stephen Heap, 1739-1827 – St Chad's old burial ground, Rochdale

4 *Samuel Heap, 1807-1873*

5 *Charles Heap, 1845-1923*

6 *William Tweedale Heap, 1832-1917*

7   The Ogden mill at Newhey c. 1910, owned by Thomas Heap

8   St Thomas's church, Newhey, built by William and James Heap, 1860

9   Memorial window to Thomas Heap, Lucy his wife, and six year-old son Thomas. St Thomas's church, Newhey

11 Gig mill with teasels for raising the nap, 1840

10 Fulling Stocks (Helmshore)

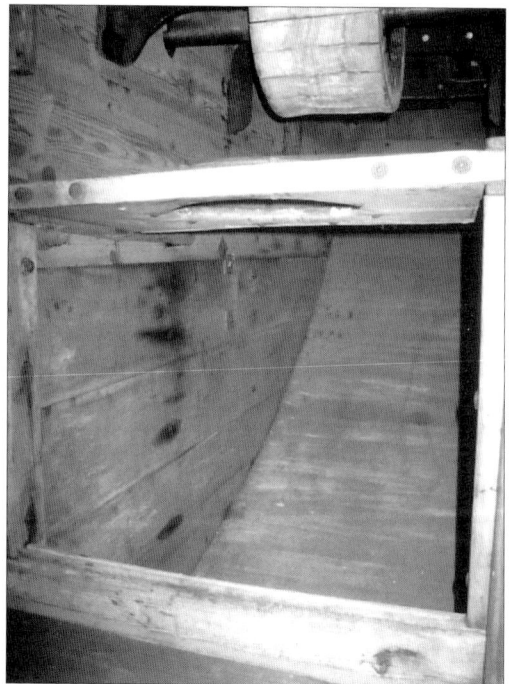

12 Rotary milling machine – exterior c.1844

13 Rotary milling machine – interior c.1844

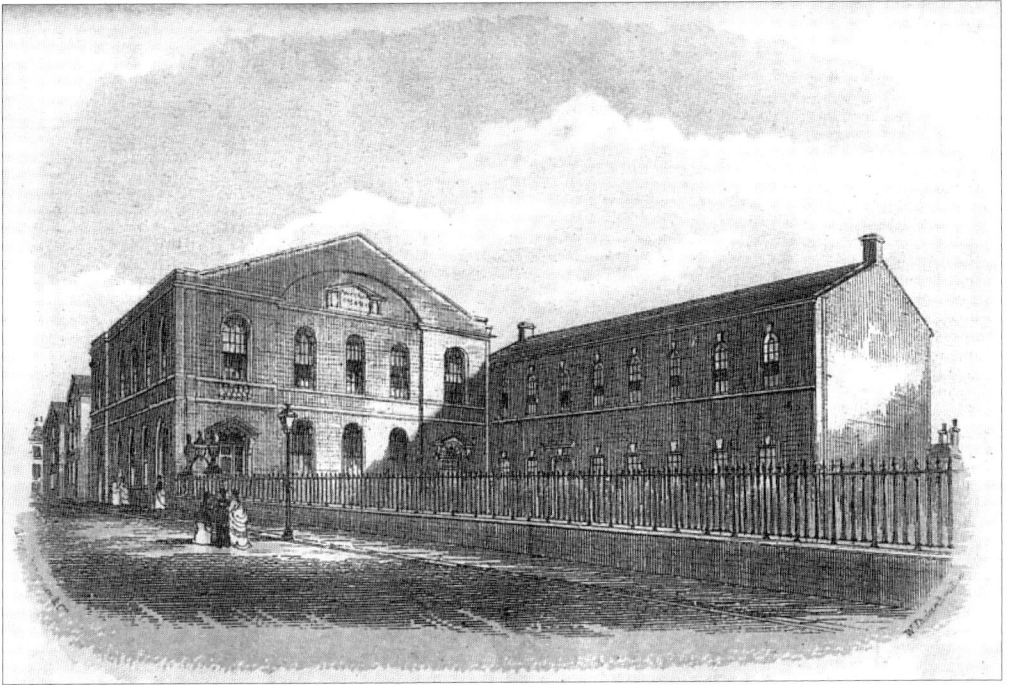

14   Union Street Wesleyan Methodist chapel, Rochdale

15   Baillie Street Wesleyan Methodist chapel, Rochdale

16 Rochdale town centre, 1780

17 Rochdale c.1900: Drake Street and the Wellington Hotel

18 Rochdale railway station, c.1840

19 Above: Samuel Heap & Son – the mill offices c.1930

20 Centre: Rooley-moor Road, c.1920

21 Below: Lanehead village with Lanehead chapel on right c.1920

22   *Charles Heap and his family, c.1900*
Back row: Fred, Billie, Jack, Helen, Sam
Front row: Annie, Charles, Jessie, Margaret (his wife), Daisy

8

JOSHUA HEAP AND THE
FENTON'S BANK AFFAIR

It is the hope of every family historian to uncover a villain lurking somewhere in the background or, failing a villain, a hero who died gloriously and needlessly on the North West frontier or some such unlikely location. But most families are full of ordinary people and such colourful characters are few and far between. However, in Joshua Heap, we find someone of whose behaviour we can disapprove and who met an early death which many would argue he richly deserved. In true biblical fashion it might even be said that his sins were 'visited' on the next generation.

Joshua was born on 15th August 1836, the third son of William Heap, the second son of William the Founder. William had left the family firm at Caldershaw and set up his own flannel manufactory at Ealees in Littleborough. His mother, Elizabeth Haslam Fielden, was the daughter of the great textile family of Fielden in Todmorden. By all accounts it must have been considered that William had made a good marriage. In 1874, at the relatively late age of 38, his son Joshua married Alice, the daughter of Edmund Leach JP. They had two sons, Stephen and Edward.

Joshua was educated at Shawforth in Yorkshire before joining his father in Littleborough, where he worked his way through the mill learning the art of fulling and flannel manufacture. He then joined his uncle Thomas at Milnrow, where he would have gained further experience in flannel manufacture before returning to join his younger brother Samuel in running the West View mills in Littleborough. He then had a stroke of luck that was to set him on the pathway to riches and establish him as one of the leading woollen manufacturers in the town.

The firm of Kelsall and Kemp was one of the oldest and largest woollen manufacturers in the town. Like nearly all the other textile concerns it began business back in 1815 when Henry Kelsall started buying in wool, had it spun for him and then supplied the yarn to the hand-loom weavers who worked for him in their own cottages. By 1835 Henry Kelsall had established his first mill and others were to follow in quick succession as the business rapidly expanded. By 1864 Henry Kelsall was in his seventy-first year and his partner, George Tawke Kemp, was troubled with his health. There were no other members of the family who were of an age to join the business, and on the recommendation of friends, Joshua Heap, a young man of 29, was invited to join the partnership in 1865 and almost immediately found himself the managing partner.

One can imagine the impact on the business of this young, capable and energetic man. He began by scrapping all the old and obsolete machinery and installing new and up to date machines which were still working fifty years later. Henry Kelsall died in 1869. The flannel trade went into decline in 1860 and 1870 but Joseph was an astute business man. He seemed to be able to predict the market and bought in raw wool when the price was at its lowest ebb and then sold the finished goods at the top of the market. A fourth mill was built in 1870, and in 1875 he purchased the old cotton bleaching mill at Woodhouse which was converted into a woollen dyeing and finishing works. Prior to this the unfinished pieces were 'put out' to be finished by outside firms of which no doubt Samuel Heap and Son of Caldershaw was one. The purchase and conversion of the Woodhouse Mill would hardly have endeared him to his cousins down at Caldershaw.

George Tawke Kemp died in 1877 when on holiday in Egypt, after which the partnership continued between Mrs Emily Lydia Kemp and Joshua Heap. In 1879 Robert Slack, aged 22, a grandson of Henry Kelsall, joined the firm where he could watch over his Aunt's interests.

The rapid expansion of the textile industry brought with it a demand for banking services and Rochdale was one of the first towns in Lancashire to open a bank. Improvements in banking facilities were urgently needed in the latter half of the 18thC. Previously business men might obtain fixed capital by borrowing from relatives or merchants or by ploughing back the profits into the business. Samuel Heap and Son provided a classic example of this. In 1825 William the Founder borrowed £1,500 from a John Elliott, a local solicitor, to provide him with the necessary funds to enlarge and modernise the old mill that he had purchased at Caldershaw. The debt to Elliott was paid off eight years later in 1833 shortly before William's death – a good indication of the success William was enjoying from his new mill. When further improvements were required William's sons put their hands into their pockets to provide the necessary funds. In 1837 the resources of the whole family were needed to take a long lease on two plots of land adjoining Caldershaw known as Gooseholds. In the same year they also bought the Tops of Spotland estate for which they paid £1,155. This was in the same year that Thomas Heap purchased the Shepherd Mill in Norden for his younger brother, John.

It is difficult to know how they managed to find the necessary finance to fund these purchases, but it seems likely they must have taken out further loans. Certainly there was the involvement of a James Booth, druggist. He was the original owner of the land and subsequently re-leased it back from the family. In 1847 they took out a lease on Catley Lane from the Trustees of Bury Grammar School which included the water rights providing the water power for their adjoining Fulling Mill.[1]

It is easy to understand why the family were willing to finance these new developments. Firstly, it was a good investment and continued to give a good return for the money invested as the business grew and flourished. Secondly, it kept the control of the business firmly in the hands of the family. Thirdly, it was part of the Wesleyan Methodist ethic that families should stick together and look after each other: family came first, others a poor second.

The family continued to invest in the business after it became a limited company in 1893 and for many years nearly all the shares were owned by members of the family. Not surprisingly they held onto their shares as year after year the company paid a dividend of over 10%. This figure may seem somewhat generous to us today but in those golden days it was not uncommon for small family concerns to pay dividends as high as 20%. In addition to the shares, the family was encouraged to make a loan to the company which guaranteed a return of 4% redeemable on demand.

Such arrangements were all very well when everything in the financial garden was lovely. But when faced with the harsher economic climate of the thirties the family began to ask for their loans to be repaid, and for a short period the company had to impose an embargo on repayment. Dividends were also falling. In several years there was no dividend at all which caused considerable hardship for family members who had no alternative source of income.

The family firm distrusted the whole idea of banks being used as a source of money and it may well have been the Fenton's Bank affair, in which one member of the family was closely involved, that was partially responsible for this. In about 1812 Messrs Rhodes, Garlick and Co. of Halifax opened a bank in Rochdale. After a few years the bank had to stop payments and it was taken over by Clement Royds and Co. It then amalgamated with the Manchester and Salford Bank which later became William Deacon's Bank in the Butts. Banking was not without its problems in those early days. A multitude of small private banks were opening all over the country, the majority of which would either fail or be taken over by the larger concerns. One such was J. and J. Fenton and Sons Bank which opened in Rochdale in 1819 and then went spectacularly bust in 1878 with some 12,000 depositors, and liabilities exceeding assets by more than £200,000.

The directors and partners of the bank consisted of various members of the Fenton family, together with Mr Jonathan Nield, a local share and stockbroker, who had been connected with the bank over many years and was one of its biggest customers. It transpired that for many years well over half the capital of the bank had been lent out to Mr Nield, the sum at risk increasing every year, with Mr Nield using the monies to invest in his own business. When the books came to be inspected it was discovered that £615,000 had been invested in the Cornwall Minerals Railway Company, in Copper Mines in Canada, and in the Baxenden Turkey Red Dyeing Co. All were found to be practically worthless, although it was argued, with some justification as was later shown, that they all had good prospects.

With most of the small investors living in Rochdale the outcry was loud and immediate action demanded. By some means, which is not made clear, Joshua Heap found himself elected as Chairman of the shareholders action group, and a very vociferous and outspoken Chairman he proved to be. It is not disclosed whether Joseph held shares in the bank, but that seems to be the only logical explanation for his involvement. Regrettably it developed into a slanging match between Joshua and Simon Nield as Chairman of the Bank, all of which was gleefully reported in minute detail by the Rochdale Observer.[2] The Chairman of the bank was quoted as having said: 'Mr Joshua Heap seems to represent a class of people who are prone to prejudge even the most important of questions, to form conclusions first and seek evidence to support them afterwards, rejecting everything which does not support their views and treating people with discourtesy and distrust who do not think as they think or say as they say'

After several exchanges of this nature it became clear that nothing other than bankruptcy or liquidation would satisfy the shareholders and so it proved when the bank went into liquidation. There is little doubt that Joseph Heap was largely instrumental in this. Had he used his leadership of the shareholders to pursue a different argument, the bank might have survived as by the time the final dividend was paid to the creditors there had been significant increases in the value of some of the shares.

Once the arrangements for the liquidation were agreed, Mr Robert Taylor Heape JP took over as chairman, a gentlemen, who it was said, possessed the esteem and confidence of all – something which could not have been said of his predecessor, Joshua Heap. Nevertheless the arrangements for the liquidation of the assets went ahead. This included the sale of Samuel Nield's collection of art and paintings which were considerable and the sale of his large Victorian Gothic mansion of Dunster on Manchester Road. To add insult to injury, Joshua Heap purchased Dunster from the Trustees at a fraction of its true value and his family continued to live there long after Joshua's premature death some years later.

Joshua didn't have many years to enjoy his new found wealth. In December of 1886, while attending the wool auctions in London with his cousin William, he collapsed and died at the Holborne Viaduct hotel following a performance of the Mikado. He was only 50 years of age and left two sons, both of whom were hardly into their teens. The funeral was held at the Rochdale Cemetery where his remains were interred in the Dissenters portion of the cemetery. It was the usual magnificent affair, the horses pulling the hearse decorated with black nodding plumes and followed by over 27 carriages. As was customary in those days not a single woman was present at the ceremony.

Joshua left an estate of £102,494.13s, a not inconsiderable sum for those days. Most of his money came from his shares in Kelsall and Kemp. Under the terms of his engagement, the firm was required to buy him out, which they duly did although not without some considerable difficulty. Robert Slack decided they could only do this by dissolving the partnership and forming a private company to take over the business. The new firm flourished, and it is an interesting footnote that in 1907 the flannel manufactory of Thomas Heap of Milnrow was acquired by Kelsall and Kemp when there were no longer any members of the family interested in carrying on the business.

Joshua Heap undoubtedly was a strong and forceful character and he cannot have been an easy man to deal with. He said what he thought and stood by his convictions. He certainly made his mark (and his fortune). He was said to be the first person in Rochdale to install his own telephone in 1881 – one wonders who he had to talk to! He was not a politician, although he favoured the Unionists. He stood briefly for Council as an Independent as he did not believe that national politics should enter into local elections. He interested himself in the workings of the Tramway Company and successfully negotiated a price reduction from the Railway Company for the transport of wool from London to Rochdale. He was an active member of the Manchester Chamber of Commerce and Director of the Equitable Fire Insurance Company. He was one of the original members of the Militia Club. Under a blunt and reserved exterior he had a kindly heart and numerous instances came to light after his death reflecting his large heartedness and charitable disposition.

That should have been the end of the story but fate wasn't done with this family yet. On 6th January 1903 the body of Captain Ernest Heap, Joshua's younger son, was found dead in the harness room in the stables attached to Dunster House. It was clear that he had shot himself with the gun lying near the body. No reason could be found for the suicide. Ernest held his commission in the Militia attached to the Lancashire Fusiliers. The Militia were the precursors of the Territorial Army of which the 6th Battalion the Lancashire Fusiliers was to become the local unit with which many of the family were to serve during the two world wars which lay just over the horizon. His brother, Stephen, died aged 49 in 1927, but we know nothing more other than that he went to Cambridge where he graduated MA and LLB.

The whole family is buried together in a large grave in the Rochdale Cemetery surmounted by a vast urn and inconveniently hidden by trees. Their mother, Alice, outlived them all and died in her eighty-third year, all they could find to inscribe on the gravestone was 'she did her best' – what an epitaph and what an end to a tragic family.

But even then fate wasn't done with this family. After Alice's death the family home of Dunster was put up for sale, but no buyer could be found for this Gothic monstrosity as it was riddled with dry rot. The house had to be demolished and the land sold for development.

References

1 Harte, Negley. Unpublished history of Samuel Heap and Son, 1964
2 *Rochdale Observer*. Numerous articles reporting the collapse of the bank, 1879

9

DR SAMUEL HEAP: 1839–1899

On 13th February 1868 John Coates, cattle dealer, sold the leasehold of a plot of land comprising 68 Spotland Road and numbers 2 and 4 Emma Street to Samuel Heap described as a fuller of Caldershaw. A similar lease was signed two days later for 70 Spotland Road. An isolated event, you might think, but one that was to become a key event in the history of our side of the family.

The plot of land was bounded by the turnpike road running between Rochdale and Edenfield to the south, Emma Street to the west and Peel Street to the north. The turnpike road is shown as Clarkes Lane on the 1851 OS map, although Clarkes Lane as we know it today runs parallel to Emma Street to the west. The turnpike road was to become Spotland Road.

The terms of the lease required Samuel 'within one year to erect with stone or brick...in a workmanlike manner and finish one good firm substantial dwelling house, the house to be set back from the turnpike road by 4 yards at least, this area to be used for garden or ornamental purposes etc. etc.' He was further required 'not to carry on any noxious business'.

So was built Leven House at 70 Spotland Road, where I was to spend my childhood and which was to remain my father's home until it was taken over in about 1964 by the Spotland Road Group Medical Practice. The house itself was well built, of two storeys at the front and three at the rear – the extra floor being added by my father to provide a waiting room for patients on the ground floor and two bedrooms in the attic for the living-in maid. My father added a small greenhouse that projected upwards through the centre section of the flat roof in which he propagated his geraniums for planting in the window boxes at the front of the house facing Spotland Road. Daffodils and crocuses in the spring were followed by geraniums and dark blue lobelia in the summer months. Later in the summer the geraniums would be attacked by caterpillars and my father would pick them off with a pair of Spencer-Wells forceps.

Behind the house was an open yard and a two-storey building with stabling for the horse and carriage. The upper floor provided storage for the large containers of drugs for use in the dispensary. The drugs would be delivered by Duncan and Flockhart, retail pharmacy suppliers. Some of the bulk liquid medicines would be delivered in large carboys enclosed in a wicker basket. They would also deliver cartons containing medicine bottles of various sizes, my particular favourites were the blue and green ribbed poison bottles. The cartons and containers would be hoisted up into the loft by means of a Weston Differential pulley system through a door which opened out above the yard. I could play quite happily for hours up in the loft, discovering all sorts of treasures which had long been discarded or placed up there for storage. There was a splendid black pram with a well in the middle so the children could sit up and dangle their feet.

These arrangements for dispensing medicines continued until the inception of the National Health Service in 1946. It may seem remarkable to us today but Insulin and Vitamin B12 for the treatment of Pernicious Anaemia only became available in the 1930s, sulphonamides a few years later, penicillin was discovered in 1943 during the war. I recall my father treating my sister with one of the first batches of penicillin which had to be administered by drip straight into the site of the infection. She had a virulent cellulitis of her thigh which was threatening to turn into septicaemia, undoubtedly without penicillin she would have died. Apart from digoxin and some of the earlier diuretics, most medicine came in bottles which amounted to little more than placebos.

The earlier OS maps show houses on both sides of Peel Street at the time Leven House was built, but after that it was open common land until you reached Falinge Road and the boundary wall of Falinge park. 'Brooklyn' at 68 Spotland Road was built at the same time as Leven House, theoretically semi-detached it was really one and the same building. The history of 68 Spotland Road is somewhat confusing, but the 1881 census shows it occupied by William Tweedale Heap and his family. Whether it had been in the possession of the family both before and after that date is not clear.

Why did Samuel purchase this plot of land and build a very substantial house which he himself would never occupy? His son, young Samuel – always known as Sam within the family, was studying medicine at Glasgow where he qualified in 1862 LFPS (Licentiate Faculty of Physicians and Surgeons) and LM (Licentiate in Midwifery). Sam then returned to Rochdale where he became an assistant to Dr Cheetham. It was not until 1869 that he set up in practice on his own account at Leven House in the property his father had built for him on the plot of land he had purchased from John Coates, the cattle dealer.

Samuel, like all the other members of the family, was born at Caldershaw in 1839 and he was to die at Leven House on 24th December 1899. Sam's wife had always been known as Annie 'Scotland' within the family, presumably because they couldn't get their tongues round her maiden name which was Ann Jane McFadyen. Annie was the daughter of Thomas Brooks McFadyen, described as 'clothier', deceased at the time of the marriage. Annie was only 17 years of age when she married Sam on 12th August 1862. They are both recorded as living at 17 Garden Street, Glasgow and the marriage took place at their home as was often the case in the Free Church of Scotland. Sam's elder brother, William Tweedale, attended as a witness. We can only make an educated guess as to what might have been behind Sam's decision to marry such a young girl so far away from his own home. Sam was said to be 'of a retiring disposition' and one wonders whether he saw this as his chance to escape the claustrophobic environment of Caldershaw with his numerous relatives and their overwhelming Wesleyan beliefs.

Annie's age and the circumstances of the marriage inevitably raises questions. Were they living together before the marriage? Was she pregnant? – but her first child Thomas was not born until 1864. Whatever the circumstances, this seventeen year old lass came down from Glasgow to Rochdale with her husband where she had to set up a new house, help to establish and run a medical practice, and cope with a host of Heap relatives. One can but admire her courage and determination.

She bore Sam a further four children, the twins William and Harry, a daughter Annie always known as Cissie, and the youngest Charles Herbert. Annie was to outlive her husband and all her children, finally dying on 21st February 1927 at the fine old age of 83.

The 1881 census describes William as a medical student and Henry, his twin brother, as a veterinary student. Sadly neither seem to have achieved his objective as by 1901 William is shown as chemist's assistant (drugs) and Henry as living on his own means. It had always been said that Dr Sam's son didn't have the necessary brain to be a doctor, and his father bought a chemist shop for him at the corner of Hudson Street and Spotland Road, close to the practice. The chemist's shop was still there when I was a lad, and

Chart 8

Descendant chart for Dr Samuel Heap

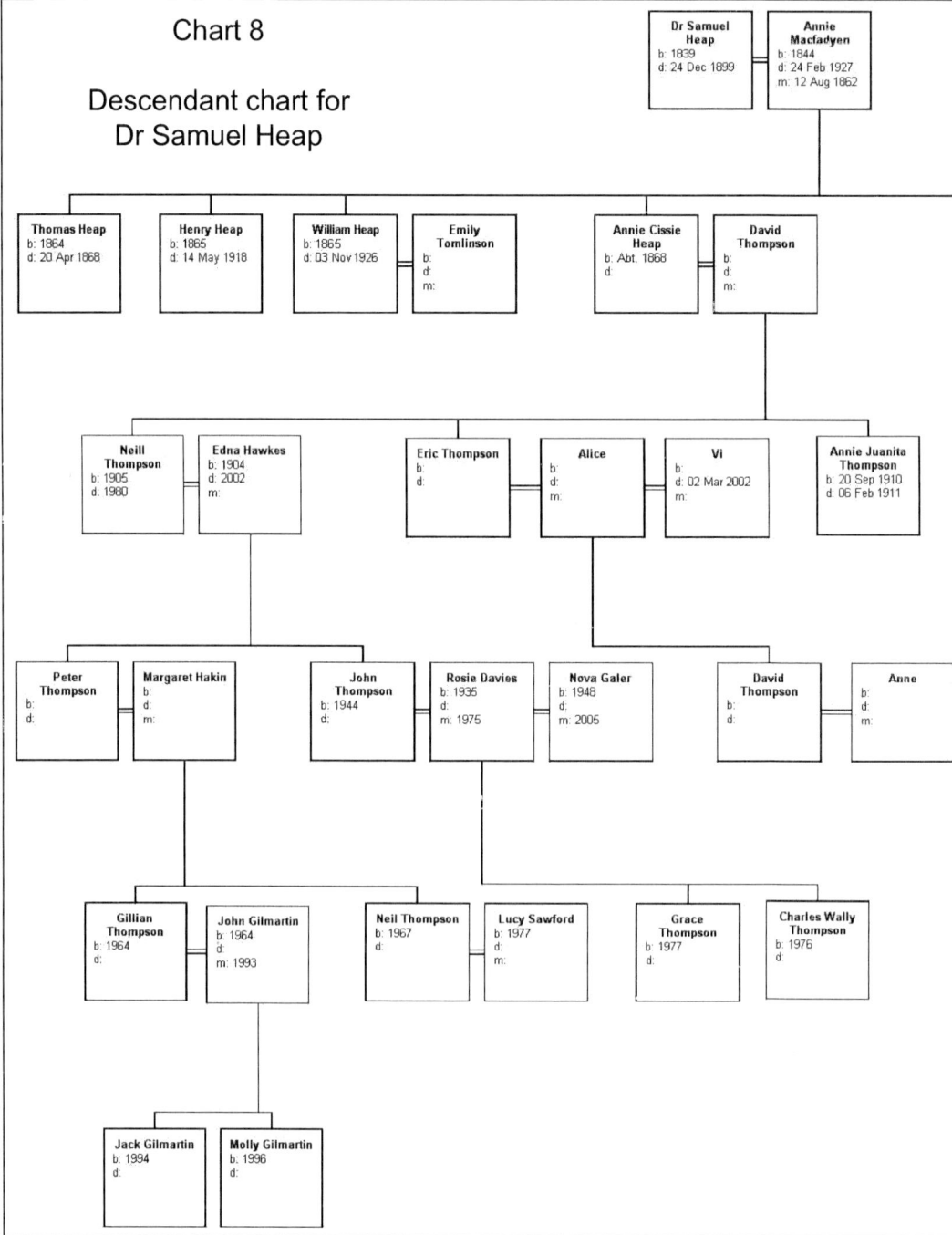

Dr Samuel Heap	Annie Macfadyen
b: 1839	b: 1844
d: 24 Dec 1899	d: 24 Feb 1927
	m: 12 Aug 1862

Thomas Heap
b: 1864
d: 20 Apr 1868

Henry Heap
b: 1865
d: 14 May 1918

William Heap
b: 1865
d: 03 Nov 1926

Emily Tomlinson
b:
d:
m:

Annie Cissie Heap
b: Abt. 1868
d:

David Thompson
b:
d:
m:

Neill Thompson
b: 1905
d: 1980

Edna Hawkes
b: 1904
d: 2002
m:

Eric Thompson
b:
d:

Alice
b:
d:
m:

Vi
b:
d: 02 Mar 2002
m:

Annie Juanita Thompson
b: 20 Sep 1910
d: 06 Feb 1911

Peter Thompson
b:
d:

Margaret Hakin
b:
d:
m:

John Thompson
b: 1944
d:

Rosie Davies
b: 1935
d:
m: 1975

Nova Galer
b: 1948
d:
m: 2005

David Thompson
b:
d:

Anne
b:
d:
m:

Gillian Thompson
b: 1964
d:

John Gilmartin
b: 1964
d:
m: 1993

Neil Thompson
b: 1967
d:

Lucy Sawford
b: 1977
d:
m:

Grace Thompson
b: 1977
d:

Charles Wally Thompson
b: 1976
d:

Jack Gilmartin
b: 1994
d:

Molly Gilmartin
b: 1996
d:

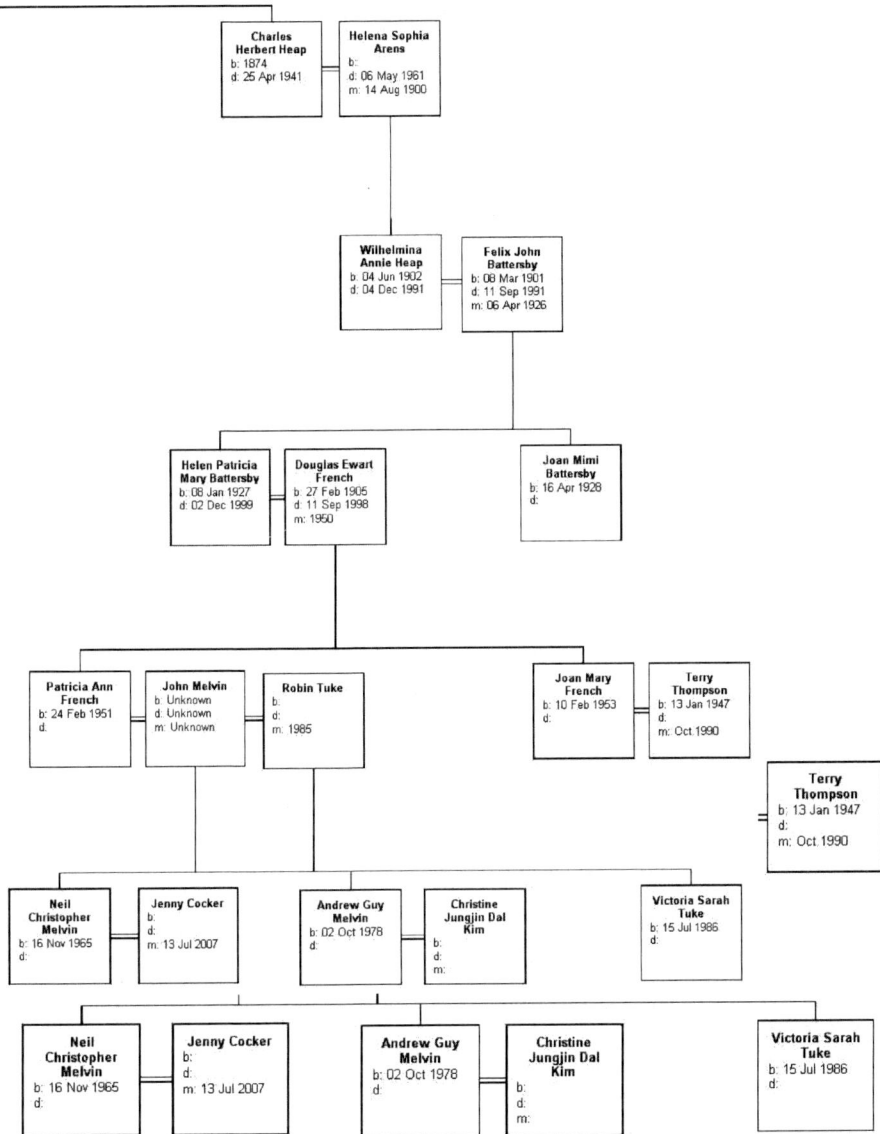

Charles Herbert Heap
b: 1874
d: 25 Apr 1941

Helena Sophia Arens
b:
d: 06 May 1961
m: 14 Aug 1900

Wilhelmina Annie Heap
b: 04 Jun 1902
d: 04 Dec 1991

Felix John Battersby
b: 08 Mar 1901
d: 11 Sep 1991
m: 06 Apr 1926

Helen Patricia Mary Battersby
b: 08 Jan 1927
d: 02 Dec 1999

Douglas Ewart French
b: 27 Feb 1905
d: 11 Sep 1998
m: 1950

Joan Mimi Battersby
b: 16 Apr 1928
d:

Patricia Ann French
b: 24 Feb 1951
d:

John Melvin
b: Unknown
d: Unknown
m: Unknown

Robin Tuke
b:
d:
m: 1985

Joan Mary French
b: 10 Feb 1953
d:

Terry Thompson
b: 13 Jan 1947
d:
m: Oct.1990

Terry Thompson
b: 13 Jan 1947
d:
m: Oct.1990

Neil Christopher Melvin
b: 16 Nov 1965
d:

Jenny Cocker
b:
d:
m: 13 Jul 2007

Andrew Guy Melvin
b: 02 Oct 1978
d:

Christine Jungjin Dal Kim
b:
d:
m:

Victoria Sarah Tuke
b: 15 Jul 1986
d:

Neil Christopher Melvin
b: 16 Nov 1965
d:

Jenny Cocker
b:
d:
m: 13 Jul 2007

Andrew Guy Melvin
b: 02 Oct 1978
d:

Christine Jungjin Dal Kim
b:
d:
m:

Victoria Sarah Tuke
b: 15 Jul 1986
d:

it was closely linked with the practice when I joined my father in 1962

His only daughter Annie 'Cissie', married a solicitor, David Thompson, who had his office in Rochdale and there are many descendants. The youngest child, Charles Herbert, known as 'Charlie', was born in 1874 and became an analytical chemist working for Coates. He met his wife to be, Helena Sophia (Zophy) Arens while she was on holiday in England. Her father, Friedrich Wilhelm Arens, is described as a general merchant on the marriage certificate and as a border guard for North Schweiburg on his daughter's birth certificate. Zophy's German ancestry caused problems for them during the 1914-18 war when they lived in constant fear that she might be interned as an enemy alien.

By all accounts it was a happy and contented household, and was to remain so until Sam's early and untimely death on 24th December 1899. His obituary said that Dr Heap '...did not accept any public office but devoted the whole of his time to his professional duties in which he took a deep interest, and he was held in high esteem by many who availed themselves of his services'. Apparently he had been in failing health for some years attributed to overwork, and for the last 18 weeks of his life was confined to his room.

Sam was laid to rest in the Rochdale cemetery after a short service held at the house. As a mark of respect all the blinds on the houses in Spotland Road and on the way to the cemetery were drawn. Twenty carriages were to follow the hearse, and there were numerous floral tributes including those from both my paternal and maternal grandparents. Curiously no women were listed amongst those attending the funeral, not even Sam's widow, presumably this was the custom in those days.

I have always had a feeling of empathy for Sam and his family, living in the same house in which I was to spend my childhood. Did Harry and William occupy the same bedroom as I did? Did they also play up in the loft amongst the new medicine bottles? It would, I think, have pleased Sam to know that when Walter Joss retired, the practice which he had started would be taken on by his great nephew, my father, Ellis Clifford Heap.

Sam's choice of career was perhaps surprising. His two elder brothers, William Tweedale and Charles, were already involved in running the family firm and his younger brother, Herbert, was destined to run the family's mills in America. Although there may not have been room for Sam in the family concern, his uncles owned mills in Norden, Littleborough and Newhey and there would surely have been a place for him had he wanted it. But medicine offered an acceptable alternative and Sam's father would have been happy to support him and find the necessary fees.

Medicine in the late 19thC didn't offer the prestigious career which it does today, and recruitment to the Victorian medical profession was from people of modest social backgrounds compared with those entering the Law and the Church. Their social origins gave them no claims to gentlemanly status and their professional activities were inimical to any such claim. This inferior status discouraged the sons of the gentry from entering the profession and thus raising its social status, but as far as Samuel was concerned, it was a step in the right direction. The social landscape of Britain was fissured by differences in class, gender and ethnicity and it was difficult in the extreme to jump from one class to another.

Sam entered medical training at an exciting and crucial stage in the development of medical services in the United Kingdom. The Medical Act of 1858 introduced the requirement for all doctors to be registered, although was not until 1886 that qualifications in all the three disciplines of medicine, surgery and obstetrics were made mandatory. The 1858 Act also set up the General Medical Council to regulate the profession and superintend the examinations required on entry. It provided and maintained a medical register and was required to publish a pharmacopoeia. However, the Act disappointed the profession in that it gave them no direct protection against the 'alternative' unqualified apothecary surgeons largely responsible for providing medical care up to that time. But it did allow the registered doctor to sue for fees, and it restricted all Public Appointments such as the Poor Law Doctors, to those on the register. Newly registered doctors found themselves in a medical market in which 'alternative' and registered practitioners were poorly differentiated (in terms of advising, prescribing for, and visiting the sick) and where keen competition meant that only the fit survived. Nevertheless a start had been made, and by the end of the century the role of the general practitioner had become firmly established, and the general practitioner had become the family doctor in effect and even in name. Movements by the general practitioners to establish their own College were to be vigorously opposed by the Consultant Specialists, who saw themselves as superior beings. A further seventy five years were to pass before the general practitioners were to have their own College and I was to sit and pass the very first examination for membership.[1,2,3]

Sam chose wisely as the training provided in the medical schools of Glasgow and Edinburgh was second to none and streets ahead of the London

Teaching Hospitals. Doctors had to have a well developed clinical sense and a questioning mind as there was little to assist him in his diagnosis other than his clinical skills. Doctors would leave College under the impression that every patient's condition could be diagnosed, which was far from the case. To be suddenly thrust into the wide world could be a traumatic experience unless you had the guiding hand of a more senior colleague to whom you would be attached as an Assistant, and from whom you would learn your trade.

The format and structure of medical training, firmly established by 1880, consisted of lectures, demonstrations, and walking the wards. It was almost identical to that to which I was subjected fifty years later. The tradition of English clinical teaching was that as much as possible should be learnt by clinical observation alone: you called in diagnostic aids only when clinical observation failed to provide an answer. The work was hard and the hours of study long, both in and out of hospital, and resulted in a search for relief in rowdiness, drunkenness and debauchery…and that hadn't changed either some fifty years later!

For the aspirant general practitioner, passing the exams and getting on the register was but the start. You had to find yourself a practice and then acquire, by fair means or foul, a following of loyal patients. Sam probably had an fairly easy course. He became an assistant to Dr Cheetham, and thus had the opportunity to learn his trade under the guidance of a wiser and older colleague. His house and surgery were waiting for him in a part of the town undergoing rapid development and expansion. Above all, he had the support and companionship of his young bride who would have an important part to play in helping her husband run the practice.

The principal challenge facing the newly qualified doctor was an over supply of trained doctors in relation to the demand for their services, a situation made worse by competition from the specialists and the large number of alternative practitioners of varying kinds. At the end of the day it was the patient who made the choice and the patient who had to pay.

The general practitioner earned his income from three sources; two thirds would come from the private fees which he charged his patients, one fifth from outside appointments, and the remainder from midwifery. For some reason Sam chose not to apply for or to hold any outside appointments. A doctor could charge whatever he chose or whatever he thought the market would bear. Most doctors would increase the fees for the middle class or more wealthy patient, and reduce the fees or accept payment in kind from the poor. By 1870 fee schedules were published in an endeavour to stop doctors competing amongst themselves and undercutting and driving down the fees as a result. Fees were correlated to household rents with patients paying less than £10 rental being provided for by the Friendly Societies or Poor Law Relief. The doctor would be paid an annual retainer by the Friendly Society which in some cases could be as low as 5/- per patient. More than 50% of the population would be covered by such a scheme.

The minimum charge for a visit would be 2/6d, with some of the shilling or sixpenny doctors charging as little as 4d for medicine and 6d if the patient was examined. Midwifery was charged at £1, with up to £10 for affluent patients. Caesareans worked out at 10-30 guineas and applying forceps 2 guineas. With these sort of charges, patient pinching was an unpleasant fact of life. A doctor couldn't afford to take much time off work for fear his patients would desert him.

Running this type of system meant that the doctor had to keep vast ledgers in which to record the fees charged. I can remember my father going through the ledger once a month when the Collector, a Mr Schofield, called to hand over the months takings. It was his thankless task to travel round the town trying to extract money from patients who hadn't paid their bills. The ledger was an enormous baize-covered book with loose leaf inserts. For all I knew, it was the same book as had been in use in Sam's day.

In these days of powerful drugs, sophisticated diagnostic procedures and advanced transplant surgery, when no disease is allowed to remain hidden and few fail to respond to modern treatment methods, and the average age of survival is in the eighties and increasing every year, it is difficult to grasp the clinical challenges that would have faced Sam on an every day basis. Infectious diseases such as scarlet fever, typhus, enteric, diphtheria, poliomyelitis and measles were rife, all of which could kill and often did. There was no water borne sanitation, infant mortality in Burnley was 54.6 %, and one in five infants died during their first year of life. Tracheotomies and post-mortems were carried out on the kitchen table, and even in the 1930s my father was still carrying out tonsillectomies in the patient's own home and asphyxiating dental patients with nitrous oxide without any access to resuscitation.

There was little understanding of the mechanism of disease and it was not until 1874 that James Lister was to introduce his carbolic acid spray as he was convinced that micro-organisms were the cause of suppuration. Apart from powdered digitalis leaf and other similar herbal based remedies, there were very few specific drugs available to the general practitioner in the latter half of the 19thC. Tradition required that they provide bottles of medicine or pills, all of which could be charged for. The dispensary shelves were loaded with large Winchesters of different coloured liquids, few of which had any proven therapeutic value, and a large pestle and mortar for the mixing and grinding up of the various ointments and unguents. The bottles were labelled with abbreviated Latin names such as Mist. Nux.Vom, most of which now escape me. It still amazes me that even as late as the 1930s this formed the basis of much of my father's practice, and I would often help the dispenser as she decanted and diluted the medicines into 6 or 8oz bottles, each of which would be clearly labelled with instructions, before being carefully wrapped in shiny white paper secured with a blob of red sealing wax before being placed on the table in the waiting room for collection by the patient.

Although the 1870s birth rate was high at about 40 to 45 births per 1,000 of the population, and Sam would have to manage three or four confinements each week, the Crude Death Rate was equally high ranging from 29 to 34 per thousand compared with 10 or so today.

Coping with all this was young Sam, newly qualified out of Glasgow, with his young 18 year-old wife and a soon to be growing family, though their eldest child, Thomas, was to die at the early age of four years. The doctor's house combined both surgery and home and Sam's family of necessity shared in the life of the practice. Nights would be disturbed by the speaking tube that connected the surgery door to the doctor's bedside (the speaking tube at Leven House remained in place until well into the 1970s although it had long since ceased to be functional) and the days punctuated by patient's calls. To the doctor's wife and children, the term 'family doctor' had a second and more basic meaning.

This was a pattern of life with which I was to become familiar during my early childhood and later adolescence, the constant peeling of the strident surgery doorbell, and later the incessant ringing of the telephone which was housed in a cubby hole in the hall where hung the hats and coats. As my sister and I started to make use of the telephone to organise and plan our own lives, we were very early on given to understand by my mother that the telephone was for passing messages only and not a means of social intercourse, gossip or the exchanging of pleasantries, 'you have been on the phone long enough, dear, someone may be waiting to talk to your father' – and thus engrained in me a habit which has persisted to this day as my own children will bear witness.

❀

Dr Walter Joss

When Dr Samuel died on 28th December 1899, Dr Walter Joss succeeded to the practice. Joss was already in partnership with Samuel at the time of Samuel's death and the records suggest that he had been taken on during Samuel's last and prolonged illness that ended in his death. Joss would have been required to purchase the practice on Samuel's death, the price forming part of Samuel's estate, unless they had already entered into some form of financial agreement during Samuel's final illness. The 1901 census shows Joss living at Leven House together with William and Harry, Samuel's twin sons.

There were three ways by which an incoming doctor could establish himself in practice. He could either 'squat' and open up a surgery where he thought he might attract sufficient patients to give him some form of living; he could take a post as an Assistant with a view to Partnership; or he could purchase a practice which had become vacant either through death or retirement of the incumbent. The buying and selling of practices was one of the more iniquitous aspects of general practice prior to the inception of the National Health Service, as you were buying the goodwill of the patients who were under no obligation to continue to attend the same surgery once the new incumbent was installed. You were also purchasing the surgery premises which usually also included the doctor's family residence. Many doctors would expect to capitalise on the sum so raised on their retirement and which, in part, would provide them with a pension.

The buying and selling of practices came to an end with the inception of the NHS and the Government agreed to place a value on all existing practices on the appointed day. The doctor was given a choice, he could either forego the payment and opt into the new NHS Pension scheme at an appropriate level, or he could choose not to participate in the pension scheme and accept payment for his practice when he retired. My father, who had purchased the practice from Dr Joss, decided to opt out of the pension scheme which was hardly worth the paper it was written on, hanging on to the theoretical value of the practice, watching its value go down year after year as inflation started to bite. Some twenty years later, the Government was forced to accept that the system was grossly unfair and all the remaining doctors in the scheme were paid out for their practices and awarded a reduced pension in compensation.

Walter Joss obtained his MA at Aberdeen University in 1888 and his MB (Medicine) and his CM (Surgery) in 1892, also at Aberdeen. He was an assistant in General Practice at Pontesbury in Shropshire in 1893/4, in Birmingham, and at Wigan before joining Samuel in Rochdale. He was to remain at Leven House running the practice until my father, Ellis Clifford Heap, qualified at St Thomas' in 1924 after which he retired back to his beloved Scotland at Meikleton of Lessendrum in Huntly.

We don't know a great deal about Dr Joss. He was to remain a bachelor, looked after by his housekeeper, Becky, who on one occasion had to help him out of the bath when he got stuck, much to the embarrassment of both of them. Immediately a much larger bath was purchased and installed so that such an event could never happen again. I well remember that bath which was indeed enormous and the cause of great concern to us during the war when you were only allowed to have six inches of bath water in order to save fuel.

Walter Joss presented an impressive figure. A large man to start with but made even more imposing by his large black beard and shiny black top hat, which must have added at least twelve inches to his overall height, as he was driven on his rounds by his coachman, William, in his open carriage. Horse and carriage were kept in the stables across the yard at the back of the house. One of his then young patients told me that he had very large hands with stiff white cuffs which used to cut into you while he was examining you. In those early days many homes were still lit by gas and when the doctor was expected to call you took the precaution of removing the gas mantle as failure to do so inevitably resulted in his topper doing the job for you, a cloud of white fragments would cascade all over the doctor's hat and coat and her mother would have to bring out the small brush to brush away the particles.

But the young Doctor Heap, she went on to say, had a way with young children, he had nicer tasting 'horrible' medicine, gentler hands and no cast iron sharp cuffs shooting out from beneath the coat sleeves; 'pear drop' medicine became a thing of the past as did hyssop tea, heaven forbid!

The Practice had a half day on Thursdays when Dr Joss would travel by train to Manchester to frequent his Club. The Club porters would see him well settled into one of the carriages on the last train and his coachmen, William, would meet the train as it drew into Rochdale station, the inebriated doctor would be helped out of the train, into his carriage and taken off home to bed.

By 1924 Walter Joss was ready to retire and my father, having passed the Conjoint examination MRCS LRCP, was summoned back to Rochdale to take over the practice before he was able to take his London degree –

something which I think he regretted later in life.

References

All three references apply to that section which describes General Practice.

1 Digby, Anne: *The evolution of General Practice 1850-1948*. Oxford University Press
2 Loudan, Irvine: *Medical Care and the General Practitioner 1750-1850*. Clarendon Press, 1986
3 Mackenzie, Sir James, a Biography. Burnley 1879-1905

10

THE VICTORIANS: WILLIAM TWEEDALE
HEAP AND CHARLES HEAP

William Tweedale was the eldest son of Samuel Heap and grandson of William the Founder. He started work in the family business age 15, his name first appearing in the wages book in October 1848 when he is recorded as having been paid the princely sum of 5s.2d. for six days work. At that time the business was being run by Samuel and his younger brother James, assisted by one of their cousins also rather confusingly named William. James left the business in 1855, having sold his share of the mill to Samuel, and in 1859 Samuel bought up the remaining shares of his brothers and sisters and the interest of the shadowy Booth. The mill and the land at Caldershaw were to be transferred for £3,600 to the name of Samuel's eldest son, William Tweedale Heap. It seems likely that Samuel and William Tweedale had been in partnership since 1855. The business was now carried on in the name of Samuel Heap and Son, a name it retained until it was finally bought out and taken over by Courtaulds in 1964.

Samuel and William Tweedale carried on the fulling business until 1867 when William Tweedale left the firm to take up a second career with William Tatham and Co, Engineers and Machinists, he was then 35 years-old. It is far from clear why William Tweedale left Samuel Heap and Son. Perhaps he had a disagreement with his father, perhaps they found they couldn't work together.

The Roach Iron Works in River Street had belonged to Robert Tempest and James Tomlinson. They manufactured carding engines and machines for breaking up shoddy. In 1862 a serious fire destroyed the works and the partnership was dissolved. Robert then built a new foundry at The Top o'the hill and named it the Sandford Works. Unfortunately the American Civil War intervened, resulting in a catastrophic loss of trade. Robert had to mortgage the works which were assigned to his wife, Hannah. Robert then died of an inflamed liver in 1866 and his widow sold out to William Tweedale Heap and William Tatham who renamed the works The Vulcan Iron Works. The business must have been on the verge of bankruptcy and no doubt the two Williams got it for a song.

It is reasonable to ask what William Tweedale was doing entering into a partnership in a foundry and engineering works, a trade about which he knew nothing. It is likely that William Tweedale saw the opportunity and went for it. He provided the cash and the business acumen, while William Tatham, essentially a hands-on engineer, provided the technical know-how. Whatever the reasons it was clearly a success. Much of the earlier work of the firm lay in converting carding engines to work cotton waste, and by 1868 they were trading with Holland, Prussia, Belgium, France and Italy and were later to export and service machinery all over the world. William Tweedale sold out and withdrew from the partnership in 1881, having no doubt made a very reasonable profit on his initial investment. He then rejoined his brother in running the family firm at Caldershaw. This was expanding rapidly, father Samuel having died in 1873.

The subsequent history of William Tathams is not essential to our story but will be of interest to those familiar with the area. In 1881 Samuel Porritt of Porritt and Sons, Bamford Woollen Mills, bought a rag-tearing machine from Tathams. Porritt's young 15 year-old grandson, Louis Porritt, had always wanted to become an engineer, and he started work at Tathams. In 1890 young Louis was taken into partnership and William Tathams remained in the ownership of the Porritt family until its eventual demise in the sixties.

In 1867 Charles Heap, one of William Tweedale's younger brothers, had entered into partnership with his father in place of William Tweedale. It was Charles Heap who took over sole control of the business when his father died six years later. It was his dynamic direction that was responsible for the growth and development of the firm over the next fifty years. William Tweedale had retained his financial share in the business and in 1889 went back into partnership with his brother. William Tweedale had never given up his involvement in the mills; he was trustee of his father's estate which legally owned the mills; and in 1887 he had joined with his brother in the purchase of the Brookside mills. No doubt to his later regret, he was also financially involved in his brother's American ventures. The partnership with Charles was relatively short-lived as in 1893 they set up a limited company retaining the name of Samuel Heap and Son. Charles received £33,700 of shares and William Tweedale £27,250

Of their father, Samuel Heap, we know little apart from his having bequeathed his name to the family firm. His picture appears to show us a kindly man if you can make such judgements from a photograph. He was born at Caldershaw on 29 June 1807, he married Ann Tweedale, and died at Caldershaw aged 67 years of diabetes mellitus on 6 November 1873. He left all his monies to his widow, having made provision for the education of his children, appointing William Tweedale, Charles and Dr Samuel as his executors. Charles, his partner in the business, was empowered to purchase his father's share of the business but until that day had to pay rent for the share that went into his estate. The total estate was valued at less than £8,000. There was no obituary in the Observer other than a bald statement in the deaths column with an added note which bizarrely said 'Friends will please accept this information'.

Samuel had been involved in various land transactions relating to the firm and had built the new mill in 1848. He seems to have been content to continue the operation of fuller, dyer and finisher along the same lines as his father. He would have replaced the old water driven hammers with steam-driven rotating machines, introduced chemical methods to bleach the cloth, and drying sheds would have been built to replace the old tenter racks and hooks, but essentially the process would have been little changed.

Samuel was a staunch Wesleyan like his father, and brought up his children in the faith. Surviving relics include a Methodist membership card issued to a Samuel Heap recognising his membership of the Union Street Chapel, and a curious entry in a local tract stating 'Mr Samuel Heap, 6 feet 2 inches in height, a local Preacher amongst the Wesleyans, was a very powerful man. He carried 960lbs in four packs of skins a distance of about 30 yards', but whether this was our Samuel or some other person by the same name is not known.[1]

With Samuel dead we come to our two Victorians, the brothers William Tweedale Heap and Charles Heap. They came to embody the very essence of the self-made, hard-headed Lancastrian businessman, dressed in his top hat and frock coat with golden Albert and chain stretched across his ample and increasing girth, liberal both in thought and politics. They had seen their family progress from the hand-powered looms and spindles that filled their ancestors cottages, through the water driven hammers of the fulling mills, and into the age of steam – making the most of the changes brought about by the Industrial Revolution

It should not be thought that William Tweedale and Charles were alone in this. They had brothers and cousins scattered across south east Lancashire, many of whom were following their example. Their younger brother, Dr Samuel Heap[2] was to escape the suffocating embrace of the family to enter one of the professions; their cousin Joshua[3] was to become Managing Director of Kelsall and Kemps; their other brother, Henry Herbert, was to be despatched to America to manage the firm's mills in the States – a venture doomed to failure.

William Tweedale and Charles represented the two sides of the family that were to provide the family firm with most of its Directors and all the Chairmen of the Board until they were taken over by Courtaulds.

Before we study the lives of William Tweedale and Charles in greater detail, we should first take a closer look at the social structure of the country at that time. By the end of the first half of the 19thC the major changes that we now recognise as the Industrial Revolution had come to fruition, and the transition from a predominantly agricultural nation to an industrial nation was almost complete. In the process there had been an enormous population shift away from the countryside to the new towns to provide the workers to man the machines and service the new industries.

The result was chaos: hundreds of workers and their families crammed together in inadequate housing, an almost total absence of a proper sewage disposal system, an impure water supply giving rise to waterborne infections and epidemics. In 1841 half the streets in the centre of the town had no sewers or drains. In the Packer Street area, if there were water closets, they would be shared between ten or more houses. The crude death rate of 45 per thousand was one of the highest in the country and Rochdale's record the worst in Lancashire. The country was in the throes of an economic depression. In Rochdale the conditions were dreadful. Weavers wages had fallen by over 40%. In 1841 Rochdale's newly elected Member of Parliament told the House of Commons that 4,000 people living in the town were trying to survive and feed their families on wages of 1s.10d per week. In response the Government passed a series of Local Improvement Acts granting powers to make improvements but little was done. The population of the town had grown to 25,000 with a further 40,000 in the surrounding villages. There was continued opposition to the new Poor law of 1834, and in John Leach they even had a Chartist Mayor.

The first Improvement Act of 1825 had established a Board of Commissioners which replaced the Parish Vestry and its five unpaid officers of Church Warden,

Parish Constable, Overseer of the Poor, Surveyor of Highways and the Field Master or Reeve. Between them they had been responsible for the town and the way the municipality was run. This Parish Vestry system dated back to Elizabethan times and had long outlived it's usefulness.

Matters were not improved when in 1840 a battle broke out over the legality of the Church rates which could only be raised with the consent of the ratepayers. The church rate was a compulsory levy raised for the repair, maintenance and running of the Parish Church of St Chad. This arrangement obviously did not suit the growing number of middle class chapel goers, amongst whom would have been Samuel Heap and other members of the family, all of whom were staunch Wesleyan Methodists. All hell was let loose as the votes were taken and counted in the churchyard with the rival factions standing on top of the tomb stones haranguing each other in a most unchristian manner. The Vicar, the high church Tory Dr Molesworth, won the first vote but by a very narrow margin, a second vote produced the same result. Further repeated votes still gave the Vicar a majority but with an even narrower margin, and the Vicar, who already enjoyed a large revenue, wisely withdrew and in 1843 the rate was dropped. If the townspeople of Rochdale could react in such a vociferous manner to such a relatively minor matter as a church rate, how would they respond to the political battles which lay ahead when they came to elect their first town council.

William Tweedale would have been 21 when the second Rochdale Improvement Act was passed in 1853. This gave the town one of the most democratic local franchises in the country. It gave the local franchise to all male owners and occupiers of rateable property in the town and incorporated clauses that reduced the number of Commissioners who had been responsible for running and administering the town. It also dealt with land belonging to the new Council, the local gas works (one of the earliest in the country), cemeteries, markets and a local police force.

In 1856 a Charter of Incorporation was granted to the town and Borough of Rochdale which now became a Municipal Corporation with its own Mayor, Aldermen, Burgesses, and elected Councillors. They took over the duties of the Commissioners and any land and possessions that had belonged to them.

A full-scale row broke out when they came to decide on the number of Wards to be represented on the new Council. The Liberal mill owners wanted eight wards, which they thought would enable them to hold a controlling vote, whereas Thomas Livsey (we shall hear more of this redoubtable fighter for local rights) leader of the Radical faction and supported by a small Tory rump, wanted only three. Eventually the dispute had to be settled by a Parliamentary Enquiry which came down on the side of the Radicals and the three-ward council. Livsey and his supporters were triumphant. But common sense and sanity were to prevail, and when Livsey put himself forward as candidate for Mayor in 1863 he was defeated by the casting vote of the Chairman, a Tory. Livsey was to die of liver failure only three months later at the early age of 48, a death brought on by his intemperate living. When Livsey died, so did radicalism, the future belonged to the reformers, the rising middle classes and Gladstonian Liberalism.

William Tweedale was born and brought up at Caldershaw. He was educated at Tulketh Hall College in Preston and then, as we have seen, started work in the family firm at the age of 15. He would have been 21 when the second Improvement Act was passed and 26 when all this bickering was taking place. One wonders what he and the family made of it, and which way they cast their votes, particularly since William Tweedale was to make his third career in local politics. Elected Councillor for East Spotland in 1881 at the age of 48, he was elected Mayor in 1889, 1890 and 1891 and Alderman for Wardleworth East in 1892, a position he was to hold until his death in 1917 at the ripe old age of 85. He had been a Magistrate since 1893.

William Tweedale lived at Eversleigh, where he and his wife, Mary Watson of Gisburn, brought up his large family. Mary predeceased him on 29 September 1896. Sadly Eversleigh, like so many of the older houses in Rochdale, has been demolished and is now the site of the BUPA Highfield Private Hospital. I remember it well, although I never managed to find an excuse to view the interior. Set back some way from Manchester Road opposite Castlemere Street, it was approached by a straight drive terminating in a circular flower bed in front of the main entrance, always filled with bright red geraniums. Prior to Eversleigh, William Tweedale had lived at 68 Spotland Road, another of these family houses where he would have had his younger brother, Dr Samuel Heap, as his next door neighbour. From Spotland Road he moved to Beech House on Manchester Road before making his final move to Eversleigh.

Like his brother Charles, he was a strict Wesleyan Methodist. He was involved in the building of the Lanehead Chapel, where for many years he was a Sunday school teacher, treasurer of the school and leader of the Society class. He worshipped at Lanehead until he moved to Eversleigh when he attended the Castlemere Street Wesleyan Chapel. He acted as circuit steward at Castlemere street where his funeral was to take place. He was a lifelong abstainer and a warm supporter of the temperance cause – an adherence that was to cause him problems in the elections of 1890 when he was opposed in the Council elections by Mr Stephen Leach Lee, landlord of the Roebuck Hotel, standing as a Conservative, and a Socialist Mr Jacob Holmes. The Publicans organised their supporters using every horse, cart and carriage they could lay their hands on … but William Tweedale retained his seat.

He was one of the founders and Director of the Crawford Spinning Co, chairman of the Boundary Spinning Co. in Oldham and chairman of the Ramie Co. at Bredbury near Stockport.

He served on the Watch and General Purposes Committee but it was as Chairman of the Waterworks Committee since 1890 that he was to play his main part. His knowledge of both the practical side and the administration was encyclopaedic, making it virtually impossible to defeat him in debate. He would go to almost any lengths to secure an adequate and clean water supply for the town, often at considerable expense through the building of reservoirs and dams.

In debate he was an effective speaker, clear, lucid, logical and often hard hitting. When he had made up his mind on a subject he was determined, not to say obstinate, but he was always respected for his honesty and integrity. A man of unusual reserve, in public he could appear dour and harsh but underneath was a kindly man, characteristics I recognise in some of his descendants. A liberal of the old school, he was in latter years out of sympathy with recent trends in democratic thought.

By the time William Tweedale was first elected to the Town Council in 1881 there had been massive improvements in the town under the guidance and direction of the new town council, first elected in 1856 following Rochdale being made a Municipal Borough. The Corporation had acquired the undertaking and property of the Rochdale Waterworks Co in 1866, Broadfield and part of the Glebe lands in 1867, and had started work on the construction of the Cowm Reservoir. They had built for themselves a magnificent Town Hall in 1871, a splendid example of Victorian Gothic and often described as one of the seven wonders of Lancashire. Unfortunately the highly decorated tower and spire caught fire in 1883 and had to be replaced by the smaller and rather more modest structure that exists today. The first public library was opened in 1872, the public baths in Smith street in 1868, the turnpike tolls were abolished, a new post office in 1875, also the year in which a Medical Officer of Health was appointed – an appointment long overdue given the appalling record of public health with typhus still rampant in the 1860s. There was still much work to be done in establishing a proper sewage disposal system.

The Rochdale system of night soil disposal was still in operation in 1870 with ten-gallon drums of deodorised waste matter collected on a daily basis and taken by cart to the treatment works on Entwistle Road.

In 1883 the inefficient Manchester, Bacup, Oldham and Rochdale Steam Tramway extended their system to Rochdale. This was replaced by a Corporation owned and operated electrical tramway in 1904. Six more parks and recreation grounds were acquired. Perhaps the most significant change was the bridging over of the River Roche as it made its through the town centre carrying with it mud, sludge and all varieties of industrial waste. This tremendous operation was carried out in four stages commencing in 1904, it was finally completed in 1926 and was to give Rochdale a magnificent town centre that acted as the transport hub for the whole area.

This would have been the Rochdale that Charles Heap would have recognised when he was first elected as a Liberal to the Town Council in his brother's constituency of Spotland East in 1903 aged 58. Charles was to spend only seven years on the council, yet he was elected Mayor in 1907 after only four years on the council, one year after he was made a Justice of the Peace. The *Observer* said 'that he filled the office of Mayor with tact, dignity and social success'. One of the highlights of his year in office was a gigantic party held at Falinge Park for all the Sunday School teachers in the town. One cannot help but wonder who paid for it all!

Charles was undoubtedly a well-informed and highly competent Councillor and the council valued his business acumen and experience. But one is left with the feeling that perhaps he didn't really think that local politics was his metier. After a successful seven years, he was glad to return to Wesleyan Methodism which was his main life interest. He was educated at Wesley College and the evangelistic spirit in him was pronounced. In 1867, at the age of 22, he became a local preacher. Six years later he was passed as a candidate for the Ministry and was accepted by Conference. Before he could take up his post his father died and he had to give up his ministerial work and return home to run the business. Despite the responsibilities of running such a large concern, he could still find time for other interests. He joined the Rochdale School Board as a Progressive and later served on the Education Committee that succeeded the Board.

He married Margaret Ellen Hudson, daughter of the late Alderman Hudson and a former Mayor of the town. Both he and William Tweedale clearly devoted the same amount of energy and effort to their families as they did their business; Charles produced nine children, including three sons who were to follow their father into the family business, and William Tweedale just capped him with ten! This splendidly fecund pair have between them given rise to over one hundred descendants who intermarried with nearly all the cotton and wool families in Rochdale.

Charles was to continue as a local preacher until his final illness. For many years the Superintendent at Lanehead, he had held nearly all the lay offices on the Circuit. He was one of the founders of the Empire Mission and later of the Rochdale Mission. It had long been his ambition to see the establishment of a Methodist Central Hall in Rochdale but there was some opposition to this, and although plans were agreed before his death, he was to die before the Champness Hall came into being.

Thomas Champness, after whom the Hall was named, had been Missionary Minister in Rochdale and Superintendent of the Rochdale (Wesley) Circuit. Champness, who died in 1905, had been one of those enigmatic gifted preachers who have come to characterise the early days of the Methodists. He spent his early years as a missionary in West Africa, where he was to lose his wife to fever, and nearly suffered the same fate himself. He was not an easy man to deal with and became a constant thorn in the side of Conference. His main claim to fame was that he 'discovered' the idea of local missionaries who would work towards converting those who had yet 'to see the light'. He started his own school of Apprentice Missionaries who could fulfil this role without the need for ordination.

Charles' son, John Hudson Heap, and his nephew by marriage, the kind and gentle Clement Coomer, were able to carry on the project after Charles' death and see it brought to fruition. They remained on its governing body.

Like his brother William Tweedale, where politics were concerned Charles was very much a Liberal of the old school and somewhat sceptical of modern developments. Charles was to be in failing health for some years before he died on 24 July 1923 aged 78 on the third anniversary of his wife's death. Margaret Ellen had died at Bridlington where they were staying while attending the annual conference being held at Hull. What better epitaph could anyone desire than the eulogy of praise heaped (an appropriate phase) on his head at the Wesleyan Conference of that year which was held at Bristol – 'one of the most devoted and saintly of men, one of God's own children, he was a praying man who really got hold of religion, a man of boundless love and devotion who has been greatly used by God'.

One cannot but admire these two men who gave so freely of their talents for the benefit of their work force and the wider community, and whose belief in a higher being was absolute. Somehow I don't think that the same will be written of us in years to come.

References

1 Robertson's political and social history of Rochdale
2 see chapter 9 – Dr Samuel Heap
3 see chapter 8 – Joshua Heap and the Fenton's Bank Affair

11

THE CHILDREN OF WILLIAM TWEEDALE HEAP AND CHARLES HEAP

Two attributes characterise the 19thC members of our family, their fecundity and their passionate belief in the Wesleyan Methodist ethic that permeated their lives. William Tweedale Heap, and his brother Charles, demonstrate these traits to the full. William Tweedale, and his wife Mary Watson of Gisburn, were to produce ten children and Charles, and his wife Margaret Ellen Hudson, nine. Both families suffered the inevitable loss of some of their children shortly after birth or in infancy, but most survived. Between them they have given rise to over one hundred descendants. The sixteen cousins would have been well known to each other, but the two families appear to have lived separate lives though within the same town. Many were to find employment with the family firm of Samuel Heap and Son, both sides of the family having their share of directors and chairmen of the board.

Two of William Tweedale's children died young, Edwin at six weeks and William Arthur aged five. His eldest daughter, Sarah Tweedale, married James Edgar Handley and her fortunes are followed in chapter 16. His second daughter, Annie Watson, was unmarried and is described as a philanthropist, suggesting she was involved in 'good works' with the Wesleyan Methodists. The next daughter, Mary Liz, married the Rev John Bicknor Edwards, one of the many Wesleyan Ministers scattered throughout the family history. There appears to have been no issue of the marriage. The Rev John preached his way across the country from the North of Scotland Mission to the Isle of Man, before returning to Saddleworth and New Mills. Next came James Henry who married a Minnie Baldwin and had four children but otherwise little is known.

His next son, Samuel, was an electrical engineer who married an Ellen

CHART 7

William Tweedale Heap's Children

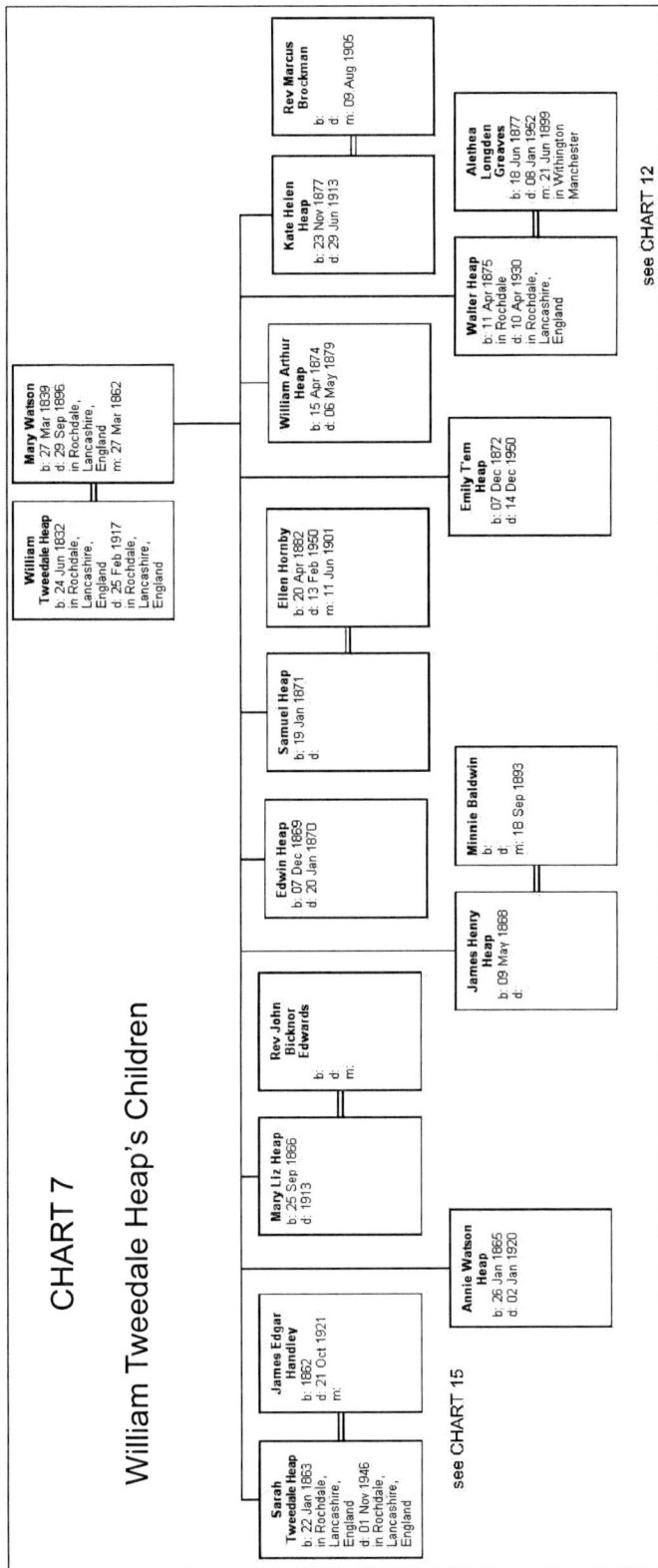

William Tweedale Heap
b: 24 Jun 1832
in Rochdale,
Lancashire,
England
d: 25 Feb 1917
in Rochdale,
Lancashire,
England

Mary Watson
b: 27 Mar 1839
d: 29 Sep 1896
in Rochdale,
Lancashire,
England
m: 27 Mar 1862

Sarah Tweedale Heap
b: 22 Jan 1863
in Rochdale,
Lancashire,
England
d: 01 Nov 1946
in Rochdale,
Lancashire,
England

James Edgar Handley
b: 1862
d: 21 Oct 1921
m:

Mary Liz Heap
b: 25 Sep 1866
d: 1913

Rev John Bicknor Edwards
b:
d:
m:

Annie Watson Heap
b: 26 Jan 1865
d: 02 Jan 1920

James Henry Heap
b: 09 May 1868
d:

Minnie Baldwin
b:
d:
m: 18 Sep 1893

Edwin Heap
b: 07 Dec 1869
d: 20 Jan 1870

Samuel Heap
b: 19 Jan 1871
d:

Ellen Hornby
b: 20 Apr 1882
d: 13 Feb 1950
m: 11 Jun 1901

Emily Tem Heap
b: 07 Dec 1872
d: 14 Dec 1950

William Arthur Heap
b: 15 Apr 1874
d: 06 May 1879

Walter Heap
b: 11 Apr 1875
in Rochdale
d: 10 Apr 1930
in Rochdale,
Lancashire,
England

Kate Helen Heap
b: 23 Nov 1877
d: 29 Jun 1913

Rev Marcus Brockman
b:
d:
m: 09 Aug 1905

Alethea Longden Greaves
b: 18 Jun 1877
d: 08 Jan 1952
m: 21 Jun 1899
in Withington
Manchester

see CHART 15

see CHART 12

109

Hornby before taking up a new post as District Assistant Superintendent of Signals and Telegraph with the London and North Western Railway based in Lancaster. They had three children, the eldest of whom, Lillian Mary, was said to have gone to sleep in a bluebell wood and woken up pregnant!

Next was Emily, always known as T'em, unmarried and lived in Tunbridge Wells. Last but one, Walter, my grandfather, destined to become chairman of the board of Samuel Heap and Son and his fortunes are followed in chapter 13. Last, but by no means least, Kate Helen, who married yet another Wesleyan Methodist Minister, the Rev. Marcus Rainsford Brockman. They had one daughter, Kate Elizabeth Rainsford, who was severely mentally handicapped and institutionalised in a long stay psychiatric hospital in Leeds. The Rev. Marcus was a prominent Rotarian and Free Mason and held the post of Past Assistant Grand Chaplain of England and Provincial Grand Chaplain. His ministry was largely in Cornwall and Yorkshire. He served as Chaplain to HM Forces in the 1914/18 war.

The history of Charles Heap's children is not dissimilar though with one or two rather more colourful characters. His eldest child, Frederick Charles, always known as 'Fred', became chairman of the board of Samuel Heap and Son after Walter's untimely death, a position he held until his death in 1937. He was educated at Pembroke House school, Lytham St Anne's, and in Germany. In 1899 he married Annie Agnes 'Dora' Brittain who was born in Walsall in 1878, the marriage taking place at Sutton Coldfield. They lived at Beightons, one of the large houses at the top of Shawclough owned by the firm, one of the director's perks that contributed to the downfall of the firm's fortunes. They had four children, Margaret Beryl, Dorothy Mary, Doreen who married Lesley Gilbert, and yet another Charles Arthur who married Molly Bowhill. He was an indefatigable worker for the Methodist church and donated a magnificent organ to the Champnesss Hall. He was treasurer of the Rochdale Mission.

Next in line was John Hudson Heap whom, it is alleged, suffered a somewhat unusual death. The history of his branch of the family is described in chapter 12. He was followed by the eldest daughter, Helen 'Nellie' Heap, who married Clement Walton Coomer and their fortunes are traced in chapter 16.

Another daughter, Annie, made two disastrous marriages. The first to Rupert Turner, son of Sir Samuel Turner who, with his brothers, had set up the Turner Brothers Asbestos Company and later the Turner and Newall Group of Companies. The main Turner factory was at Spotland, just across the Spodden from Samuel Heap and Son. The business flourished until the dangers of working with asbestos became more widely known, and many were the cases

CHART 10

≡r)

Children of Charles Heap and Margaret Ellen Hudson
(note: children not necessarily in date order)

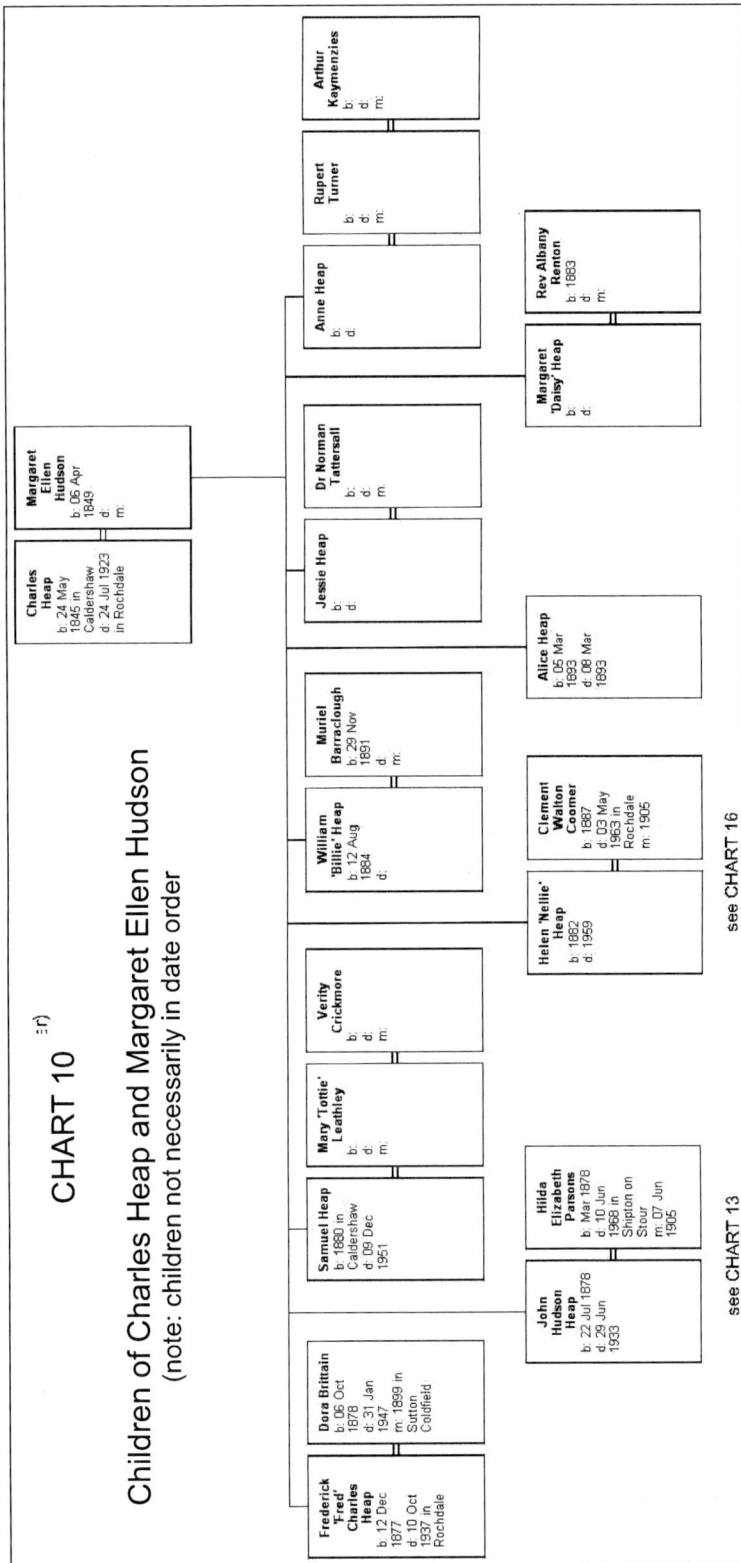

Charles Heap
b: 24 May 1845 in Caldershaw
d: 24 Jul 1923 in Rochdale

Margaret Ellen Hudson
b: 06 Apr 1849
d:
m:

Frederick 'Fred' Charles Heap
b: 12 Dec 1877
d: 10 Oct 1937 in Rochdale

Dora Brittain
b: 06 Oct 1878
d: 31 Jan 1947
m: 1899 in Sutton Coldfield

Samuel Heap
b: 1880 in Caldershaw
d: 09 Dec 1951

Mary 'Tottie' Leathley
b:
d:
m:

Verity Crickmore
b:
d:
m:

William 'Billie' Heap
b: 12 Aug 1884
d:

Muriel Barraclough
b: 29 Nov 1891
d:
m:

Anne Heap
b:
d:

Rupert Turner
b:
d:
m:

Arthur Kaymenzies
b:
d:
m:

Jessie Heap
b:
d:

Dr Norman Tattersall
b:
d:
m:

Margaret 'Daisy' Heap
b:
d:

Rev Albany Renton
b: 1883
d:
m:

John Hudson Heap
b: 22 Jul 1878
d: 29 Jun 1933

Hilda Elizabeth Parsons
b: Mar 1878 in
d: 10 Jun 1968 in Shipton on Stour
m: 07 Jun 1905

Helen 'Nellie' Heap
b: 1882
d: 1959

Clement Walton Coomer
b: 1887
d: 03 May 1963 in Rochdale
m: 1905

Alice Heap
b: 05 Mar 1893
d: 08 Mar 1893

see CHART 13

see CHART 16

111

of mesothelioma of the pleura and asbestosis that I was to see during my years as a general practitioner. I can recall as a child, drawing pictures in the dust on the wooden fencing bordering the public footpath that ran alongside the factory, so inadequate were the control measures.

Rupert was a rogue. He drank heavily, and Annie finally divorced him, but not before having borne him three sons, Gordon, Ivan and Charles. She was well rid of him. He became involved with numerous women and many were the drunken escapades reported in the local press. He was apprehended by HM Customs and Excise bringing thousands of pounds worth of jewellery into the country for one of his many wives, an episode that nearly landed him in prison. Annie didn't fare much better. After divorcing Rupert she married Arthur Kaymenzies, but the marriage was annulled almost immediately when Arthur went off with a chambermaid. Money may have its compensations but it doesn't always bring happiness.

Next came Samuel who succeeded Fred as chairman of the board, a post he held until his death in 1951. Samuel married first Mary Leathley, known as 'Tottie', and by whom he had two children, Sibyl Mary who married Arthur James Baron, and Charles Herbert 'Bert' Leathley who was killed in Normandy shortly after D-Day in 1944, serving with the Lancashire Fusiliers. Charles Herbert could reasonably have expected to 'inherit' the chairmanship of the board. After Tottie died, Samuel married Verity Crickmore who had worked as a journalist. She could talk the hind leg off a donkey and addressed everyone as 'Darling'!

Next in line was Margaret 'Daisy' who married the Rev Albany Renton, yet another Wesleyan Methodist Minister who was always on hand to marry or bury members of the family. His Ministry was mainly in the north of England and included a period as Chaplain to the Forces in the 1914/18 war. Their daughter died young whilst in her twenties, her brother Peter served as a medical officer in the RAMC during the 1939/45 war before joining the Blood Transfusion service in Manchester, where he met his wife Jeanne Hancock.

William 'Billie' was born on 12 August 1884. Educated at Royal Mount School and Manchester University, he followed other members of the family to Neuwied in Germany. He was a chemist and manager of the Ramie Company at Bredbury, near Stockport that consisted of a spinning mill and an incandescent mantle factory. He was also a non-executive director of Samuel Heap and Son. During the 1939-45 war he set up a factory in Wandsworth to manufacture thorium nitrate which he developed for use in an incandescent

CHART 11

William 'Billie' Heap Descendants

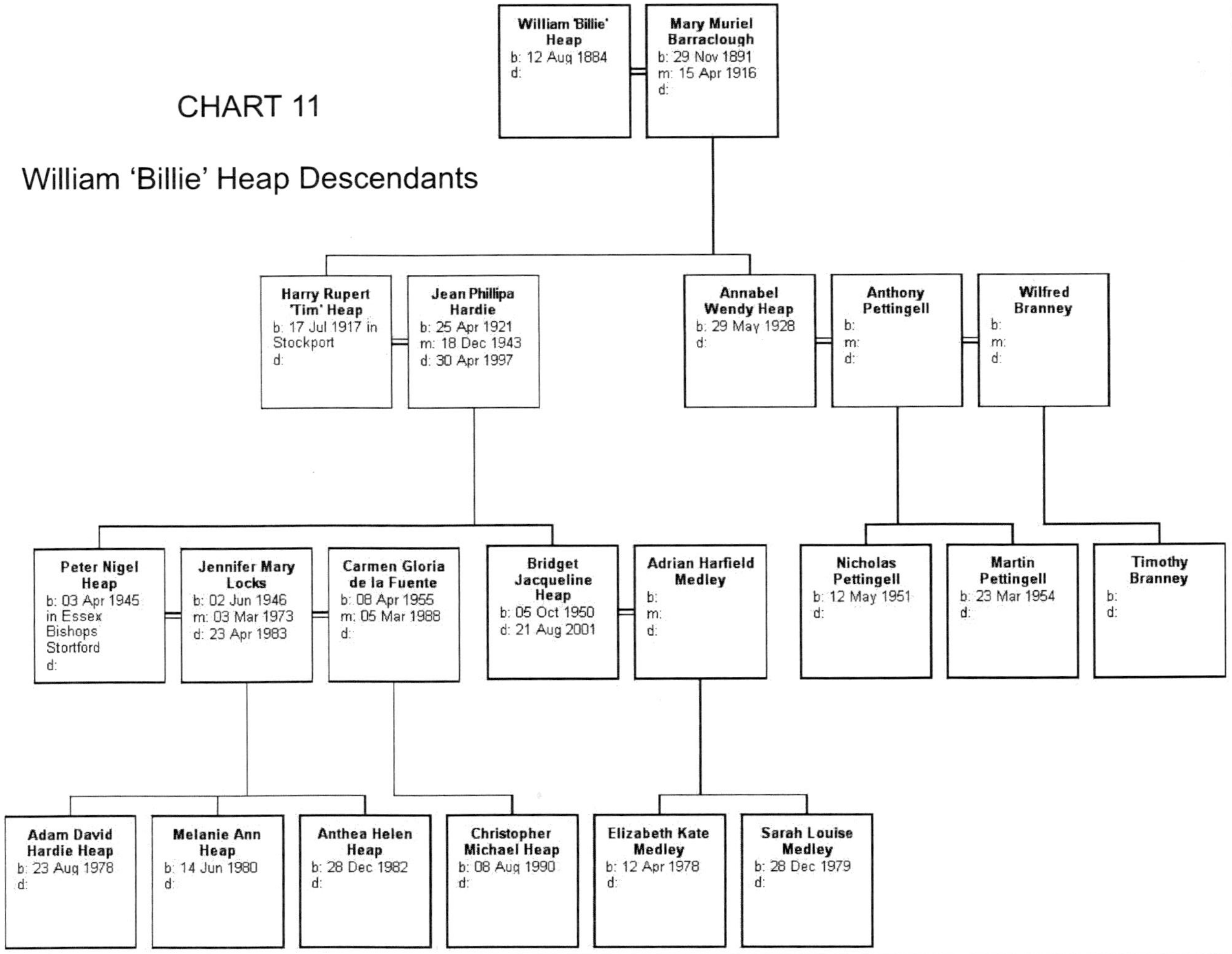

William 'Billie' Heap
b: 12 Aug 1884
d:

Mary Muriel Barraclough
b: 29 Nov 1891
m: 15 Apr 1916
d:

Harry Rupert 'Tim' Heap
b: 17 Jul 1917 in Stockport
d:

Jean Phillipa Hardie
b: 25 Apr 1921
m: 18 Dec 1943
d: 30 Apr 1997

Annabel Wendy Heap
b: 29 May 1928
d:

Anthony Pettingell
b:
m:
d:

Wilfred Branney
b:
m:
d:

Peter Nigel Heap
b: 03 Apr 1945 in Essex Bishops Stortford
d:

Jennifer Mary Locks
b: 02 Jun 1946
m: 03 Mar 1973
d: 23 Apr 1983

Carmen Gloria de la Fuente
b: 08 Apr 1955
m: 05 Mar 1988
d:

Bridget Jacqueline Heap
b: 05 Oct 1950
d: 21 Aug 2001

Adrian Harfield Medley
b:
m:
d:

Nicholas Pettingell
b: 12 May 1951
d:

Martin Pettingell
b: 23 Mar 1954
d:

Timothy Branney
b:
d:

Adam David Hardie Heap
b: 23 Aug 1978
d:

Melanie Ann Heap
b: 14 Jun 1980
d:

Anthea Helen Heap
b: 28 Dec 1982
d:

Christopher Michael Heap
b: 08 Aug 1990
d:

Elizabeth Kate Medley
b: 12 Apr 1978
d:

Sarah Louise Medley
b: 28 Dec 1979
d:

mantle. The business was taken over by ICI and Billie remained in their employment for the rest of his working life. His son, Harry Rupert 'Tim', was also a chemical engineer. He graduated at St Andrews University and worked for Crompton Parkinson in Chelmsford. His grandson, Peter Nigel Heap, now lives at Manuden near Bishop's Stortford.

Alice died shortly after birth in 1893.

Last but not least was Jessie, who may have been the youngest of Charles' children, and who married Dr Norman Tattersall.

23   Leven House, 70 Spotland Road – the Practice house

24   Dr Walter Joss outside Leven House – setting out on house calls c.1910

25   Walter Heap, 1875-1930

26   Alethea Longden Heap (née Greaves), 1877-1952

27   The Heap Men at the marriage of Kenneth Heap and Cynthia Cartwright, 30 June 1939
?, Dr Clifford Heap, Dr Michael Heap, Kenneth Heap, ?, ? And in front Derek Heap, aged 8

28   *Marriage of Walter Heap and Alethea Longden Greaves, 1899*

Back row: Jack Greaves, ? , Robert Greaves, Arthur Moon, ? , ? , Elizabeth Greaves

Front row: Emily Greaves, Kate Helen Heap, Rev. John Clapham Greaves, Mary Eliz Greaves, William Tweedale Heap, ? , ? , Emily T'Em Heap, Ethel Greaves

29 Rochdale town hall square and St Chad's c.1903

30 Rochdale town centre before bridging over of River Roach, 1903

31 Rochdale town hall and the Angel, 1903

32   Marriage of Felix Battersby and Mimi Heap, 1926
Tom Rigg next to bridegroom. Kenneth Heap far right and to his left Kathleen Heap.

33   Helen and Clement Coomer, 1952

34   Left: James Edgar Handley and Sarah Tweedale (née Heap) Handley and their five sons.

From left to right: Bernard, Leslie, Edgar, Donald, Alan

35   Below: The Handley boys go for a ride: Hubert Leslie and Donald

36 The Family Gathering, June 1952: Helen Coomer's 70th birthday

Top row: George Heap, Leslie Handley, Anne Handley, Graham Coomer, Doris Radcliffe, John Baron

Fourth row: Sheila Coomer, Ruth Coomer, Bee Kirk, Elizabeth Heap, Stockdale Heap

Third row: Peter Renton, Norman Tattersall, Edith Heap, Albany Renton, Daisy Renton, Jessie Tattersall, Sybil Baron, Dorothy Heap

Second row: Grace Litton, Anne Turner, Helen Coomer, Clement Coomer

First row: Marjorie Coomer, Helen Redmayne, Phil Tattersall, Margaret Renton, Frieda Coomer

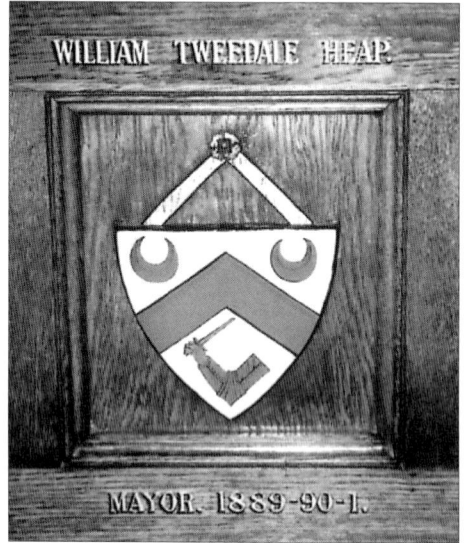

37 Left: Richard Henry Greaves, 'Bad Uncle Dick', 1870-1937

38 Right: The Heap coat of arms as displayed in the Mayor's Parlour, Rochdale town hall

39 SS Arabic, torpedoed off Kinsale Head, 1915

12

JOHN HUDSON HEAP
AND HIS DESCENDANTS

by Richard Heap

John Hudson Heap was the second son of Charles Heap and always known within the family as Jack. Born on 22 July 1878 and educated at Pembroke House school, he completed his technical education at Neuwied in Germany. He joined the family firm as a young man, becoming a director on the woollen side where he was known as a capable business man with progressive views. He was in charge of the finishing branch of the works and the dyeing and finishing of knitted goods and artificial silks. He married Hilda Elizabeth Parsons on 7 June 1905 at Wylde Green, Birmingham. They had four children – George Hudson, Audrey, John Stockdale and Charles Deryk. He could have expected to succeed his elder brother, Fred, as chairman of the board had he not succumbed to an early death.

A staunch Wesleyan Methodist and member of the chapel committee of the Wesleyan church, his real interest was in the Champness Hall. Together with his brother Fred, he endeavoured to finish the work his father had started and bring the project to a successful conclusion. It was said that his main interest in life was in the Kingdom of God in Rochdale.

He died on 29 June 1933, aged 54, at the Grand Hotel in Cromer where he had been staying while visiting his two sons who were at school at Greshams on the Norfolk coast. The cause of death was given as acute streptococcal laryngitis resulting in heart failure. A quarter of a century later his grandchildren were brought up to believe he had died a hero's death saving a workman, either from drowning in a vat of dye or from exposure to sewer gas. Sadly, much as we would like it to be true, we have been unable to find any evidence to support

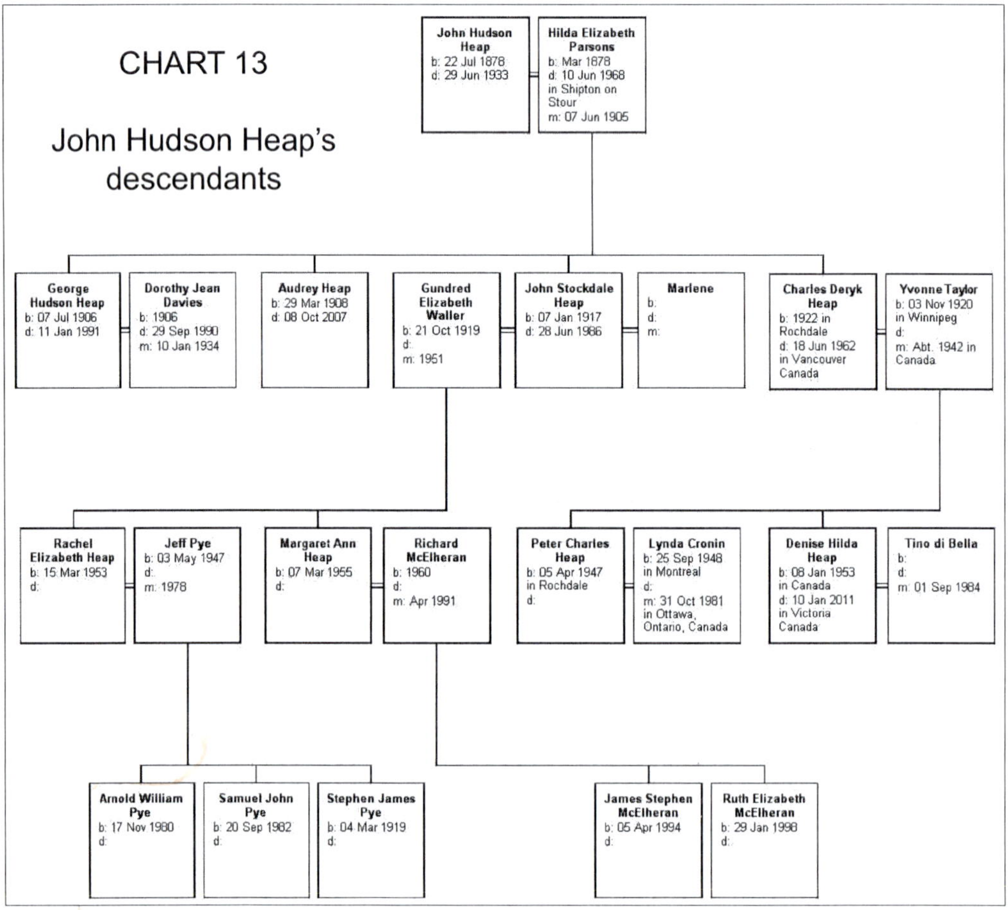

CHART 13

John Hudson Heap's descendants

John Hudson Heap
b: 22 Jul 1878
d: 29 Jun 1933

Hilda Elizabeth Parsons
b: Mar 1878
d: 10 Jun 1968 in Shipton on Stour
m: 07 Jun 1905

George Hudson Heap
b: 07 Jul 1906
d: 11 Jan 1991

Dorothy Jean Davies
b: 1906
d: 29 Sep 1990
m: 10 Jan 1934

Audrey Heap
b: 29 Mar 1908
d: 08 Oct 2007

Gundred Elizabeth Waller
b: 21 Oct 1919
d:
m: 1951

John Stockdale Heap
b: 07 Jan 1917
d: 28 Jun 1986

Marlene
b:
d:
m:

Charles Deryk Heap
b: 1922 in Rochdale
d: 18 Jun 1962 in Vancouver Canada

Yvonne Taylor
b: 03 Nov 1920 in Winnipeg
d:
m: Abt. 1942 in Canada

Rachel Elizabeth Heap
b: 15 Mar 1953
d:

Jeff Pye
b: 03 May 1947
d:
m: 1978

Margaret Ann Heap
b: 07 Mar 1955
d:

Richard McElheran
b: 1960
d:
m: Apr 1991

Peter Charles Heap
b: 05 Apr 1947 in Rochdale
d:

Lynda Cronin
b: 25 Sep 1948 in Montreal
d:
m: 31 Oct 1981 in Ottawa, Ontario, Canada

Denise Hilda Heap
b: 08 Jan 1953 in Canada
d: 10 Jan 2011 in Victoria Canada

Tino di Bella
b:
d:
m: 01 Sep 1984

Arnold William Pye
b: 17 Nov 1980
d:

Samuel John Pye
b: 20 Sep 1982
d:

Stephen James Pye
b: 04 Mar 1919
d:

James Stephen McElheran
b: 05 Apr 1994
d:

Ruth Elizabeth McElheran
b: 29 Jan 1998
d:

116

their story. There was no Coroner's inquest held into his death and no report of an industrial accident.

Hilda survived him by a further 35 years until her death in 1968 at Shipton on Stour where she had been cared for by her daughter Audrey. She enjoyed playing the piano despite being affected latterly with arthritis of her fingers.

George Hudson Heap, their eldest son, was born 7 July 1906. After finishing his schooling at Greshams he joined the family firm. He became chairman of the board in 1951 by right of primogeniture, as had been the practice since the company was set up in 1923, and he held the post until the take-over by Courtaulds in 1965. A tall man, he is described by those who knew him as somewhat aloof and condescending. He was a magistrate on the Rochdale County Bench and Commandant of the Special Constabulary of the Rochdale Borough force. There were no children of the marriage, but they kept a succession of Airedale terriers. He died on 11 January 1991.

His wife, Dorothy Jean Davies, came from Reigate where they were married on 10 January 1934. She made up for the lack of children of her own by throwing herself enthusiastically into every aspect of youth activity. Divisional Commissioner of the Rochdale Girl Guides, she was awarded the medal of merit. Chairman of the Lancashire standing committee of voluntary youth organisations, and a founder member of the Rochdale Music and Drama group. She was appointed a JP in 1952 and was for many years a member of the juvenile or youth panel. When the County and Borough benches were amalgamated she was appointed chairman, and in 1971 was awarded the OBE in recognition of her services.

'A formidable lady', she is remembered with great affection by members of the court staff even twenty years after her death. She always wore a hat when sitting on the bench. She is reputed to have blocked the appointment to the bench of the redoubtable Cyril Smith (one of Rochdale's most colourful characters and MP for Rochdale) having expressed doubts about his moral integrity. She predeceased George by a few months, dying on 29 September 1990. Between them they maintained the Liberal-Methodist-textile magnate tradition, living in a succession of large houses before moving into a small cottage on the Shawclough road.

George's sister Audrey was born in March 1908. Brought up in the family tradition of Methodism, she trained in the Montessori method of education before joining the Manchester and Salford Methodist Mission, after which she worked as a Deaconess in South Wales and later in the East End of London. She never married but gave up her vocation to care for her aged mother in

Shipton on Stour. She is remembered for her great sense of humour as well as her self-discipline, and her ability to inspire others to achieve her own high standards. She lived to be over 99 years of age, thereby narrowly missing becoming the first Heap centenarian, singing to the end.

John Stockdale Heap, George's younger brother, was born 7 January 1917 and was one of the two brothers away at boarding school when their father died. As an impressionable teenager, he may have blamed himself for the death. Thereafter, for a Heap, his biography is atypical. He was a Conscientious Objector during the 1939-45 war which he spent working as a farm labourer. He married Gundred Elizabeth Waller in late 1951 in Kensington. Gundred was a Quaker and her children were brought up as Quakers though later they reverted to the Church of England. He made a career for himself in social work with the local authority for which he was later awarded an OBE. During the course of his work he met Marlene, an American Buddhist, whom he subsequently married, having divorced Gundred in 1970. He died on 28 June 1986, having progressed from Methodism to Quakerism and finally to Buddhism. His funeral was a mixture of Methodist hymns set in a Buddhist ritual.

The youngest son, Charles Deryk, was born in Rochdale in 1922 and was only nine when his father died. He joined the RAF during the war and was posted to Canada as part of the Commonwealth Air Training Plan, stationed at Moose Jaw, Saskatchewan. Whilst in Canada he met and married Yvonne Taylor in Vancouver and immediately afterwards was posted to India. The young couple didn't see each other again until after the war. Meanwhile Yvonne had travelled to England and was staying with her new family pending Charles' return. Charles spent a short stint at Cambridge before the family emigrated to Vancouver in 1947, six weeks after the birth of their first child, Peter Charles, who like so many of the family was born at Birch Hill hospital in Rochdale. Denise Hilda, their second child, was born in Vancouver on 8 January 1953. Peter is the proud possessor of the oil portrait of William The Founder which hung on the wall of the boardroom at Caldershaw.

Charles Deryk worked as a newspaperman and in advertising before joining Western Canada Steel where he spent most of his career, rising to become the sales manager. He was a keen cricketer and field hockey player, latterly coaching juniors in both sports.

After Charles' premature death from a brain tumour in 1962, Yvonne went back to work to support the family, and spent the better part of 25 years as a research assistant at the neurophysiology laboratory at the University of British

Columbia. Both children rewarded their parents efforts, Denise became a lawyer specialising in family and poverty law and training young lawyers at the Law Centre at the University of Victoria. She married Tino di Bella in 1984. Tino is a prominent private sector lawyer in Victoria. Denise died in January 2011. Peter attained a PhD in history at Yale and later held senior positions in both the Canadian and British Columbia governments. In more recent years he held the post of senior research assistant at the centre for Global Studies at the University of Victoria.

13

WALTER'S CHILDREN

by Derek Heap and Richard Heap

Walter Heap was born at 68 Spotland Road on 11 April 1875, the youngest son of William Tweedale Heap. Almost certainly his uncle, Dr Samuel Heap, would have attended the birth since he had set up in practice in the house next door at 70 Spotland Road, both houses having been built by Dr Samuel's father – Samuel Heap of Caldershaw.

Walter Heap married Alethea Longden Greaves on 21 June 1899 at the Wesleyan Chapel in Withington. The service was conducted by her father, the Rev John Clapham Greaves, popular Superintendent of the Oxford Road Circuit, a rather fierce looking gentleman judging by the wedding photograph. It was said he had 'by his earnest piety and large heartedness, won for himself a perfect host of Christian and social friends. His family all round have willingly and affectionately supplemented his pastoral efforts with the result that they severally and collectively enjoy the affectionate esteem of all whom duty and pleasure have brought them in contact'.

So the Wesleyan ethic continued to weave its way through the family and entwine its members. I sometimes wonder whether our own lives might have been improved had we followed their example. Although my sister and I were baptised into the Wesleyan faith, mother had other ideas. She chose to worship at the Anglican Parish Church of St Chad which looks down over the Rochdale town centre. Every day we had to laboriously climb the church steps on our way to and from school at Miss Humphreys in William Street.

There was nothing new in this return to the Anglican fold. We already have the example of Thomas Heap (eldest son of William the Founder) whose sons, James and William, were to finance the building of the Parish Church of St Thomas in Newhey in memory of their father, yet all were baptised into the

Wesleyan faith. Despite an increasing respect for non-conformity, particularly in the industrial towns of south-east Lancashire, there was more prestige attached to membership of the Anglican church. It was not uncommon for wealthy non-conformists to desert their chapels and join the church proper, where they could more easily mix with the upper middle classes for social and political reasons. So to the Parish Church we went every Sunday, though as children we were allowed to escape before the sermon. For a brief period we attended the Sunday school held in one of the side aisles but mother soon decided that Sunday school was not for us, she felt she was quite capable of bringing us up in the Christian faith, aided by the religious education provided at our kindergarten

Over a period of time we came to see the non-conformist churches as not quite right for us though many of my parents' friends and contemporaries retained their allegiance to their nonconformists background. A similar attitude was instilled into us about Roman Catholicism. This smacked of popery, candlesticks, the need to bend the knee and cross oneself, and their churches reeked of incense. Not at all suitable places for people with a north country Wesleyan background. It all seems very petty now in this age of religious indifference where the debate is more likely to be between Muslim and Christian than between the different branches of the Christian church. It is no longer about faith and belief but more probably about political aspirations and the demand for Muslim rights within a largely secular state.

Grandmother was attended at her wedding by four 'maids' in pretty dresses of yellow silk covered with *mousseline de soie*, carrying bouquets of yellow roses and wearing sapphire and pearl brooches, a gift from the Bridegroom. The quartet were prominent figures in the remarkably pretty scene as the bridal party took up its position before the officiating Ministers. The four attendant maids were the bride's sisters, Emily Dearlove and Ethel Greaves, Emily Heap – always known as T'Em who later lived in Tonbridge Wells, and Kate Helen Heap – sisters of the groom. Kate Helen was the only one of the four to secure a husband, the Rev Marcus Brockman, a Methodist Minister, a severe looking man with a pince-nez. Kate Helen died in 1913 and Brockman married a second time to Edith Mary Holmes. There was another elder sister, Elizabeth, perhaps considered too old to be a bridesmaid. She appears in the back row in the wedding photograph.

Walter was William Tweedale's youngest son and destined to follow him into the family business after completing his training at the Bradford School of Technology. After working his way up through the Mill he was appointed a

Director in 1902 age 27, such things are possible in a family run concern. In 1921 he succeeded his uncle Charles as Managing Director and Chairman of the Board. He was also Chairman of the Board of the Boarshaw Raising and Finishing Company when the company was taken over by Samuel Heap and Son in 1924. Like all the family before him, he was a Liberal and a member of the Reform Club in Manchester. Unlike his Uncles he took no part in public affairs, being more interested in Freemasonry.

Freemasonry has been described as an international all male movement devoted to charitable and social activities and the secret practice of certain rituals. It is not a religion though in most countries masons must acknowledge a Supreme Being venerated as the Great Architect of the Universe. Members of a Masonic Lodge take 'three degrees' which are conferred with impressive rituals dramatizing the soul's progress from darkness to spiritual light and rebirth. Orthodox freemasonry has been notable for its generous charities and its respectability.

Freemasonry flourished in Rochdale since the latter part of the 18thC. Nationally the Fraternity received a boost when the Prince of Wales became Grand Master in 1876. Walter joined the Rochdale Lodge of Harmony no: 298 in 1906 and the Chapter of Unity later the same year. For some reason he resigned from both in 1912, possibly following a business dispute with another Brother. He remained unattached until 1918, when he is recorded as a Petitioner for a new lodge, King William's no: 3883 in Castleton on the Isle of Man, of which he became a Founder and later Master in 1922. Earlier in 1918 he joined the Minnehaha lodge in Manchester and the Rochdale Lodge of Probity and Freedom in 1923. He became Provincial Senior Grand Warden in East Lancashire in 1928, deputising on numerous occasions for the Earl of Derby. He joined the East Lancashire Provincial Grand Officer's Lodge in 1929

Walter was a Trustee of the Memorial Home for Crippled Children in Norden and of the Union Street Wesleyan Chapel. A keen cricket player, he was Vice President of the Castleton Cricket Club and Treasurer of the Whittaker Golf Club, where my parents used to play in later years, a dreadful course high up on the moors above Littleborough where the players had to cope not just with the coarse moorland grass, but frequently also with the elements as the driving rain swept across the course.

Walter died on 10 April 1930 aged 54. He had attended the East Lancs. Provincial Grand Officers Lodge Masonic meeting on the previous evening, came home, went to bed and was found dead the next morning when his wife went in to wake him. Presumably he suffered a massive coronary or cerebral haemorrhage, possibly brought on by over-indulgence the previous evening. Walter must have been under increasing stress since the firm was beginning to run into financial difficulties and had made a loss for the first time for many years. As Chairman of the Board he would have felt responsible and this may have been a contributory factor in his premature death.

His funeral was an occasion to be remembered, they did things properly in those days. The hearse set off from Chamber House followed by six flat wagons belonging to Samuel Heap and Son loaded with the 125 floral tributes, our grandfather's empty car, the leading car with my father and mother, Kathleen, Kenneth and a Miss Heap (T'em), followed by forty cars carrying the mourners. Grandmother's name doesn't feature among the mourners – it was still the custom in many families that women didn't attend the funeral.

Sadly neither of us knew our grandfather as he died before we were born.

His premature death presented the family with a problem. Chamber House, along with the other Directors' houses, was owned by Samuel Heap and Son although it had been purchased specifically for Walter's use in 1920. His Chairman's salary would have ceased on death, though presumably there would have been some form of widow's pension. Such other monies as they possessed would either have been invested in the Loan Accounts issued by the firm, or in shares in the same company. Samuel Heap and Son was already in financial difficulty and matters were going to get worse. The heady days of the earlier part of the century, when the shares were paying dividends of over 20%, were long since gone never to return. Grandmother had to vacate Chamber House and bought Edensor, 496 Manchester Road, half a mile away across the valley, there she stayed until her death in 1952, looked after by Kathleen and giving a home to Kenneth until he married, and to Michael after he qualified and returned home from the war to join his elder brother, Clifford, in General Practice on Spotland Road.

The sale of Chamber House was protracted and difficult. The housing market was at a low ebb and the value was well below the purchase price. Few people were interested in buying what many would see as a Victorian Gothic monstrosity and it was not until 1934 that the property was sold to Fletcher Bolton who used the garden and surrounding land to provide stabling for his horses. There were several references to the sale in the mill safe, 'under no circumstances should any prospective purchaser be given details of the cost of coke for heating or of the number of gardeners employed, unless they specifically asked for this information'. This was an expensive house to run, not that this would have been any concern to Walter and his family as the firm undertook to pay all the running costs. Walter had employed three gardeners and six indoor staff, the garden was renowned for its colourful display of flowers and included a croquet lawn and tennis court.

After Fletcher Bolton the story was all downhill. It was taken over by the Rochdale Corporation as an old people's home and I can recall visiting several of my patients living out their old age in a degree of comfort they had not previously enjoyed, and admiring the family coat of arms recorded in stained glass in one of the windows. It later became a nightclub of sorts, giving rise to complaints from the neighbours due to noise and rowdiness late at night. Thereafter it fell into a state of disrepair until severely damaged by fire in 1996. It was eventually demolished in 1999.

Curiously my maternal grandfather, George Walker, and his family had also lived at Edensor as when my mother married in 1927, she was described as 'of Rydal Mount, Ilkley and previously of Edensor, 496 Manchester Road'. George had left Edensor before 1926 so presumably there had been an intermediate owner before my grandmother bought the house after Walter's death.

Alethea Longden Greaves was born in 1877 at 2 Watt Place in Birmingham during her father's Ministry there. She married in 1899 at Withington during another Ministry, and died in 1952 at Rochdale. Although a diminutive five feet in height she successfully brought up her four children and educated them to take their rightful places within the community. In 1940 she suffered a severe injury to her right hand due to a boiler explosion, resulting in a loss of function of the hand, not that she allowed this to interfere with her life. She continued to play the role of Raksha, Mother Wolf, with the Cubs and to play one handed cricket with her grandchildren. Very much the matriarch in her later years, she could demonstrate an almost Victorian formality in her relations with others but her grandchildren could do no wrong.

Walter and Alethea had five children, Ellis Clifford, Kathleen Mary, Walter Kenneth, Raymond, and Geoffrey Michael. Raymond only lived for ten days, nursed night and day by Rachel Morritt who had been in service with the family for over thirty years. The older children spent their childhood at Passmonds House, one of a row of houses adjacent to the mill. Passmonds lies on Edenfield road just beyond the junction with Sandy Lane. It must have been an idyllic spot for the children, free to roam for miles across the fields. It had, however, the disadvantage of being close to the mill which was very noisy, particularly in the summer when the doors would be left open. Passmonds was a mule-spinning mill with machinery much of which had changed little since the early days of the industrial revolution. The mule travels backwards and forwards as the cotton thread twists and spins, winding onto a row of bobbins. Spinning mules always had a fascination for me and we would peer inside to watch the men at work until we were chased out by the foreman.

This was not to be my only acquaintance with the Passmonds mill. The front of the mule had a wooden bar soaked in oil which had seeped out from the machinery. As the mule trundled backwards and forwards on its wheels, rumbling its way across the wooden floors, the operator's scrotum would come into contact with the bar as he leaned over to repair the broken threads. Unfortunately the mineral oils used at that time were carcinogenic, and prolonged exposure resulted in some of the operatives developing cancer of the scrotum. Once the problem was recognised the oils were changed. The mules at Passmonds must have been some of the last machines still in operation and I had the delight in seeing what must have been one of the last cases of mule spinners carcinoma of the scrotum in my capacity as Factory Doctor for the County Borough of Rochdale.

From Passmonds the family moved to Woodville on Falinge Road where they lived from 1909 to 1920 before moving to Chamber House when Walter became Chairman of the board.

The children began their schooling at Miss Cramp's near 'The Angel' at the bottom of Bury Road. There they were taught the three Rs with two or three classes held in one large room, the classes sitting back to back. Woe betide you if you were not attending. The ruler would be brought smack down across the back of your hands. This chastisement must have served its purpose since all the boys went on to King William's College in the Isle of Man and Kathleen to Harrogate College.

My father was a bright lad by all accounts, a Praepositor at King William's before leaving to study medicine at St Thomas Hospital in London where he qualified MRCS LRGP in 1924. He should have stayed a further year to get his London MB BS but Dr Joss, the current occupant of the practice, was anxious to retire and return to his beloved Scotland.

My father was a born General Practitioner. He loved his work which kept him fully occupied from morning until late in the evening. He was held in high esteem and affectionate regard by his patients – the only losers were his children, who seldom saw him. Hidden behind his newspaper at breakfast – he had a special rack to hold the *Daily Mail* which provided an effective screen behind which he would retire, and he was still at work in the surgery until long past our bedtime. I loved this man but he was difficult to know, being

CHART 12

Walter Heap's Children

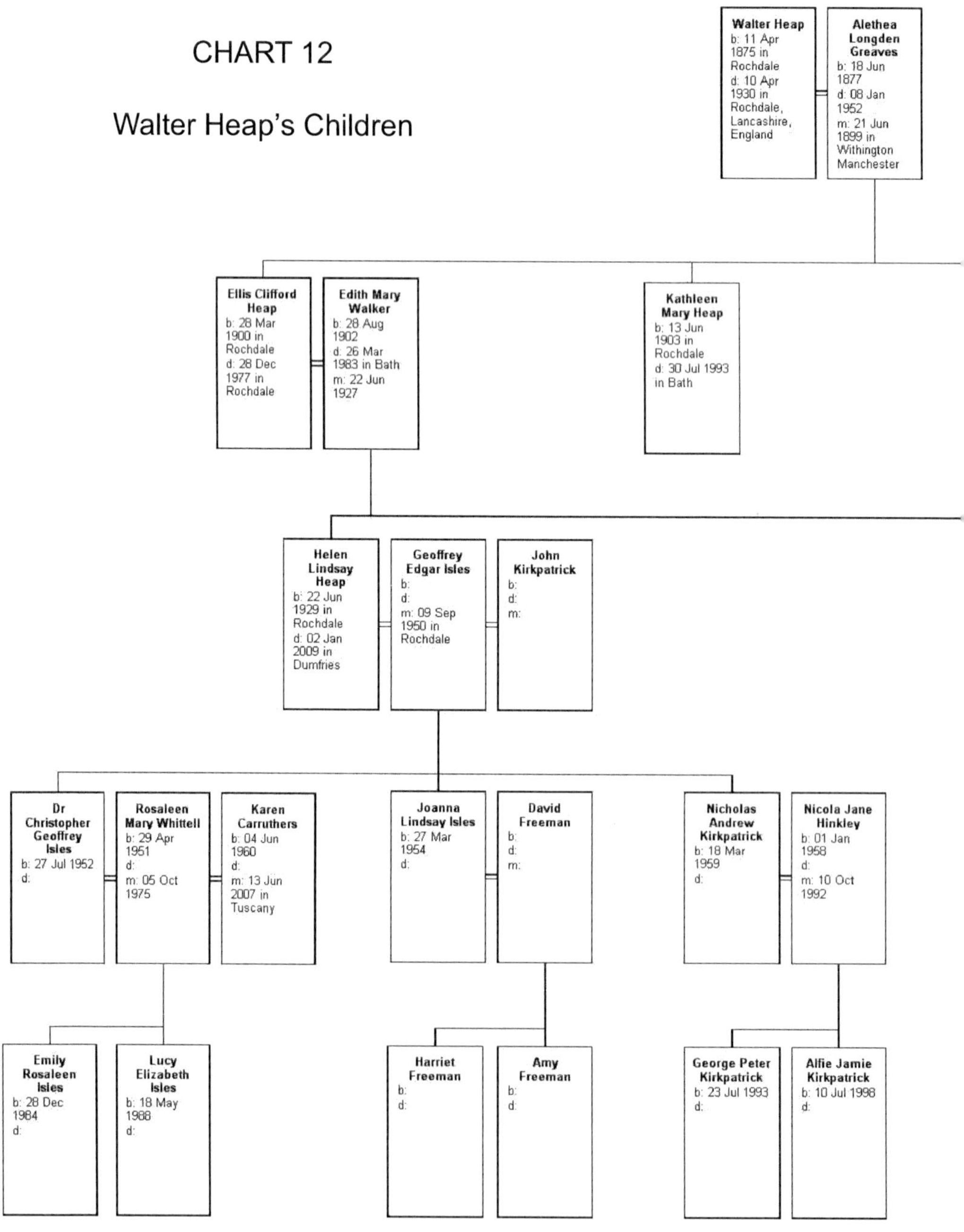

Walter Heap
b: 11 Apr 1875 in Rochdale
d: 10 Apr 1930 in Rochdale, Lancashire, England

Alethea Longden Greaves
b: 18 Jun 1877
d: 08 Jan 1952
m: 21 Jun 1899 in Withington Manchester

Ellis Clifford Heap
b: 28 Mar 1900 in Rochdale
d: 28 Dec 1977 in Rochdale

Edith Mary Walker
b: 28 Aug 1902
d: 26 Mar 1983 in Bath
m: 22 Jun 1927

Kathleen Mary Heap
b: 13 Jun 1903 in Rochdale
d: 30 Jul 1993 in Bath

Helen Lindsay Heap
b: 22 Jun 1929 in Rochdale
d: 02 Jan 2009 in Dumfries

Geoffrey Edgar Isles
b:
d:
m: 09 Sep 1950 in Rochdale

John Kirkpatrick
b:
d:
m:

Dr Christopher Geoffrey Isles
b: 27 Jul 1952
d:

Rosaleen Mary Whittell
b: 29 Apr 1951
d:
m: 05 Oct 1975

Karen Carruthers
b: 04 Jun 1960
d:
m: 13 Jun 2007 in Tuscany

Joanna Lindsay Isles
b: 27 Mar 1954
d:

David Freeman
b:
d:
m:

Nicholas Andrew Kirkpatrick
b: 18 Mar 1959
d:

Nicola Jane Hinkley
b: 01 Jan 1958
d:
m: 10 Oct 1992

Emily Rosaleen Isles
b: 28 Dec 1984
d:

Lucy Elizabeth Isles
b: 18 May 1988
d:

Harriet Freeman
b:
d:

Amy Freeman
b:
d:

George Peter Kirkpatrick
b: 23 Jul 1993
d:

Alfie Jamie Kirkpatrick
b: 10 Jul 1998
d:

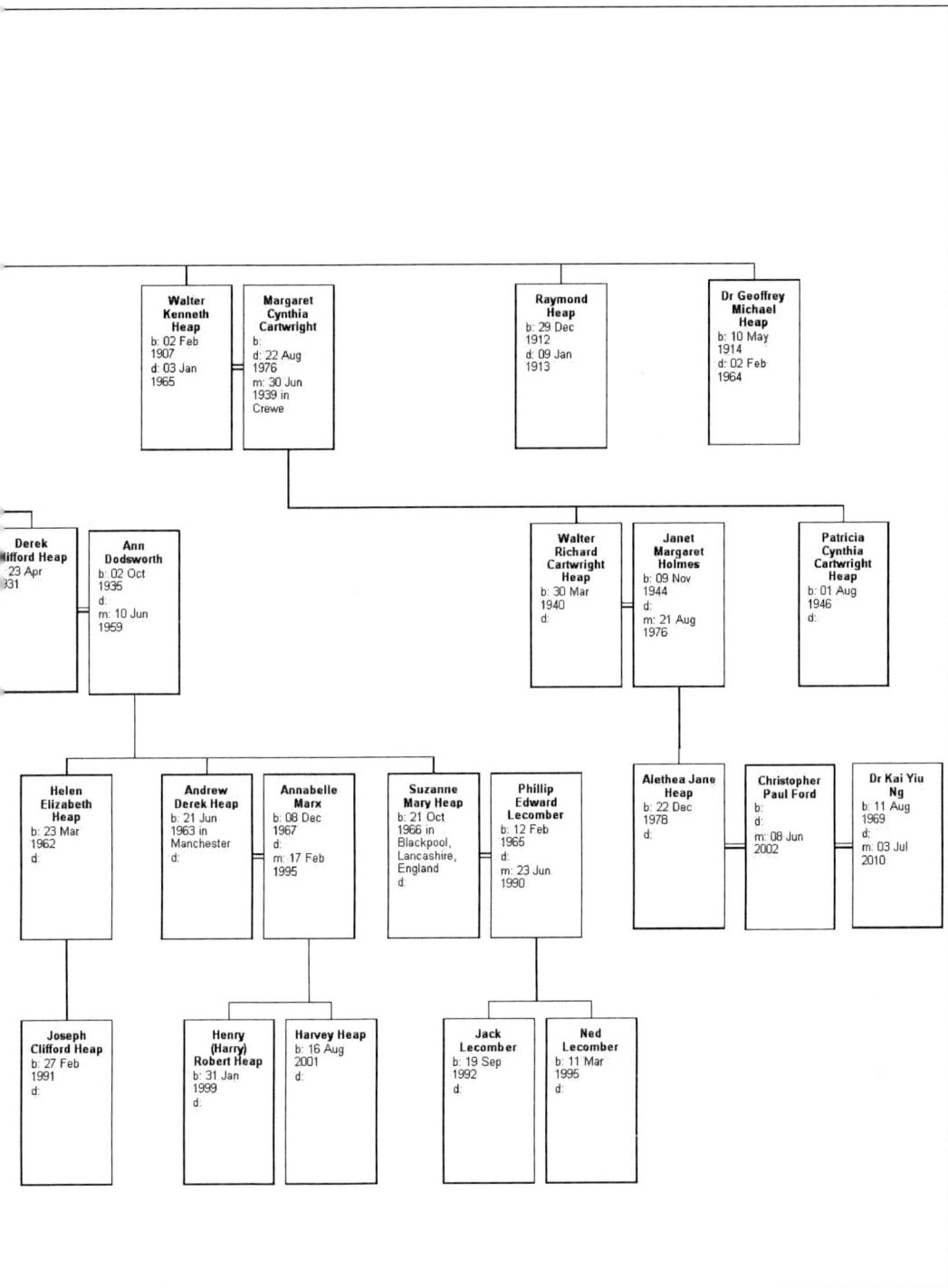

Walter Kenneth Heap
b: 02 Feb 1907
d: 03 Jan 1965

Margaret Cynthia Cartwright
b:
d: 22 Aug 1976
m: 30 Jun 1939 in Crewe

Raymond Heap
b: 29 Dec 1912
d: 09 Jan 1913

Dr Geoffrey Michael Heap
b: 10 May 1914
d: 02 Feb 1964

Derek Clifford Heap
b: 23 Apr 1931

Ann Dodsworth
b: 02 Oct 1935
d:
m: 10 Jun 1959

Walter Richard Cartwright Heap
b: 30 Mar 1940
d:

Janet Margaret Holmes
b: 09 Nov 1944
d:
m: 21 Aug 1976

Patricia Cynthia Cartwright Heap
b: 01 Aug 1946
d:

Helen Elizabeth Heap
b: 23 Mar 1962
d:

Andrew Derek Heap
b: 21 Jun 1963 in Manchester
d:

Annabelle Marx
b: 08 Dec 1967
d:
m: 17 Feb 1995

Suzanne Mary Heap
b: 21 Oct 1966 in Blackpool, Lancashire, England
d:

Phillip Edward Lecomber
b: 12 Feb 1965
d:
m: 23 Jun 1990

Alethea Jane Heap
b: 22 Dec 1978
d:

Christopher Paul Ford
b:
d:
m: 08 Jun 2002

Dr Kai Yiu Ng
b: 11 Aug 1969
d:
m: 03 Jul 2010

Joseph Clifford Heap
b: 27 Feb 1991
d:

Henry (Harry) Robert Heap
b: 31 Jan 1999
d:

Harvey Heap
b: 16 Aug 2001
d:

Jack Lecomber
b: 19 Sep 1992
d:

Ned Lecomber
b: 11 Mar 1995
d:

somewhat shy and retiring. I really only came to know him when we were on holiday in early September each year, usually in the Lake District.

Father married Edith Mary Walker on 22 June 1927 at the Presbyterian Church in the centre of Rochdale just across the road from 'The Angel' (the church was later demolished to make way for a road improvement scheme). The Walkers were another Rochdale family engaged in the wool trade and their children would have grown up together. George Walker had two daughters, the elder Winifred Ann and my mother Edith Mary, named after her great Aunt on the Best side of the family. It was said that my father was courting both daughters at the same time and was unable to make up his mind as to which he should marry until eventually their Father was forced to intervene and demand that he either desist or chose one or the other and make an honest woman of her. My father chose the younger daughter Edith. Winifred promptly took herself off to India where she had obtained employment as Governess to an Indian Army family and thus did not have to suffer the embarrassment of having to attend her younger sister's wedding.

Kathleen Mary was born at Passmonds on 13 June 1903 and would have been 27 when her father died. She was a pretty and vivacious girl and could reasonably have expected to be married by this time. The 1914-18 War had killed off many of the eligible males and like so many of her generation she was destined to remain a spinster all her life. One wonders how she occupied her time. Like many of the upper middle class she had not been expected to have to work and earn her living and as a result she was not trained in any skills. Although my Grandmother was now head of the family and took on a matriarchal role, it was Kathleen who ran the house and provided a home for her two younger brothers and she was to play an increasing role in caring for her ageing Mother.

Kathleen's opportunity came with the 1939/45 war. Kenneth was now married and both he and Michael were called up for military service. The whole country was mobilising itself and many of the unattached women and wives whose husbands were serving overseas in the forces, either joined the services or found other work with the Land Army, in factories, or driving buses – taking on work which had been done by men. Kathleen did none of these things. She remained at home where she considered it her duty to look after her mother. She then took the extraordinary decision to take on and run her younger brother's Scout Troop.

Michael had always been passionately interested in the Boy Scout movement and set up a Scout Troop wherever he happened to be. Before he was called-up he had established the 37th Rochdale Scout troop with its prominent purple neck scarf. Devoted to her brothers, Kathleen decided it was her duty to take on and run the troop, a task for which she had no training and no previous experience other than as a Girl Guide at school. It was unheard of for a woman to be a Scout Master, but the Association was prepared give her a trial, and she set about the task with vigour having at last found an outlet for her undoubted talents. She had always wanted children and here at last was her opportunity, not just to have one or two children but a band of twenty or more, and all of them boys!

She soon found herself in difficulty as she had no funds. So she set about collecting waste paper (much to the horror of her family, who hardly approved of her turning into a refuse collector). She was soon a familiar sight round the commercial part of the town in her Scout uniform (which she had designed herself!) complete with the classic Baden-Powell pointed hat, assisted by a small band of Scouts collecting and loading the waste paper into the Scout trek cart. Waste paper was in constant demand as part of the war effort and brought a reasonable return in cash. She first taught herself all she needed to know about Scouting and then passed on her knowledge to the boys, even to taking them on their annual camp in the summer. She not only taught them Scouting, she taught them what she considered to be good manners, she showed them what they could achieve in life if they were willing to try. For the boys – some of whom came from a very poor background – this was quite an eye-opener. The Scouts christened her 'Skip', a term of endearment by which she was known by countless generations of boys up to her death.

When her brother returned from the war she proudly handed over the troop and set about establishing a Wolf Cub pack (which women were allowed to run) providing a constant stream of recruits for the Scouts when they reached the appropriate age.

She was a strict disciplinarian and this excerpt from Sir David Trippier's autobiography sums it up beautifully 'my most vivid recollection of those earlier days is of my career in the 37th Rochdale Wolf Cubs which met in a converted church hall surrounded by fields. Its leading light was our respected Akela, Miss Kathleen Heap, sister of our local Doctor. Although relatively small, Miss Heap was buxom in build, thoroughly prim and proper with a back straight as a ramrod. She had a steely glare which was all the more alarming as it was accentuated by her horn-rimmed spectacles. That famous glare was guaranteed to reduce any grown man at whom it was directed within a ten yard radius to a gibbering idiot.

In my stupidity I actually believed my career in the Cubs was blossoming. I had already gained one stripe and thought I was well on the way to gaining my second which would make me a Sixer, I might even then gain my third which would turn me into the top Cub, senior to all the others. Then came my downfall in the form of a telephone call to my mother from Miss Heap. 'I have decided to strip him of his rank. He is grossly ill disciplined. When I blow the whistle for the Cubs to rally round he invariably fails to respond as he is always fighting. Not that he is much good as he is constantly picking on someone bigger and stronger than himself.'

But I learnt my lesson and I suffered at the hand of my father who was exceedingly angry although I was later able to crawl back into Miss Heap's affections and I did gain that third stripe!'

Kathleen was to receive the award of the Silver Acorn from the Boy Scout's Association in recognition of her service. When she died at the advanced age of ninety, preserved by nicotine and gin, her Scouts and Cubs came from far and wide to pay homage at her memorial service and to give thanks for all she had taught them.

Next came Walter Kenneth Clapham born 2nd February 1907, again at Passmonds. Saddled with the Greaves family name of Clapham, he wisely ditched this before going off to King William's to join his brother because, as he said, he had no wish to be 'confused with a railway junction!' Totally dissimilar from his brothers at nearly six feet tall and weighing over 17 stone at his heaviest, he excelled on the rugger field where he was a member of the first fifteen, and as a CSM in the school Cadet force. He later played for Manchester 1st XV. Commissioned into the 2/6th Territorial Army battalion of the Lancashire Fusiliers, he attended Manchester University College of Technology from 1926 to 1928 before joining the family firm of Samuel Heap and Son, of which he was a Director.

Several members of the family served with the Territorials between the two wars, usually in the local battalion of one of the line Regiments. They were required to undergo basic infantry training and attend a certain number of days camp each year. Officers were required to ride and one of my earliest memories of my uncle was of him astride a white horse at the head of his company at the annual review – horses were probably his least favourite animal! The local connection was intended to foster camaraderie between the participants, many of whom would already know each other. But it was to have disastrous effects during the 1914–18 war when the battalion went to war as a unit. During the first battle of the Somme the Accrington Pals Battalion suffered 585 casualties, including 235 killed, all within the first twenty minutes with disastrous consequences for the town.

Between the two wars the TA was very much a social activity in the East Lancashire towns with the Officer's Ball a highlight of the winter season, along with the Hunt Ball. The photograph of Felix Battersby's wedding in 1926 shows them all in uniform. It includes Kenneth who was acting as a steward and formed part of the Guard of Honour outside the church. I am sure it never occurred to any of them that 14 years later they would all be involved in a terrible war, happily they all survived.

Kenneth married Cynthia Cartwright on 30th June 1939. He had met her on a cruise travelling with her widowed mother. They set up home together at Buckley Hill House in Milnrow but it was not long before their lives became engulfed in the 1939/45 war. Kenneth's unit was mobilised and he was to spend his war years as a Training Officer in Aberystwyth, being awarded his TD in 1943. He died on 3 January 1965 during the negotiations for the take-over of Samuel Heap and Son by Courtaulds, and is buried in the family grave in Rochdale.

Geoffrey Michael, the youngest member of the family, was born at Woodville on Falinge Road on 10 May 1914. He followed in his brother's footsteps to King William's College in the Isle of Man and then on to St Thomas Hospital in London where he qualified MRCS LRCP in 1938. As a medical student in London he joined the Black Shirts and marched with Oswald Mosley through the streets of London. An interesting insight into the attitudes of the intelligent and educated youth of the day who had grown up during the recession of the early thirties and who were rebelling against the failure of the Government to right what they saw as the many wrongs of society at that time.

After qualifying he joined his elder brother in practice at Spotland Road for a brief period before being called-up to join the RAMC with whom he served throughout the 1939-45 War. Posted to Malta, he travelled out on one of the Malta Convoys. Lucky to be a passenger on a cruiser, he survived the voyage and landed on this embattled Island. There he found himself Medical Officer to the Tigne Garrison where he set about establishing a Scout Troop for the garrison's boys which kept him occupied during those few leisure hours when he wasn't being chased by the bombs. Unfortunately he developed Amoebic dysentery and had to be evacuated to Cairo. Following his recovery he was posted to an ammunition storage facility in Palestine where he always said he was able to pay his mess bills with his poker winnings ... one of the many skills which he acquired during his time in the army. He also became a dab hand at snooker.

Michael remained a bachelor all his life, living with his sister, Kathleen, at Edensor until his early death from a coronary on the golf course at Bagslate in 1964. His one great interest in life was his Boy Scouts. A shy and retiring man, he came to life when among his boys and was never happier than when he was sitting round the camp fire during the summer camp, leading the singing and constantly devising new games and activities. Scout Master, Group Scout Master, and eventually District Commissioner, his memory still lives on. Holidays were spent fishing in Ireland. He was the proud owner of two Jaguar sports cars with almost identical number plates to confuse the observer. His religious beliefs and practices were unlike any of his ancestors – a high anglocatholic who would only eat fish on Fridays, he caused consternation by genuflecting and kissing the Episcopal ring during his niece's confirmation by the Bishop of St Asaph.

Walter's five children begat only four children of their own, Helen and Derek Heap and Richard and Patricia Heap. None of them knew their grandfather Walter who died before they were born, but there are seven great grandchildren and eleven great great grandchildren, three of whom still carry the name of Heap…

Notes

The Masonic Million Memorial Fund of 1919 was instituted to raise the funds to build a Temple in memory of those brethren who gave all for King and Country, Peace and Victory, Liberty and Brotherhood. Work on the Masonic Peace Memorial, later to be called the Freemason's Hall, was started in 1927 and completed in 1933. Walter Heap was one of the many who donated generously to the fund and received in recognition of his gift the gold version of the Commemorative Jewel indicating that he contributed 100 guineas or more. The medal is worn as a personal breast jewel suspended on a dark blue ribbon.

14

THE THIRTIES

The Lowry like figures queued up outside the UCP Tripe shop across the road with its red and gold sign above the shop window, dressed in black, woollen shawls covering their heads, feet shod with black wooden clogs which clattered on the pavements as they walked, some bright with rows of highly polished brass studs. I had always wanted a pair of clogs. There was a clog shop further down Spotland Road and on the top shelf behind the counter was a pair of pale blue clogs on which I had set my heart. The Doctor's children don't wear clogs I was told, nor do they eat tripe, end of discussion – not that there ever was any discussion, my mother and our nurse ruled our small world and what they said, went.

Small and trivial events in a child's life, yet the memory remains as clear as the day they were witnessed, conjuring up the immense social divide separating the upper middle classes from the working class in the days before the war. The doctor's family in a south east Lancashire cotton town was one of the privileged, particularly if the doctor had 'inherited' his position, with cotton or wool money behind him and generations brought up in the town, owing their living to the mills and other successful enterprises on which their lives depended. In those days the doctor had to 'live on the job' and he and his family occupied the practice house usually to be found in the centre of the area of the town that provided his patients. This had the disadvantage in that there was usually no garden attached to the house and he lived apart from his friends, most of whom lived in the more affluent parts of the town.

As children we were happy and contented living in a large and comfortable house in the centre of the town. We were discouraged from mixing with the local children who played out their games in the back streets adjacent to the practice house. I watched with envy as young Jackie Greenwood from across the road would make use of Emma Street as his football pitch. How I could have benefited from his football skills once I went away to school. Our friends were scattered across the town and relatively inaccessible until in later years we became the proud possessors of bicycles. We weren't allowed on the main roads, considered too dangerous even in those pre-war days, but soon found our way round the back streets and 'ginnels' that gave us access to any part of the town, often using mill yards as part of our through routes. Boys were destined for boarding school from the age of eight, their sisters following them two years later. We made the most of our freedom.

This may sound very restrictive but mother knew exactly what she was doing. In those days before the war regional accents were not acceptable if you were to progress in life. Her children were destined for boarding school and greater things to come. If ever a word of dialect or accent crept into our speech we were made to repeat the word or phrase until we were word 'King's English' perfect.

Deprived of the company of our friends, my sister and I had devised for ourselves a complex system of games and each morning we would decide what was to be played and which roles we would take. When my sister started at school I was bored and lonely, and made increasing use of the company of the servants. A full time living-in maid who lived up in the attic, dark black haired Irish Mary who served us well until one day I came into the kitchen and found her coughing up her lungs and the scrubbed wooden surface of the kitchen table covered with bright red arterial blood … Mary disappeared rapidly but not before, no doubt, she had given us both our primary dose of tuberculosis. Mary was replaced by Winnie, a delightful well-endowed Geordie from Durham to whom no doubt I would have lost my virginity had I been a few years older, and the onset of war had not packed Winnie off to a munitions factory. My father's chauffeur was a tall lugubrious individual by the name of Woolfenden who must have been near retirement age. Woolfenden was replaced by Allen, a much younger man, soon to be gobbled up by the forces and my father had to drive himself on his rounds – not that he minded, I think he preferred it as it gave him freedom to go where and when he wanted.

Even so, the household was not complete. There was Susie Sharrocks who lived up Bentmeadows and came every Monday to do the weekly wash. She had a terrible hacking cough which cannot have been improved by the ice cold damp working conditions in the cellar which would certainly not be tolerated today. Above stairs, so to speak, was my father's dispenser who worked out of the surgery, answering the telephone and the surgery bell. Her job was to make out the visiting lists and to prepare and dispense the bottles of coloured medicines. I would happily assist her in the task and spent many a happy hour in her company, washing bottles, crushing up tablets, and manufacturing ointments with pestle and mortar.

Standing apart from the household servants and very much their social superior was the nanny. No upper middle class family was complete without its nanny. We all had them, from the up-market Princess Christian Nannies dressed in brown, some in uniform and others, including our own, with no specific uniform which identified them as belonging to some professional group or training college, but dressed in clothing of their own choice.

It was nanny's job to look after the children and bring them up. They lived-in and in many cases, including our own, had to share their bedroom with the youngest child. It was their job to see the children were washed and dressed and when the occasion demanded brought downstairs and shown off to the visitors. They were essentially part of the family but yet not as equals, a relationship which we might find difficulty in understanding today. They would even come on holiday with us (otherwise who would look after the children whilst their parents played golf?). Afternoons being spent on the beach or on a picnic up in the lakes. Today we are more used to the au-pair dressed in jeans, with her own room and her own life one or two days a week. Nannies were something quite different, they were essentially professionals, in most cases devoted to the children left in their care and, it has to be said, not infrequently displacing the parents in the affection of the child.

We did not have a nanny but instead she was known as 'Nurse', a title more befitting in a doctor's household. Nurse Ellam from Lancaster stayed with us until I was about 4yrs old. I loved her dearly, as ugly as sin but with a heart of gold. She was followed by Nurse Seymour, Mary Augusta Seymour from Wantage. Again I loved her dearly and it was she who was largely responsible for bringing me up. It was part of my mother's remit to interview and chose the nanny and I suspect she selected the ugly ones so that my father's roving eye might not have cause to rest, not that my father was so inclined as far as I am aware.

This raises the question what did the mothers do with their time if nanny had the job of bringing up the children. None of the mothers worked, upper middle class mothers were not expected to work. They supervised the running of the household, did the shopping, played bridge in the afternoons, did a little of the cooking such as cake making. Mother also had the task of ensuring that the surgeries were kept clean and tidy, not that she was expected to do the cleaning, that was the job of the daily help. But she would see to the arranging of the flowers on the waiting room table!

Nanny would take the children for a walk each day. In our case, in the absence of a garden, this usually meant up the Edenfield Road or across the common behind the house to Falinge Park, once the home of Clement Royds one of the rich textile magnates in the town. Our nurse would usually arrange to meet Nurse Naylor in the park where they would sit gossiping and knitting while the children played on the grass making daisy chains.

When we were older and started school at Miss Humphreys in William Street, our nurse would walk us to school and then collect us again when the school day was over. We had to walk along Spotland Road, down Blackwater where you could still see the tram lines imbedded between the setts, across the town centre, up the church steps (110 steps each way) and across the graveyard around the Parish Church of St Chad, each day I would unknowingly pass the grave of my great-great-great-grandfather, something I discovered many years later. Miss Humphreys acted as the local kindergarten and primary school for the upper middle classes. Children began school at the age of five, boys left at the age of eight for prep school whilst girls stayed on until they were eleven or twelve. There were three classes in the converted outbuildings with a 'sixth form' for the girls in the main house. The main purpose was to teach you to read and write, add, subtract, multiply and divide. So far as I was concerned they succeeded, and when I went to my prep school I went straight into the second form whilst those who had yet to master the three Rs went into the bottom form. The one subject which I never could master was copper plate handwriting for which you had to copy meticulously the writing in the line above.

As schools went it was probably no better or worse than many others, but most of us were happy and contented. But as we left for our prep schools there were ominous signs, a large trench lined with concrete was built in the garden and then roofed over, and a new game was invented to be played once a week during the morning break … air raid shelters!

Memories of early childhood are notoriously fickle, and it is often difficult to distinguish between fact and what one has read or been told. I remember the lamplighter who came round as dusk fell, using his long pole to turn the pilot light inside the lantern allowing ignition of the main gas supply. He must have returned each morning to turn the gas off. The main roads were soon to be lit by electricity but the old gas 'lanterns', persisted for many years in the back streets behind the surgery. I like to think that I can also remember the 'knocker-up-er' with her long pole, attached to the top of which was a bunch of umbrella wires that she used to tap on the bedroom window of the cotton workers to rouse them from their beds … but surely I was too young and would still have been asleep. One clear memory was the raucous call of the rag and bone man. It was years before I discovered that the loud and strident call 'AG-OH' could be interpreted as 'rag-bone'. Bring out enough rags or bones and you would be rewarded with a block of soap stone to colour the edges of the pennant stone steps in front of your house.

Milk was delivered daily in a yellow milk float with two large wheels and drawn by one of the farm horses. Our milk came from the Greave Farm, one of the few Tuberculin Tested herds, a problem still with us today as our badger population is learning to its disadvantage. The milk was transported in a large churn with a brass tap at the bottom carried at the back of the float perched perilously on the lower step. When the milkman stepped up onto the float (it had steps at the back to assist him) the float would tip up and down. The milk would be drawn off into a pint or gill can and then tipped into the householder's jug or container.

Gradually the churns and the milk floats disappeared and were replaced by bottles which are still in use today. The early bottles had a cardboard 'lid' which fitted into the neck of the bottle. If you pressed down too hard on the disc when opening the bottle, the milk spurted upwards into your face.

Living in Spotland Road was like living in a small village, everyone knew everyone else. I spent my Saturday penny at Fred Kitchen's newspaper shop, usually on sweets, further down the road was Mathews the greengrocer, his fruit and vegetables arranged in open racks on either side as you entered the shop. Further still on the same side was the chemist shop thought to have been built by Dr Samuel Heap for his son who failed to make the grade into medical school. On the other side of Hudson Street, a branch of Duckworths the grocers. Although mother would shop at Duckworths in the centre of the town, she would buy her day to day groceries from Burgons just across the road from the practice house. The walls were tiled and long counters stretched on either side of the shop. Tea was still measured out and weighed, as was butter and sugar. The shelves behind the counter were stacked high with biscuit tins and other packaged goods. On the other side of Spotland road was a mysterious shop with a large window of opaque glass above which could just be seen large gas lamps covered with inverted glass domes. We never did discover what went on inside, a subject about which our nurse was curiously reticent.

Spotland road was one of the main arterial highways leading out of town. After Spotland Bridge it became Edenfield Road which took you right up into Norden and then onto the moors, passed 'Owd Betts' and ultimately to

Blackpool! Come Wakes Week and the whole town went on holiday, most of it to Blackpool and the Lancashire coast. There was an agreed schedule of dates so that no two towns would be on holiday at the same time. Most people travelled by bus or 'charabancs' as they were known in those days. All the buses started from the town centre which meant they all had to drive along Spotland Road. My sister and I would sit glued to the window, watching the charabancs that came from all over Lancashire, blue ones, red ones, green ones, buses with gaily coloured patterns, multicoloured buses, interspersed with the local buses from Yelloway and the white and red of Ellen Smith. After the exodus the town was deserted and unnaturally quiet for a week, all the mills and most of the shops were closed. Peace reigned until a week later when the whole process was reversed.

It was not only buses that used Spotland Road. Many of the funeral processions would use Spotland Road to reach the cemetery. In those days there was still some respect for the dead, traffic came to a standstill, walkers stood silently having doffed their caps, and still one or two people would draw their curtains or pull down their blinds. Most of the hearses were motorised but there was still the odd horse-drawn vehicle, the horses wearing black plumes on their heads and delicately carved tracery on the hearse itself.

No account of life in Edwardian England would be complete without some description of Christmas. Christmas at Edensor (the home of my maternal grandmother) followed a never changing pattern. One week before the appointed day my sister and I would be summoned to Edensor to decorate the Christmas tree in the bay window in the lounge. On the day before the great event, out came the family dinner service and the large canteen of cutlery. Everything had to be washed, the silver cleaned, the knives sharpened in the rotary knife cleaner, the table laid. The youngest grandchild had the place of honour next to my Aunt Kathleen, perched uncomfortably on top of a Victorian child's chair. After the meal the younger children would distribute the presents from under the tree. The King's speech was listened to in silence and then everyone stood to attention during the playing of the National Anthem. Tradition required that after the presents had been opened the children would kiss the great aunts and thank them for their present, something I dreaded as even at an early age I was repulsed by these nicotine-stained moustaches so one year I decided that I would not! Alas! our nurse soon detected my ploy, I was taken on one side, firmly admonished and forced to go through the ritual to my humiliation and disgust.

Why devote a chapter to this one short period in the life of our family?

There were no momentous family events, there were few marriages and even fewer deaths, although the great aunts and great uncles were soon to shuffle off this 'mortal coil'. It describes a way of life which is quite foreign to us today and is probably incomprehensible to today's youth. But it was a way of life which would still have been recognisable by William the Founder and his generation and as such it forms a bridge between two quite different ideologies.

While we were growing up inside our protected and privileged cocoon alarming events were taking place in the outside world. The decade had begun with a deep financial recession and rising unemployment that had little immediate effect on our lives. But much worse was to come with the rise of Hitler's Germany which annexed the Sudetenland, marched into Austria and then invaded Poland and on 3rd September 1939 Britain found itself at war with Germany, a war which was soon to involve nearly the whole world.

Although we, as children, had little understanding in the early years of what was happening, it had a profound effect on our lives. Our servants disappeared almost overnight, not that this had much effect on my sister and I as we were away at boarding school although it did mean that the restrictions on travel and a shortage of petrol meant that we would only see our parents once a term, and then only for one brief day out. Food was in short supply and severely rationed. Our uncles were called up for military service and over four years were to elapse before we saw them again.

Of far greater effect on our lives were the sweeping social changes which resulted from the war, the Welfare State, a National Health Service that totally altered the pattern my father's work although he was young enough to adapt, and the erosion of the class barriers that had determined the pattern of our lives before the war … an increasingly egalitarian Britain had arrived.

15

TRANSATLANTIC CONNECTIONS

Three thousand miles of potentially turbulent sea separate us from the Americas, but ever since Columbus discovered the New World our sailors have claimed the Atlantic as their own. Not many years were to pass before we laid claim to the eastern seaboard of America and Canada, albeit not without competition from the French in Canada and North America, and Spain further to the south. By the early part of the 18thC there were thirteen well established American Colonies belonging to Britain and the parent nation derived great benefit from trading with the colonies until the Americans demanded their Independence. This they fought for and won in the American War of Independence and our armies and navy were ignominiously evicted. However we retained control of Canada which was garrisoned with a large army, one of whose tasks being to maintain and defend the border with America to the south against any possible incursions by this young and vigorous new nation. They were also there should there be further problems with the French who were in a majority in Quebec and other counties on the eastern seaboard. Serving with that army in Canada was the first of our ancestors to cross the Atlantic, one Richard Howarth, who served in the Corps of Royal Artillery Drivers from 1803 to 1814.

Richard Howarth was nephew by marriage to William The Founder through his wife Betty Howarth. Richard was born in Bury in 1785 and joined the army in 1803 where he served as a Driver in Chief with the Royal Artillery. Unfortunately we do not have a copy of his service record except we know he took his own discharge whilst serving in Canada.[1]

At the time Richard was serving in the Niagara District of Canada and when he left the army he set himself up as a farmer, clearly he thought that Canada had more to offer him than a return to industrial Lancashire. His cousins, Thomas and William Heap, kept in touch by mail and we have copies of their letters from 1817 until 1851 when the correspondence ceased, perhaps Richard Howarth had died.[2] Unfortunately we do not have copies of the letters Richard wrote in return although it would seem that he was making a reasonable living for himself as a farmer, firstly near St Thomas in the London District and later at Ten Mile Creek in the Township of Grantham in the district of Niagara. It seems likely that the Stamm sisters[3] had traced the connection between their family and Richard Howarth's descendants but unfortunately we have no record of this.

Thomas and William's letters would have been carried to Canada by the packet boats which operated out of Falmouth on a regular scheduled service. They held the contract to carry the Royal Mail.[4] The packets operated more than a mail service, merchants entrusted their money to them, and they carried official despatches and bullion to pay the British troops. They were fast and operated outside any convoy system. In war time the attrition rate was high, both from enemy action and privateers, and anyone else who might think they were fair game. In addition to this there were frequent sailings by merchant vessels as trade with the American colonies and Canada increased year by year, particularly after the brief 1812 war with the newly fledged American United States. Richard would probably have travelled out to Canada on a merchant ship chartered to carry troop reinforcements.

This increase in trade resulted in an increasing demand for some form of scheduled passenger service and in 1818 the sailing packet *James Monroe*, left New York for Liverpool carrying eight passengers, 71 cotton bales, 14 bales of wool, and small quantities of cranberries and turpentine. A few days earlier a similar vessel had left Liverpool for New York, and the Black Ball Line was born. The packets established an average time of 22 days on the outward voyage and 40 days on the more difficult return journey. The service was a success and it was not long before competition arrived with the Red Star Line, the Swallow Tail Line and the London Line.[5]

In 1837 Isambard Kingdom Brunel began his first Atlantic crossing with the Great Western which combined steam and sail and cut the journey time down to 15 days. In 1840 Cunard began its first regular cargo and passenger steamship service between Boston and Liverpool, and by 1870 the White Star's Oceanic set a new standard of comfort with large portholes, electricity, and running water in all the first class cabins. By the time Herbert Heap and his family set off for North America to manage Samuel Heap and Son's new American venture, he could be assured that he would not only travel in comfort but on a regular service that would stick to a rigid timetable regardless of weather and

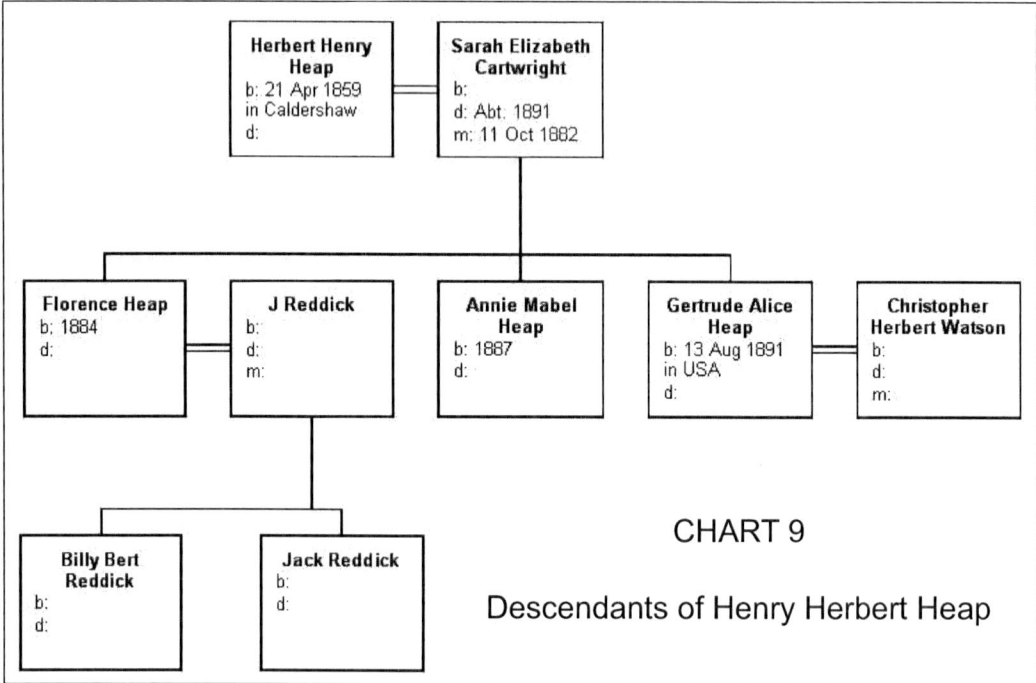

Herbert Henry Heap
b: 21 Apr 1859
in Caldershaw
d:

Sarah Elizabeth Cartwright
b:
d: Abt. 1891
m: 11 Oct 1882

Florence Heap
b: 1884
d:

J Reddick
b:
d:
m:

Annie Mabel Heap
b: 1887
d:

Gertrude Alice Heap
b: 13 Aug 1891
in USA
d:

Christopher Herbert Watson
b:
d:
m:

Billy Bert Reddick
b:
d:

Jack Reddick
b:
d:

CHART 9

Descendants of Henry Herbert Heap

cargo availability.

Herbert Henry Heap was born at Caldershaw on 26 April 1859, a younger brother to the redoubtable Charles and his elder brother William Tweedale Heap. He is recorded on the 1861 and 1871 census as living in Spotland, presumably at Caldershaw. He married Sarah Elizabeth Cartwright at Madeley in South Cheshire on 11 October 1882 and on the marriage certificate Herbert is described as a farmer living in Shropshire. With the benefit of hindsight it hardly seems this was an appropriate background for anyone destined to be sent out to North America to manage and control Samuel Heap and Son's American business. By all accounts Herbert was a 'hail fellow, well met' type of individual and perhaps he welcomed the challenge.

There were three daughters of the marriage, Florence born in 1884 who married a J. Reddick, Annie Mabel born at Cound in Shropshire in 1887, and Gertrude Alice born in 1891 possibly in the USA as the UK 1911 Census describes her as USA Resident. Herbert is described as a widower on the 1911 census and Sarah is not shown on the US 1910 census so presumably she died after the family arrived in the USA or shortly before they sailed.

In the 1880s Charles Heap, always on the look-out for new machinery and new processes to keep one step ahead of the competition, introduced the Moser Grosselin raising machine to Britain which enabled him to manufacture a new type of raised cotton cloth known as 'flannelette'. Most woollen and some cotton cloths had to have the 'nap' raised as part of the finishing process and this had always been done with a machine fitted with natural teazles. This gave the cloth a fur-like appearance which could then be trimmed or 'sheared' to the required length. The new Moser machines mechanised the process. They were infinitely more efficient and enabled output to be doubled.

In 1888 Charles paid Moser £2,500 which gave him the sole right to sell the machine in the USA where it was protected by an American patent negotiated by Grosselin and Moser. Charles began exporting the machine to the USA and in 1892 set up the American Napping Machine Company registered in Maine to begin construction of the machines. Grosselin and Moser, together with Charles' wife and brother William Tweedale, owning the stock between them. Herbert had been sent out to the States, probably in 1888, to manage what was hoped would be a rapidly expanding and profitable business.

Not satisfied with this, Charles decided to build a finishing works in Williamstown, Massachusetts, and a contract exists dated August 1892 to build a new bleaching and dying works on the Green River at Williamstown for $27,375, to be known as the 'Boston Finishing Works'. Charles, William

Tweedale, and their brother-in-law Christopher Watson, a Liverpool wool broker, all paid several visits to the States and expressed themselves satisfied with the outcome and returned home waiting to rake in the profits.

Alas! it was not to be. Both businesses were already in difficulties by 1892. Apart from disagreements between Moser and Grosselin, the American machine makers challenged the right of the incomers to operate and the American Napping Machine company soon went out of business. The Boston Finishing Works never made a profit and one can only assume that the Americans discouraged their own cloth manufacturers from making use of the interloper. The Heaps knew the finishing business probably as well, if not better, than anyone else in the world at that time so technical inability is unlikely to have been a factor. Further, American law had the effect of discouraging foreign competitors and making life difficult for them. The situation was not made any easier when their tax advisers told them that they couldn't offset the American losses against their English profits.

Charles blamed Herbert for lack of drive and dynamism, and the business was sold and closed down and Herbert returned to England under a cloud. The 1911 census shows him living at 108 Sheriff Street with his two younger unmarried daughters and working as a bleacher and dyer, presumably at Samuel Heap and Son – the family always looked after its own. He died at Crosby, Liverpool, in 1935. Florence had left home to marry a J. Reddick by whom she had two boys, Billy Bert and Jack.

This was not to be the end of the family's involvement with the Americas. Richard Henry Greaves[6] was serving as a Unitarian Minister in the USA from 1897 to 1902, and was living in New Jersey when his daughter, Margaret Elizabeth Cowell, was born in 1912. Margaret Elizabeth and her mother were attempting to rejoin her husband when they were torpedoed off the coast of Ireland by a German submarine in 1915 … after that experience they decided to remain in the United Kingdom!

One of the more recent crossings was made by Charles Deryk Heap, the youngest son of John Hudson Heap and grandson of the entrepreneurial Charles Heap. He was serving in the RAF during the 1939-45 war and was posted out to Canada to train Canadian pilots where he met his wife Yvonne Taylor. Their eldest child Peter Charles was born in Rochdale in 1947 and six weeks later the family emigrated to Vancouver where they remain to this day.

Crossing the Atlantic today is no more difficult than flying to anywhere else in Europe. Eight hours of acute discomfort and boredom crammed into the rear cabin of an aircraft with scarce room to breathe, only to be discharged the other end disorientated for time and space. It would almost have been preferable to have travelled steerage along with other immigrants to the new world. It certainly would have been a great deal more comfortable travelling with Herbert Heap in one of the upper class cabins on a transatlantic liner, when he would have had time to reflect on the problems which would face him when he landed in the Americas, or to think what he was going to say to an irate Charles Heap when he landed at Liverpool.

References

1 Attestation records with duplicate discharge certificate. Corps of Royal Artillery records
2 see appendix 4
3 see Lye Stamm papers appendix 3
4 Mallinson, Howard. Send it by Semaphore. pub Crowood Press 2005. p 20
5 Wikipedia – Transatlantic Crossing
6 The Greaves Family – see chapter

16

THE HANDLEYS AND THE COOMERS

The family was connected by marriage to many of the textile families in Rochdale, a reflection of the social structure of the upper middle classes in the latter half of the 19thC which endured up to the 1914-18 war. But the loss of a generation of young men in the war opened up opportunities for those who had survived, and the younger post-war generation expected more as their right. Employment in the cotton and woollen mills had little attraction for many of them, and they sought employment outside the industry, forging careers in the professional classes for which their education had fitted them. Even their wives and girl friends were demanding the right to vote and earn their own living.

The Lancashire County Boroughs were fiercely independent self-governing units of local government with their own Mayors, Chief Constables, Aldermen and Town Councillors, many of whom were mill owners who lived in the town in the larger houses on the outskirts. They still came to work at the mill each day or occupied themselves with the buying and selling of wool and cotton at the Exchange in Manchester. But change was coming, and many would say it was long overdue.

Living and working in the town, the mill owners families and their supporting cast of doctors, solicitors, accountants had tended to look for wives and husbands from among their own class. Hence the relatively high rate of intermarriage within a small group of families. But the field of opportunity was widening, and the history of the Handleys and the Coomers illustrates this. Sarah Tweedale Heap, the eldest daughter of William Tweedale Heap, was to marry James Edgar Handley and her cousin Helen (Nellie) Heap, the eldest daughter of William Tweedale Heap's younger brother, Charles, was to marry Clement Walton Coomer. The Handleys were tradesmen and retailers from the West Riding of Yorkshire. The Coomers were bankers and accountants from

Liverpool and Cheshire. There was however one element of their lives which they shared, and that was their Wesleyan Methodist faith, a faith that brought them together to worship on Sundays and provided a structure within which they could mix freely regardless of their background. The young would occupy the gallery above the main chapel concourse and it is said that assignations were made and notes passed, concealed between the pages of their prayer books. But even here the social divide operated. The Baillie Street chapel was patronised by the wealthy upper strata of society, whereas the Union Street chapel was favoured by the tradesmen and the working class. No such distinction could operate in the smaller chapels which were springing up on the periphery of the town, providing a service for the outlying communities. The Lanehead chapel, situated on the edge of the moor above Caldershaw, was one such and was patronised both by the Heaps of Caldershaw and the Handleys. Both families held office in the chapel. Unfortunately most of the records of the Lanehead chapel have disappeared and the chapel itself was demolished in the late sixties. Probably both families had contributed towards the cost of the building.

❀

The Handleys

The Handleys were cattle traders who came to Rochdale from Middleham in Wensleydale in the early part of the 19thC. William Handley and his two younger brothers, Peter and Robert, would have brought their cattle to the livestock market in Rochdale, held each week on the wide open space where the new police station now stands. One side of the market was bordered by the River Roche into which all the effluent would have been hosed down at the end of the day's business. There had been a thriving market in Rochdale for more than a hundred years and it continued well into the 20thC. On market days my sister and would try to persuade our nurse to divert our morning walk so that we passed by the market. There we would hang over the raised wall surrounding it, and drink in the scene laid out below: the constantly moving beasts, the raucous shouts of the auctioneer, the steaming piles of dung, the lowing of cattle and bleating of sheep and lambs as they were herded off to slaughter or into the custody of the purchaser.

William Handley, the eldest of the three brothers, was born in Middleham on 23 May 1798 and was married three times, firstly to Mary Dawson, mother of all his children, subsequently to Sarah Lister, and then to Martha Binks, the latter two wives being without issue. Mary Dawson died on 17 September 1836 and was buried in St Chad's New Burial Ground across the road from the Parish church.

William must have liked the look of Rochdale as he set up in business as a butcher at 6 The Shambles in the centre of the town (also given as 4 Shamples House, The Baum). His son, Joseph Handley, born 1827, married twice, first to Ellen Taylor and then to Frances Bevan who named her eldest son James Edgar Handley, born 26 March 1862. James Edgar married Sarah Tweedale Heap, the eldest daughter of William Tweedale Heap. It was these two who were to form the bond between the two families that continues to this day.

Joseph was the third son of William Handley, now described as of Shaw Hill. He began business as a grocer and provisions dealer at 33 Yorkshire Street, soon making a name for himself as one of the finest judges of tea in the North of England. He also had premises at Hanging Ditch and Church Street in Manchester. He was chairman of the Rochdale and District Commercial Loan and Discount Co., afterwards known as the Rochdale Stock Bank. Joseph represented Castleton Ward as a Liberal Town Councillor for 22 years from 1865, although curiously he never made it onto the Aldermanic bench or held the post of Mayor. He was an ardent Wesleyan Methodist attending the Union Street Chapel, of which he became treasurer in 1877. He died after a short illness at the Victoria Lodge, Birkdale in Southport in February 1900, aged 73.

Anyone who attempts to unravel the history of the Handley family soon becomes entangled with the descendants of William's two brothers, Peter and Robert, both of whom settled in Rochdale. Nearly all of them were engaged in the shop trade. We know of a Robert Handley, tailor of Oldham Road, a John Handley, butcher, of 132 Yorkshire Street, another Robert who was a butcher, Joseph the flannel merchant of Acker Street, another Joseph, draper of 77 Yorkshire Street, George a linen and stocking merchant … confusion reigns since nearly all of them named at least one of their sons Joseph. This came to light in 1955 when a gravestone was discovered in the long disused cellars at 77 Yorkshire street. On the stone was engraved the name Joseph Handley, draper, 1866 and the initials A.H. and H.H. which refer to his two sons, Arthur and Herbert, who died in infancy. The mystery remains as to how the gravestone got there in the first place, and why they were buried in unconsecrated ground – if indeed their bodies lie beneath the slab …

When Joseph Handley died his flourishing business passed to his son, James

Edgar, who was to marry Sarah Tweedale Heap on 14 August 1889. Sarah was to bear him five sons, Edgar Bevan, Bernard Watson, Donald Clifford, Hubert Lesley and Allan Tweedale. Sadly the marriage was not a success. James Edgar had always wanted to be an artist and had no interest in the business even though it provided him with a very reasonable income. He became an alcoholic, lived apart from his wife and dissociated himself from his children, eventually dying of cirrhosis of the liver in 1921. He left an estate valued at £50,000 but disinherited his family. The money was left to the Rochdale Infirmary and for the establishment of a trust fund to purchase works of art for the Rochdale Art Gallery.

A broken marriage was not to be the only problem facing Sarah Tweedale. As the century advanced the clouds of war began to darken the horizon and of Sarah's five sons, four were the right age to be caught up in the war. The eldest Edgar Bevan, born 26 May 1890, was a private in the army but his unit is unknown. He survived the war after being badly gassed during the early years. Edgar was to join William Tatham and Son, manufacturers of cotton machinery, after the war and subsequently worked for the English Card Spinning Co. Ltd. He married Marie Sommerville Gabb, always known as 'Bee'. Bee's sister, Amy, was a nurse and they may have met Edgar during his convalescence after being gassed and discharged from the army. Edgar died in 1956.

They had one child, Catherine Frances Handley, who may have served in the WRNS during the 1939-45 war. Unfortunately the family lost touch with her although it is known she was living alone in Sidmouth in her latter years and subsequently died in a Nursing Home in Honiton aged 86 in September 2006. She was unmarried but had one son, Christopher, whose present whereabouts are unknown.

The second son, Bernard Watson Handley, born 23 Aug 1892, a sapper in the Royal Engineers, was killed at Ypres when a shell landed in the trench he was occupying. Bernard was an artist and caricaturist of great promise. Trained at the local art school, he had many of his drawings published in the *Manchester Evening News* and he had begun to branch out into the political sphere.

The third son, Donald Clifford, followed his brothers into the army serving in the Army Cyclists Corps in Salonika. The cyclists was seldom deployed as a separate unit. They were more usually attached to larger formations at battalion level and served as messengers. The Allies had despatched an army corps to Macedonia early in 1915 made up of British and French units, but it arrived too late to help the Serbs. It was not until the latter part of the war that it was engaged against the Bulgarians and the Austrians when it attempted to

CHART 15

The Handley Family

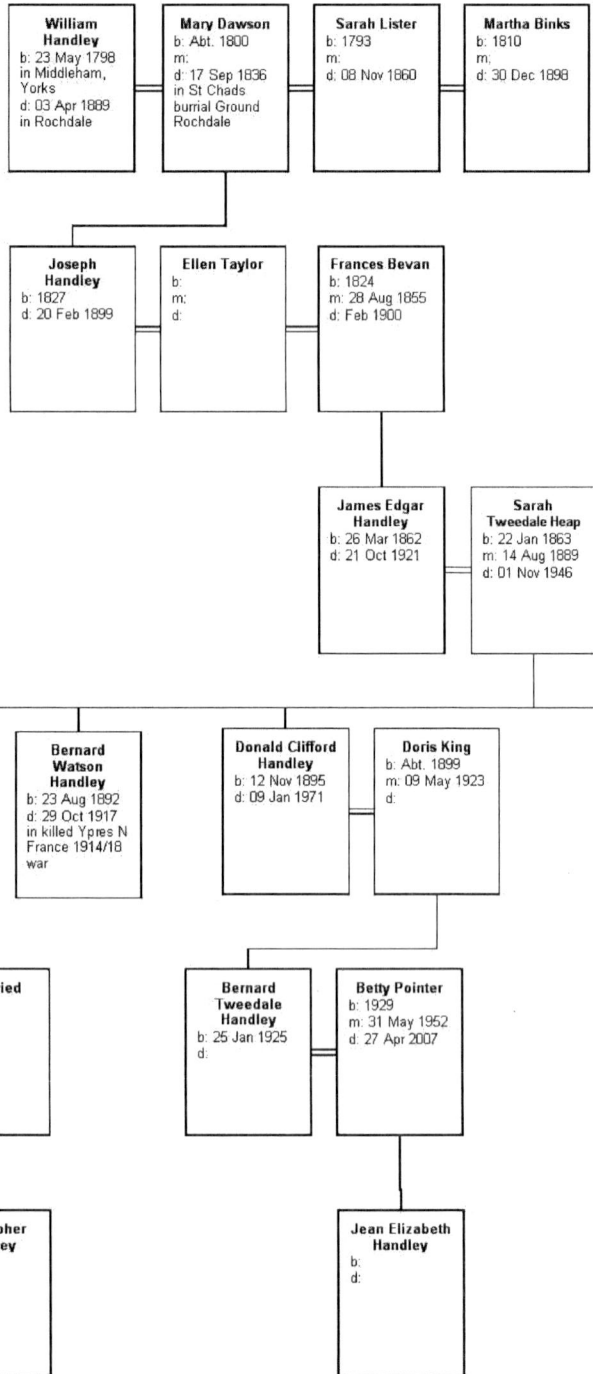

William Handley
b: 23 May 1798 in Middleham, Yorks
d: 03 Apr 1889 in Rochdale

Mary Dawson
b: Abt. 1800
m:
d: 17 Sep 1836 in St Chads burrial Ground Rochdale

Sarah Lister
b: 1793
m:
d: 08 Nov 1860

Martha Binks
b: 1810
m:
d: 30 Dec 1898

Joseph Handley
b: 1827
d: 20 Feb 1899

Ellen Taylor
b:
m:
d:

Frances Bevan
b: 1824
m: 28 Aug 1855
d: Feb 1900

James Edgar Handley
b: 26 Mar 1862
d: 21 Oct 1921

Sarah Tweedale Heap
b: 22 Jan 1863
m: 14 Aug 1889
d: 01 Nov 1946

Edgar Bevan Handley
b: 26 May 1890
d: 1956

Bee Marie Somerville
b: 1980
m: 08 Jan 1919
d: 1961

Bernard Watson Handley
b: 23 Aug 1892
d: 29 Oct 1917 in killed Ypres N France 1914/18 war

Donald Clifford Handley
b: 12 Nov 1895
d: 09 Jan 1971

Doris King
b: Abt. 1899
m: 09 May 1923
d:

Catherine Frances Handley
b: 09 Jan 1920
d:

unmarried
b:
m:
d:

Bernard Tweedale Handley
b: 25 Jan 1925
d:

Betty Pointer
b: 1929
m: 31 May 1952
d: 27 Apr 2007

Christopher Handley
b:
d:

Jean Elizabeth Handley
b:
d:

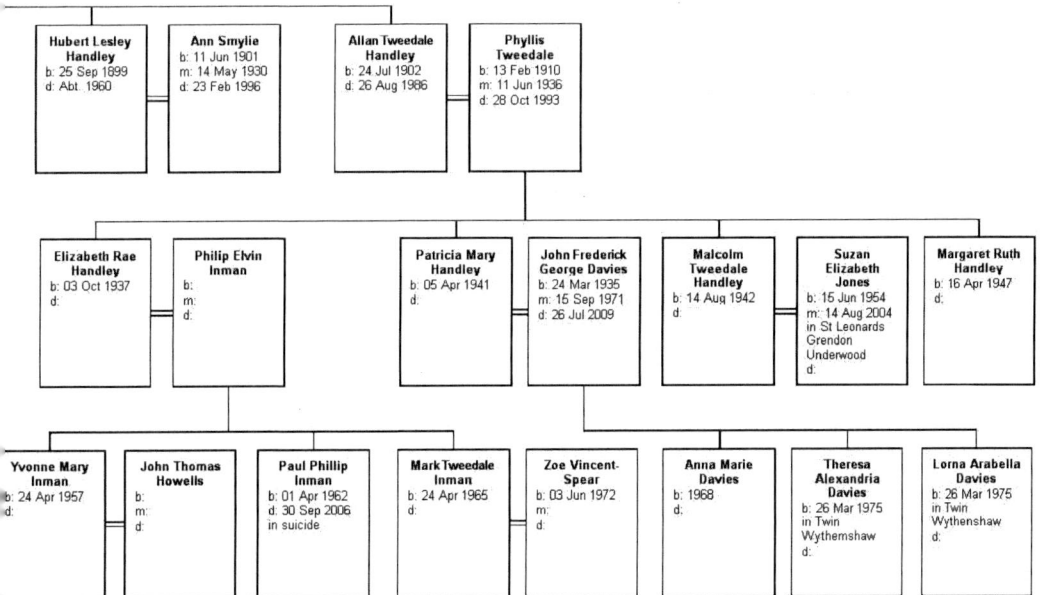

Hubert Lesley Handley
b: 25 Sep 1899
d: Abt. 1960

Ann Smylie
b: 11 Jun 1901
m: 14 May 1930
d: 23 Feb 1996

Allan Tweedale Handley
b: 24 Jul 1902
d: 26 Aug 1986

Phyllis Tweedale
b: 13 Feb 1910
m: 11 Jun 1936
d: 28 Oct 1993

Elizabeth Rae Handley
b: 03 Oct 1937
d:

Philip Elvin Inman
b:
m:
d:

Patricia Mary Handley
b: 05 Apr 1941
d:

John Frederick George Davies
b: 24 Mar 1935
m: 15 Sep 1971
d: 26 Jul 2009

Malcolm Tweedale Handley
b: 14 Aug 1942
d:

Suzan Elizabeth Jones
b: 15 Jun 1954
m: 14 Aug 2004
in St Leonards Grendon Underwood
d:

Margaret Ruth Handley
b: 16 Apr 1947
d:

Yvonne Mary Inman
b: 24 Apr 1957
d:

John Thomas Howells
b:
m:
d:

Paul Phillip Inman
b: 01 Apr 1962
d: 30 Sep 2006
in suicide

Mark Tweedale Inman
b: 24 Apr 1965
d:

Zoe Vincent-Spear
b: 03 Jun 1972
m:
d:

Anna Marie Davies
b: 1968
d:

Theresa Alexandria Davies
b: 26 Mar 1975
in Twin Wythemshaw
d:

Lorna Arabella Davies
b: 26 Mar 1975
in Twin Wythenshaw
d:

storm the heavily fortified heights around Lake Doiran, with disastrous results and very heavy casualties. It was only saved by the armistice in 1918. If Donald had been engaged in the fighting on the Pip ridge he was lucky to have survived. After the war he joined the District Bank, rising to become manager of the Chorlton-cum-Hardy branch. His son, Bernard Tweedale, served in the RASC during the 1939-45 war and fought his way up Italy. He survived to become manager of the Nat West Bank in Alderley Edge.

The fourth son, Hubert Lesley, joined the Royal Flying Corps as a Cadet in 1917 but happily survived. Although trained as an engineer, he started work at Samuel Heap and Son after he was demobilised. He remained in employment with the family firm for the rest of his working life. Lesley, as he was more commonly known, was a jovial soul with a red face and a large hooked nose, and looked just like Mr Punch. They had no children but I was privileged to attend his silver wedding when the Handleys and the Heaps gathered to celebrate the occasion on a hot summer afternoon, fires blazing in every grate, the tables groaning with food and the drink flowing liberally, and everyone over dressed. George Heap, Chairman of the board, stood aloof from the rest but would condescend to discuss frivolities if you take the conversation to him.

The youngest son, Allan Tweedale Handley, had his brother's artistic streak and went into photography. He worked with Lafayettes in Manchester and also with W.H. Carter of 43 Drake Street in Rochdale – a business which he subsequently acquired. He also owned studios in Bury and Oldham. He took over Guttenbergs, the society photographers in Manchester, and took the official photographs when Royalty and other important persons visited Manchester. Successful although his photography business was, it is rumoured he made most of his money on the Stock Exchange. He married Phyllis Tweedale at the Baptist Hope Chapel in Rochdale on 11 June 1936, with the Rev Albany Renton officiating. They had four children, Elizabeth Rae, Malcolm Tweedale, Margaret Ruth and Patricia Mary. All the male Handleys take Tweedale as their second name in memory of their great grandmother Ann Tweedale. The youngest son, Allan Tweedale Handley also married a Tweedale, Phyllis Tweedale and it is thought that the two families share a common origin.

✻

The Coomers

The Coomers were contemporaneous with the Handleys, the connecting link in each case being the wives – Helen 'Nellie' Heap marrying Clement Walton Coomer and her cousin, Sarah Tweedale Heap marrying James Edgar Handley. Both Clement Coomer and one of the Handley boys, Leslie, were to find employment with the family firm of Samuel Heap and Son but in rather different capacities. They were all Wesleyan Methodists. I don't doubt that they were all required to attend chapel on Sundays. One wonders which came first, romance, chapel attendance, or work.

The Coomers are recorded as living in Cheshire from the early part of the 18thC at Audlem, Hough, Wybunbury and Basford. Several are listed as farmers. Clement Coomer's father, John Coomer, who married Lydia Durant, was born at Basford Hall to the south of Crewe. He became a banker with the North and South Wales Bank, later taken over by the Midland Bank. He worked out of the head office in Liverpool before moving to Walton where his alphabetical children, Albert, Beatrice, Clement and Duncan were born. Both Clement and Albert bear the second name Walton thought to be a reference to their place of birth. Albert was described as a retired bank inspector in 1941.

John Coomer left the bank when he was 35 and moved to Nantwich. He went into the cotton trade with an office in Manchester and then in 1903 formed the Norden Cotton Co. Ltd. in partnership with Edward Tattersall. The firm changed its name to Cords Ltd. in 1906. He later moved to Rochdale where he built Bamford Dene. He died at Southport in 1923.

Clement Coomer was born on 14 August 1877 at Walton, Liverpool, and went to school at Nantwich before joining the Manchester Warehousemen and Clerks School at Cheadle Hulme. He qualified as a chartered accountant, then set himself up in business as a stockbroker with offices in Rochdale. He specialised in cotton mill shares and it must have been in this capacity that he probably managed the share capital of Samuel Heap and Son and also the family loan scheme of which Ernest Muehleck, who had been brought in as Manager and Director, was so highly critical. Unfortunately we have been unable to access the Samuel Heap and Son archives dealing with Clement Coomer and his and their business interests. From what we do know his influence in that sphere was more than just superficial. He became Chairman of the Oldham Stock Exchange, an office that he held over a twenty-year period. He was also secretary of the Rochdale Steam Tramway and Secretary and Director of Cords Ltd.

CHART 16

Coomer Family Tree

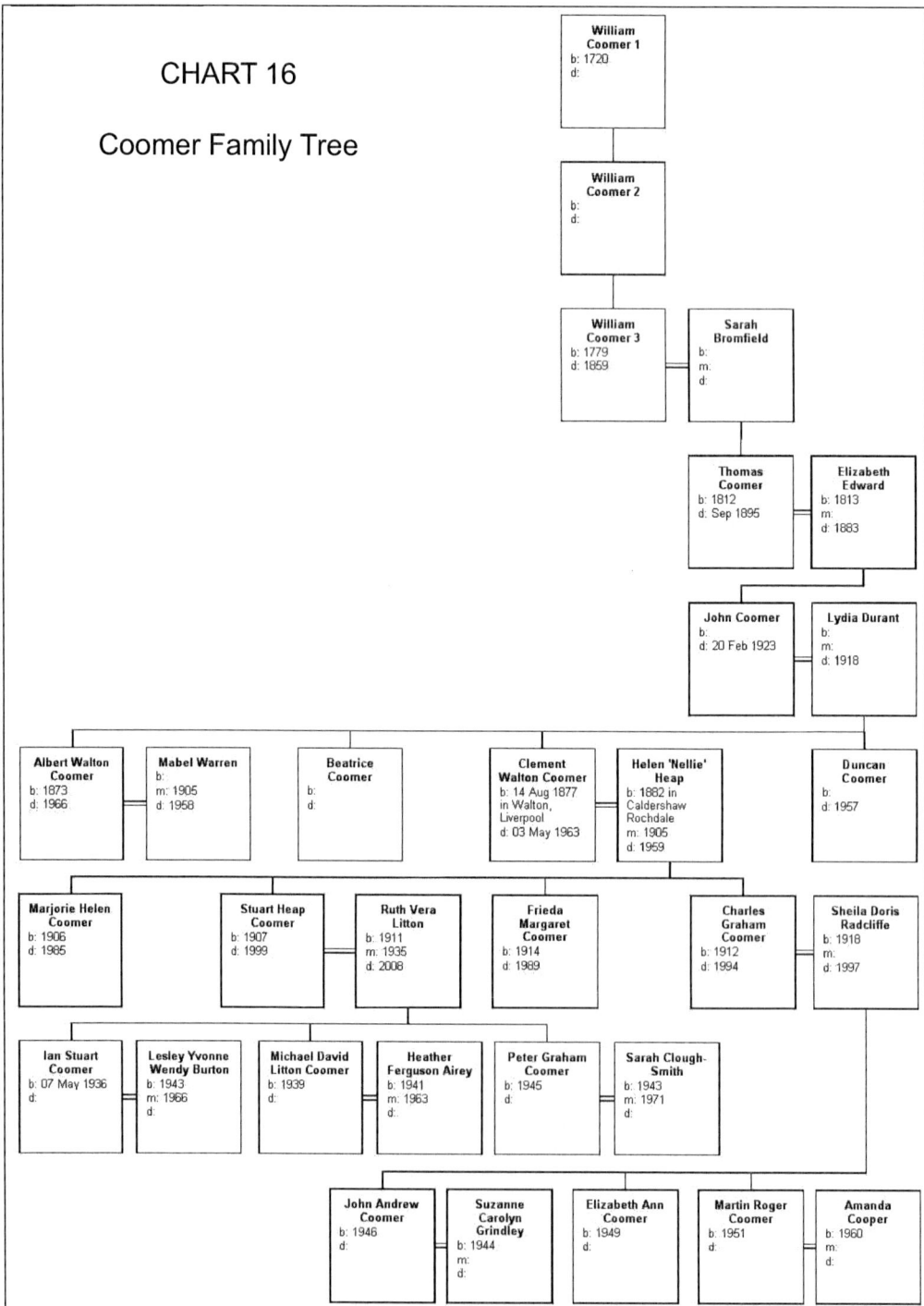

William Coomer 1
b: 1720
d:

William Coomer 2
b:
d:

William Coomer 3
b: 1779
d: 1859

Sarah Bromfield
b:
m:
d:

Thomas Coomer
b: 1812
d: Sep 1895

Elizabeth Edward
b: 1813
m:
d: 1883

John Coomer
b:
d: 20 Feb 1923

Lydia Durant
b:
m:
d: 1918

Albert Walton Coomer
b: 1873
d: 1966

Mabel Warren
b:
m: 1905
d: 1958

Beatrice Coomer
b:
d:

Clement Walton Coomer
b: 14 Aug 1877 in Walton, Liverpool
d: 03 May 1963

Helen 'Nellie' Heap
b: 1882 in Caldershaw Rochdale
m: 1905
d: 1959

Duncan Coomer
b:
d: 1957

Marjorie Helen Coomer
b: 1906
d: 1985

Stuart Heap Coomer
b: 1907
d: 1999

Ruth Vera Litton
b: 1911
m: 1935
d: 2008

Frieda Margaret Coomer
b: 1914
d: 1989

Charles Graham Coomer
b: 1912
d: 1994

Sheila Doris Radcliffe
b: 1918
m:
d: 1997

Ian Stuart Coomer
b: 07 May 1936
d:

Lesley Yvonne Wendy Burton
b: 1943
m: 1966
d:

Michael David Litton Coomer
b: 1939
d:

Heather Ferguson Airey
b: 1941
m: 1963
d:

Peter Graham Coomer
b: 1945
d:

Sarah Clough-Smith
b: 1943
m: 1971
d:

John Andrew Coomer
b: 1946
d:

Suzanne Carolyn Grindley
b: 1944
m:
d:

Elizabeth Ann Coomer
b: 1949
d:

Martin Roger Coomer
b: 1951
d:

Amanda Cooper
b: 1960
m:
d:

Like the rest of the family, he was ardent adherent of the Wesleyan Methodist faith and was one of the prime movers in setting up of the Rochdale Mission and the building of the Champness Hall[1,2], particularly after the untimely death of Charles Heap. It had been one of Charles Heap's lifelong ambitions to build a Wesleyan Mission Hall in the centre of the town as a lasting memorial to his faith. He had for many years rented the Empire Theatre for this purpose but wanted to see a permanent purpose built structure in his lifetime. Although he would not live long enough to see the project brought to fruition, the Champness Hall was finally completed in 1925 due to the generosity of J Arthur Rank of cinematic fame. There was 'accommodation for one thousand scholars', seating for two thousand in the main hall and many other offices. Sadly, it was all too late. The days of large urban Mission were coming to an end. It is said the main hall was never filled to capacity, attendances declined year by year and the building was finally closed down in. It was an ignominious end for what that scurrilous publication the 'Rochdale Alternative Paper' described as a 'mausoleumistic monstrosity' with, it has to be said, some degree of justification.

Clement and Helen Coomer lived at the top end of Upper Sheriff Street, further up the street from Leslie and Ann Handley. In his latter years Clement became a jigsaw fanatic, receiving jigsaws by post. I recall him as a kind and gentle soul, the perfect gentleman, very retiring in his ways, always ensuring that others stood in the limelight while he worked patiently behind the scenes. It was Mrs Helen Coomer who 'declared the Champness Hall open' on 8 September 1925, Clement doesn't even appear amongst the worthies standing on the steps.

Clement Coomer died in 1963 aged 86. I can do no better than quote from the Rochdale Mission:

'Clement Coomer, the last of the great warriors. His death was a serious loss to the Mission. His meticulous care and guidance brought the Mission through many difficult times. His love for the work was shown by his great generosity and unassuming help and advice constantly given. We thank God upon every remembrance of him.'

Clement and Helen Coomer had four children: Marjorie Helen and Frieda Margaret, neither of whom married; and Stuart Heap Coomer and Charles Graham Coomer who have kept the name very much alive with six children, ten grandchildren and nine great grandchildren. Stuart was a chartered accountant with the District Bank of which he became Joint General Manager at the Head Office in Manchester, he served with the Home Guard during the last war. The younger brother, Charles Graham, was a Flt. Lieut. RAFVR in Coastal Command, stationed at Sullom Voe in the Shetlands, during the last war, and was awarded an MBE in recognition of his service.

Stuart Heap Coomer's elder son, Ian Stuart, is a retired chartered surveyor; Michael David Litton Coomer a retired chartered accountant who had worked for TAC Construction Materials – part of the Turner and Newall Group; Peter Graham still in practice as a solicitor.

There is not a single member of the Heap family or a Coomer or a Handley now resident in the Rochdale. All have left the town, presumably seeking a better life elsewhere … inevitably posing the question why?

Acknowledgements

I am indebted to Michael Coomer and Malcolm Handley for the wealth of information they have provided about their two families.

References

1 Champness, Eliza. *Life story of Thomas Champness.* Chas Kelly: London, 1907
2 Barker, John E. *The Rochdale Mission 1905-1965* from The Champness Inheritance. p 60

17

THE GREAVES FAMILY

by Richard Heap

The family's connection with the Greaves Family begins with Alethea Longden Greaves, my paternal grandmother, who married Walter Heap in 1899. Alethea was the third daughter of the Rev. John Clapham Greaves. His parents were Thomas and Mary Greaves, both born in 1799, and he had an elder sister, Ann.[1] John Clapham was born on 11 December 1842 at Birstall in Yorkshire and educated at Batley Grammar school. At the age of 18 years he 'found peace with God' and entered the Methodist ministry in 1863 and was appointed to Tunbridge Wells.[3,4] The next year he was translated to Windsor,[3,4] and in 1867 to Islington, London[3,4] On August 6 1867 he married Mary Elizabeth Cowell at Birstall.[5]

Mary Cowell was born on 1 December 1839. The 1901 census gives her birthplace as York whereas the 1911 census has her born in Leeds. She died on 30 January 1915 and is buried alongside her husband in Manchester Southern Cemetery. Family legend has it that she was South African, had nine brothers, and brought with her a dowry of loose diamonds. These were sold from time to time to fund their living expenses. The last one remaining diamond was thought to have been lost for many years until it was found by Alethea. It was passed from her to her daughter Kathleen, who bequeathed it to her niece Helen, since when it has again disappeared.

John Clapham was to become the Patriarch of the Tribe, begetting ten children. Two were born in Dalston[5] – Mary Elizabeth on 24 May 1868 and William Henry on 7 June 1869 who died the same day – this was during John Clapham's Ministry in Islington[3,4]. Richard Henry was born at Birstall on 26 August 1870[5] before the family moved yet again to New Street in York[3] where Robert Walkington was born on 6 February 1872[5] and Arthur Clapham on 3

June 1873[5]. No trace remains of the manse in York, or of the chapel which was closed in 1908 and subsequently occupied by a furniture dealer and remover. It was converted to a cinema in 1920 and demolished in 1967.

1873 found the family moving to Carver street in Sheffield[3,4] where Emily Dearlove (Mem) was born 15 August 1874 and Charles Elam on 8 April 1876. A move to Birmingham in 1876 saw the birth of Alethea Longden on 18 June 1877 and Ethel (Ek) on 21 June 1878.[5] A further move to Liverpool in 1879[3,4] was marked by the birth of John Cowell, 2 May 1880, the last and youngest of the family.[5]

Anyone reading an account of the life of John Clapham Greaves will be struck by two things: first – his undoubted fecundity, and second – the number of moves made by Wesleyan Methodist ministers. The first attribute is shared by the Heap family into which one of his daughters, Alethea, was to marry some thirty years later. Families of up to ten or more children were not uncommon in the latter half of the 19thC, and we can accredit this in part at least to improvements in child care and in the nation's health. Infant mortality rates had fallen dramatically as a result. Life was lived at a much more leisurely pace, middle class wives were not expected to work – it was their job to run the household and to bring up the children, and there was no television to keep them occupied in the evenings! So far as John Clapham was concerned, it was almost as if he felt the need to imprint his genes on the locality at the start of each new ministry, or was he merely following the Old Testament instruction 'to be fruitful. and multiply'?

The rapid turn-round in Methodist Ministers is a matter of historical and current fact. It dates from the early days when the itinerant Preachers had no fixed base but moved around on their circuit, preaching as they went. From time to time they were required to change onto a different circuit. By the mid 19thC all Methodist ministers were 'ordained' and appointed to 'livings' for a fixed term after which they were required to move. There were obvious drawbacks to the system. The minister had only a limited time to get to know his congregation, and the ever-increasing costs of re-housing and moving were a growing burden on central funds. When the minister moved, so did his family. If, like Walter Heap, you were wooing the minister's daughter, you had to look sharp otherwise she would have moved on.

In 1882 John Clapham was transferred to London (Mostyn Road).[3,4] In the same year Richard and Robert were away at school at The Grove (now Woodhouse Grove), the junior school for Kingswood to which they went the following year.[6] Kingswood was then essentially for the sons of Methodist ministers, financed by donations from their congregations. There is no record in the school history of the other three boys attending.

After Bradford (1885)[3,4] the next move was to Haworth and Oakworth in 1888.[3,4] Whilst at Haworth he laid one of the foundation stones for the Bridgehouse Wesleyan Sunday school. After spells in Liverpool chapels (1891 and 1894),[3,4] the family moved to Manchester in 1897.[3,4]

In the local press account of Alethea Greaves' marriage to Walter Heap on 21 June 1899, John Clapham is described as 'the popular superintendent of the Oxford Road circuit'. He was living at Wesley House, Withington and was one of the officiating Ministers at the service. The bride was given away by her brother Robert, and Mem and Ek were two of the many bridesmaids. Although the press account ran to 19½ column inches there is no mention of any other Greaves relatives, other perhaps than a 'Miss Walkington from Edmonton'. Who was this woman who bears the Walkington name given to the bride's elder brother – Robert Walkington Greaves – and was this Edmonton in north London?

The Kingswood school records for 1898[6] describe Richard as being 'Methodist minister at Montreal in Canada' but he doesn't appear in any British list of Methodist ministers. If this is correct he must have been ordained in Canada or the USA. Robert is described as 'architect and surveyor, Liverpool'. It seems probable he was still living in Manchester and commuted daily to Liverpool.

1900 saw John Clapham moving to Manchester Victoria.[3,4] It was also the year his son, Charles Elam, entered the Ministry at Altrincham having trained at Didsbury.[3,4] In the same year was born the first grandson, Ellis Clifford Heap, eldest son of Alethea and Walter. Alethea was the only one of his children to rival his fecundity but managed only five children, one of whom died in infancy.

The 1901 census is as illuminating for it's omissions as for it's inclusions. It has the majority of the family living at 259 Cheetham Hill Road, father, mother, Elizabeth, Robert, Arthur. Emily was a teacher at a private boarding school in Southport; Charles was exercising his ministry at Altrincham; Ethel was living with Walter and Alethea and Clifford, which leaves Richard and John unaccounted for. John was probably at sea.

Somewhat unusually, John Clapham returned to Withington in 1903, living at 17 Heaton Road. His health failed in 1906, resulting in a stay at Grange over Sands for some time. He died on 28 March 1908. Tributes referred to his writings and to his preaching, he was described as '…very lovable, gentle

CHART 14

The Greaves Family

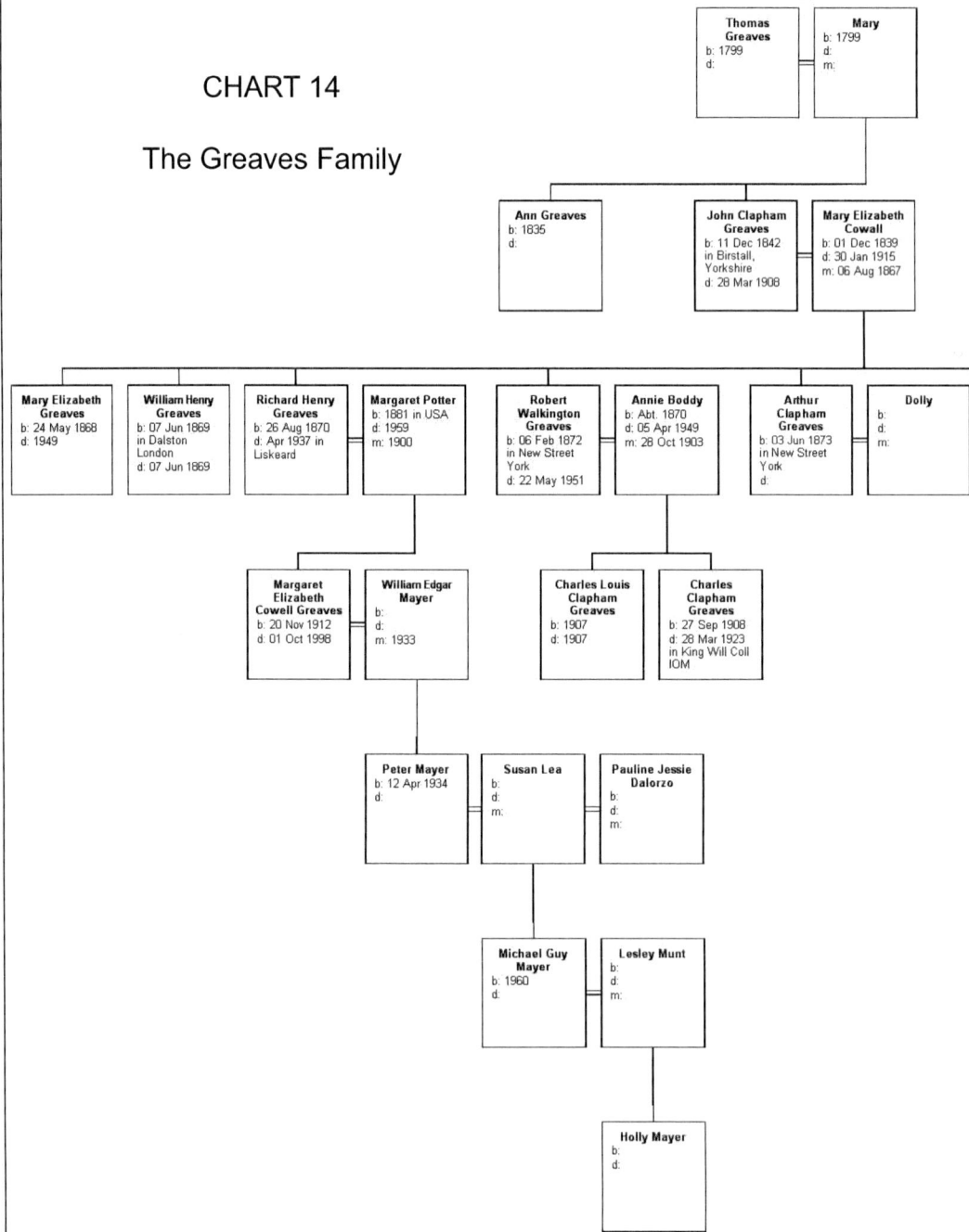

```
                                              Thomas          Mary
                                              Greaves         b: 1799
                                              b: 1799         d:
                                              d:              m:


                              Ann Greaves     John Clapham    Mary Elizabeth
                              b: 1835         Greaves         Cowall
                              d:              b: 11 Dec 1842  b: 01 Dec 1839
                                              in Birstall,    d: 30 Jan 1915
                                              Yorkshire       m: 06 Aug 1867
                                              d: 28 Mar 1908
```

Mary Elizabeth Greaves	William Henry Greaves	Richard Henry Greaves	Margaret Potter	Robert Walkington Greaves	Annie Boddy	Arthur Clapham Greaves	Dolly
b: 24 May 1868	b: 07 Jun 1869	b: 26 Aug 1870	b: 1881 in USA	b: 06 Feb 1872	b: Abt. 1870	b: 03 Jun 1873	b:
d: 1949	in Dalston	d: Apr 1937 in	d: 1959	in New Street	d: 05 Apr 1949	in New Street	d:
	London	Liskeard	m: 1900	York	m: 28 Oct 1903	York	m:
	d: 07 Jun 1869			d: 22 May 1951		d:	

Margaret Elizabeth Cowell Greaves	William Edgar Mayer	Charles Louis Clapham Greaves	Charles Clapham Greaves
b: 20 Nov 1912	b:	b: 1907	b: 27 Sep 1908
d: 01 Oct 1998	d:	d: 1907	d: 28 Mar 1923
	m: 1933		in King Will Coll IOM

Peter Mayer	Susan Lea	Pauline Jessie Dalorzo
b: 12 Apr 1934	b:	b:
d:	d:	d:
	m:	m:

Michael Guy Mayer	Lesley Munt
b: 1960	b:
d:	d:
	m:

Holly Mayer
b:
d:

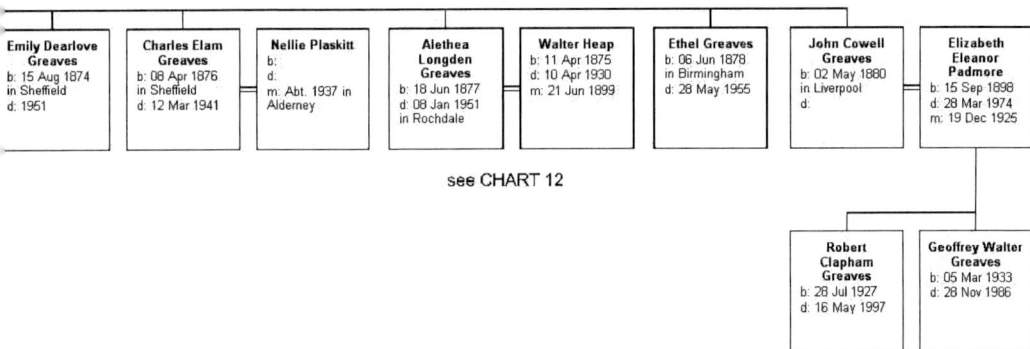

Emily Dearlove Greaves	Charles Elam Greaves	Nellie Plaskitt	Alethea Longden Greaves	Walter Heap	Ethel Greaves	John Cowell Greaves	Elizabeth Eleanor Padmore
b: 15 Aug 1874 in Sheffield d: 1951	b: 08 Apr 1876 in Sheffield d: 12 Mar 1941	b: d: m: Abt. 1937 in Alderney	b: 18 Jun 1877 d: 08 Jan 1951 in Rochdale	b: 11 Apr 1875 d: 10 Apr 1930 m: 21 Jun 1899	b: 06 Jun 1878 in Birmingham d: 28 May 1955	b: 02 May 1880 in Liverpool d:	b: 15 Sep 1898 d: 28 Mar 1974 m: 19 Dec 1925

see CHART 12

Robert Clapham Greaves	Geoffrey Walter Greaves
b: 28 Jul 1927 d: 16 May 1997	b: 05 Mar 1933 d: 28 Nov 1986

161

without being weak, friendly without reserve, dignified without a trace of pride, firm when firmness was needed, tender as a woman whenever tenderness could be the balm of a wounded spirit'.[7]

With John Clapham Greaves gone to his maker we can follow the somewhat varied fortunes of his ten children, beginning with the eldest, Mary Elizabeth Greaves.

Mary Elizabeth Greaves was described as 'Lizzie' on a Wesleyan quarterly ticket of membership dated 1895. Latterly she was always known as 'Pompey' to the younger members of the family, though what occasioned this unusual sobriquet is not known. The 1901 census described her as a Teacher of Music and as a Professor of Music in 1911, a title assumed by music teachers at that time. In Slaters Directory 1912[8] she is listed as LRAM, practising out of Century Buildings in Deansgate, but there was no entry for the following year. She may well have to escaped to London when her mother bought 2 St Aldwyns Road, Withington. She was certainly living in London in 1920 when she would entertain her nephew, Clifford Heap, to lunch on Sundays with apple pie. Clifford was a medical student at St Thomas Hospital and would shortly follow his great uncle into General Practice in Rochdale. Tradition has it that 'Pompey' lived in the Notting Hill/Holland Park area and was working as a secretary/translator at the Foreign Office. She would join the family Christmas at Edensor. My sister Patricia, then aged two years, remembers her as the old lady with black teeth who terrified her because she knew witches had black teeth.[9] She died in 1949.

Richard Henry Greaves was born 16 August 1870 at Moat Hill, Birstall. In 1882 he was a pupil at The Grove School (now known as Woodhouse Grove) and in 1883-86 at Kingswood School in Bath.[6] The Kingswood School records describe him as 'Methodist minister, Montreal'. There is no record of him being ordained in England but he may well have been ordained in Canada or the USA. He married Margaret Potter c1900. The 1901 census records her as living with her 'in-laws' at 259 Cheetham Hill Road, Manchester aged 20. Her place of birth is given as 'Ches Chtm' in USA. Her grandson Peter Mayer, remembers her telling him of going on sleigh rides by the Hudson river.[10]

Ruston[11] states that he was a former Methodist, but practiced as a Unitarian Minister in the USA 1897-1902, after which he returned to the UK. He was appointed 'Minister and Preacher' of the St Saviourgate Unitarian congregation in York in 1905 when he was described as being 'of London'.[12]

The St Saviourgate Chapel is a late 17thC building of considerable architectural importance. His appointment was confirmed and in November 1907 he was re-appointed on a permanent basis. It was a successful and innovative Ministry, the congregation had doubled, he formed a Ladies Guild and introduced a special children's service … and then, suddenly, he resigned on December 26th 1908 – the date may well be significant. Writing to his congregation he confessed 'I have collapsed in every way, even my mind seems paralysed … I must have complete rest and change. I have no other work to go to but I am going to see old friends and lie quiet till I am able to go in for a complete change of occupation.'

It is interesting to speculate what caused this breakdown. The most likely explanation is that he lost his faith. Unitarianism is a branch of Christianity that rejects the doctrine of the Trinity and the Divinity of Jesus Christ. It could be that he could no longer accept this rejection, hence perhaps his developing interest in Spiritualism in his later years.

Richard and Margaret returned to the USA where their daughter Margaret Elisabeth Cowell, always known to the family as Peggy, was born on 20 November 1912 at Cresswell, New Jersey. By 1915 the marriage was in difficulties. The couple separated and mother and daughter returned to England. Social ostracism was often the fate of a divorced or separated woman, and Margaret would not have found life easy in England. Later the same year she determined to return to the USA, probably to make another attempt to repair her marriage, or if that failed, to seek the support of her family.

It was not to be. Margaret and her three year old daughter sailed out of Liverpool on the White Star liner SS *Arabic* (15,800 tons) bound for New York. Nearly all New York bound liners called at Queens Town (the port for Cork) to pick up their lucrative Irish immigrant passengers. As they left the harbour they had to pass close to the Old Head of Kinsale where the U–Boats lay in wait. Sure enough on that fateful day, 19 August 1915, the SS *Arabic* was torpedoed by U24. She went down in 11 minutes with the loss of 44 lives, including two Americans. Margaret and her small daughter were rescued after clinging to a life raft and being hauled into a lifeboat.

The sinking of passenger liners bound to or from the Americas in the early part of the war illustrates vividly the problems of fighting 'total war'. President Wilson had declared American neutrality on the outbreak of war and in 1915 Germany declared submarine warfare under the quaintly named 'cruiser rules'. America had made it clear that any loss of American lives or US ships would bring it into the war on the side of the Allies. Germany was desperate to keep

America neutral. US firms were doing good business keeping Britain supplied, but there was a strong pro-German and pro-Irish lobby in the States. The first trigger was the sinking of the *Lusitania* on 7 May 1915 by U20 with severe loss of life including 100 Americans. German jubilation was short-lived as neutral opinion, headed by the Pope, castigated Germany. The U-boat commander was reprimanded by the Kaiser and U-boat Captains were given strict orders to be more careful in the future … to little avail.

After the rescue Margaret and her small daughter returned to England where 'Peggy' went to live with her uncle Walter in Rochdale. She was brought up as a member of the family along with Clifford, Kathleen, Kenneth and Michael. Her mother, Margaret, eked out a precarious existence hand painting china and later running a boarding house in Old Colwyn. Peggy married Edgar (Bill) Mayer in 1933.[10]

Richard Henry moved down to Cornwall where he became a recluse, living the life of a hermit in Polperro in 1925. An attempt on his life took place in late 1933 by a man who subsequently committed suicide. The event attracted coverage in the national press. Richard, having survived this attempt on his life, died in 1937. His death was registered at Liskeard.

During the 1939-45 war Peggy worked in Admiralty Censorship, leaving Peter with his grandmother as she had separated from Edgar. Around 1945 Peggy moved to Shropshire, first to a property belonging to a cousin of her mother and finally to Green Pastures in High Ercall, where she remained until her death. There she worked as a home teacher for the blind. She also worked with guide dogs for the blind. Her mother moved to join her in the mid-1950s and died in 1959.[10] Peggy died on 1 October 1998 – the last member of the family to have borne the name of Greaves.

Family legends abound over Richard Henry who was known as 'Bad Uncle Dick'. He did not, as legend has it, live in a cave in Polperro, but in a small cottage which my father, Kenneth, found when on holiday in 1955. It is true he dabbled in Spiritualism but Peggy always denied that he practiced Black Magic. Items which mysteriously disappeared and then reappeared in the same place were attributed to him functioning as a poltergeist.

Robert Walkington Greaves was the Rev John Clapham's third child. He married Elizabeth Anne (Annie) Boddy in October 1903, and it is thought they lived at 20 Alan Road, Withington. Annie's father, Charles Boddy, is described as a builder on the marriage certificate. Their first born son, Charles Louis Clapham Greaves, was born and died July/September 1907. Their younger son, Charles Clapham Greaves, usually known as 'Sonny', was born on 27 September 1908. There has always been some confusion over the name 'Louis', and it was not until the 1911 census revealed that Annie and Robert, unknown to us, had an older son who was born and died before the 1911 census that the pieces began to fall into place.

From 1902 to 1908 Robert practised as an architect and surveyor in what appears to have been a one-man business at 20 Cross Street, Manchester.[8] The family were certainly living at 20 Alan Road at the time of the 1911 census in which Robert is described as a builder's manager and Charles Boddy as a joiner and builder. By the next year the family had moved to 19 Victoria Avenue,[8] where they lived until their deaths. Charles Boddy had premises on Oxford Road and at Ardwick Island.[8] It seems probable that Robert's practice was unsuccessful and father-in-law had to bail him out.

'Sonny' entered King William's College, Isle of Man, in May 1922 but died there on March 28 1923, aged 14 years.[13] The cause of death is stated as pneumonia following influenza. Sadly his parents were unable to reach him before he died.

Robert was a keen stamp collector but parsimonious – he used out of date Chamber of Commerce forms, presumably provided by Ethel, as album pages.

During the 1920s ownership of 19 Victoria Avenue was transferred to Annie. Annie died on 5 April 1949 and Robert followed soon after on 22 May 1951.

Arthur Clapham Greaves was recorded in the 1901 census as living at 259 Cheetham Hill Road, Manchester, described as an Architectural Draughtsman – status 'worker'. It is possible he was working for his brother. He is missing from the 1911 census, and probably emigrated to South Africa between 1901 and 1911. At some stage he married Dolly but we have no further information about her. He attended his brother in law Walter Heap's funeral in 1930. He kept in touch with his sister Alethea, and in 1950 was still alive in Pietermaritzberg. His emigration to South Africa may support the theory that this is where his Mother came from.

Charles Elam Greaves was born at Sheffield in 1876.[5] Having followed his father into the ministry he received his training at Didsbury College. He followed an apparently uneventful life, ministering from Northumberland to Cornwall with a spell in the Isle of Man, and finally to Alderney. While on Alderney he married his then housekeeper, Nellie Plaskitt. He left Alderney in 1938.[3,4] His successor arrived in 1939, only to be evacuated before the arrival of the Germans. Butes Chapel did not reopen after the war.

Charles Elam died on 12 March 1941 and was the subject of an appropriately eulogistic obituary in the *Methodist Recorder*,[2] which said '…in the pulpit he was a man inspired and spoke with charm and power. Preaching was his chief delight. He was of an exceptionally quiet and unassuming disposition but those who penetrated this barrier of reserve discovered a rare soul whose friendship was a constant benediction. The memory of his loving nature and gentle ways, seasoned with the salt of humour, will long be cherished…'.

Alethea Longden Greaves Alethea Longden Greaves's story more properly belongs to the Heap Family following her marriage to Walter Heap in 1899. Her first grandchild, Helen, was born on 22 June 1929 only a few months before Walter died in 1930. Thereafter she seems to have acquired the role of Matriarch of the Family, extending this role to include her siblings. Christmas Day at Edensor in the late 1940s was a tribal gathering in more ways than one. My cousin, Derek, as a small boy was convinced that the aged great aunts (and great uncle Rob) were brought out of the store cupboard along with the Christmas decorations, dusted off, parked on chairs, given glasses of gin, and all the children were then required to kiss them in thanks for their present. Alethea died after a short illness on 8 January 1952.

Great Grandmother Mary Elizabeth Greaves and the Great Aunts – Emily Dearlove and Ethel Emily Dearlove and Ethel were always affectionately known as 'Mem' and 'Ek', and often more generally as 'The Aunts'. After the death of John Clapham in 1908, the domestic lives of his widow, Mary Elizabeth, and her two daughters, Mem and Ek, became inseparable. When John Clapham became incapacitated in 1906 the family had moved to 24 Oak Road, Fallowfield, a large semi-detached Victorian house opposite what is now Christie's hospital. It is currently (June 2009) derelict and it is not clear whether it is to be renovated or demolished. They were all living there at the time of the 1911 census, Mary as head of the household aged 71. Mem's flirtation with teaching at Southport in 1901 has ceased and she has no occupation recorded, Ek is shown as aged 32 and private secretary to the Manchester Chamber of Commerce. Mary's birthplace is recorded as Leeds

In 1912 Mary purchased 2 St Aldwyn's road, Withington, a substantial newly built semi-detached house which was to remain their home until they had all died. Mary died in 1915 and the house was then transferred to Mem.

Then in December 1931 came a bombshell. Ek, having been effectively side-lined by her employer, was sacked by the Chamber of Commerce. Family folklore had it that she had been private secretary to (Sir) Raymond Streat in his capacity as secretary to the Manchester Chamber of Commerce, or so she described herself in the 1911 census. Raymond Streat, a compromise candidate, had been appointed in 1920 at the age of 22. He rose to become Chairman of the Cotton Board and was Knighted. Sir Raymond's diaries for 1931[14] give the names of his secretaries as a Miss Seddon and a Miss Pullin; Ek, it would seem, had been sidelined into the post of office manager. Redundancies and economies were called for and the axe fell on Ek, but she was only prepared to leave on her own terms. The diary records 'all the Directors felt that the figures proposed were too high ... especially in the case of Miss Greaves; faced with the further fact that Miss Greaves would only go willingly if her figures were met, in the long run the Board gave in.'

'I had some painful and watery interviews with Miss Greaves who did not seem to realise quite how lucky she was to be treated so handsomely,' recorded Raymond Streat. 'Miss Greaves' desire not to defer her departure until the end of January ... her emotions were such that on the whole she was better out of the way.' The diary goes on to record the hiring of two office boys. Another senior member of staff left at the same time somewhat under a cloud.

There was little or no employment legislation at that time and no Industrial Tribunals so Ek was forced to fight her own battles. At the age of 53 she faced down the leaders of Manchester business and left on her own terms. What a woman!

The spinster sisters must have been 'as poor as church – or rather chapel – mice'. Even with her pension, they were obliged to seek gainful employment compatible with their position in the social hierarchy. It was then that their love of bridge paid off, and in 1934 The Central Bridge Club (proprietress Miss Emily Greaves) at 81 Central Road was opened for business. This was a substantial semi-detached building less than two hundred yards from St Aldwyns Road. Although Mem was the Proprietress, Ek was the business woman. I suspect the club may have been financed by fellow card players. I remember visiting the house in the late 1940s and being fascinated by a totally illegal 'one armed bandit' whose presence would never have been suspected on premises run by two highly respectable Methodist maiden ladies. The club has now moved to 30 Palatine Road and become the Manchester Bridge Club, with members of international standing.

Mem died in 1951 but Ek soldiered on. My parents used to visit them on a weekly basis, often accompanied by my sister, who used to play the piano while the grown-ups talked. Prior to her death on 28 May 1955 she told of two dreams in which one of her deceased friends called down to her 'Come up here and make a fourth hand!', the other involved of a calendar rotating the days and stopping on the day she was due to die.[9] Was Uncle Dick looking after his little sister?

John Cowell Greaves The youngest of the family and about whom we know very little. He joined the Merchant Navy and his cap badge still survives. In the 1911 census he was on leave at 24 Oak Road,[1] described as 'Mariner, Merchant Navy, quartermaster'. A search in the National Archives Merchant Navy records, known to be incomplete, proved fruitless.

In 1915 he had already started courting Elizabeth Eleanor Padmore – a 16 year-old who was 18 years younger than himself! A letter to her from Nantes dated 22 April said that he was to be mate on the Saint Winifred for the rest of the voyage to Baltimore to collect grain, and then probably back to France. They eventually married more than ten years later, on 19 December 1925 in the South Manchester Registry Office, with his brother Robert and sister Ethel acting as witnesses. What would his father have said?

Kelly's Directory for 1928 describes him as 'clerk', but on his son's birth certificate in 1933 he is described as 'building contractor', possibly in partnership with his brother Robert.

Their first son, Robert Clapham Greaves (known as Bob) was born on 28 July 1927, their second son Geoffrey Walter Greaves (known as Geoff) on 5 March 1933. In 1927 the family moved to a newly built house at 51 Thornley Lane, Denton.

John Cowell was 45 years of age at the time of his marriage. Neither of his sons married – Geoff was briefly engaged, but Ella did not approve. Bob had two careers, the first at Mather and Platt and then latterly in the Registrar's Dept at Manchester University. At the time of his retirement we were introduced to a widow with whom he was associating, but nothing came of it. A jazz enthusiast like his brother, Bob was a card carrying Labour Party member, and an appalling punster. He died 16 May 1997, the last member of the family to bear the Greaves surname.

John's disappearance/death left Ella to bring up the two boys in comparative poverty in a terraced house at 42 Braemar Road, Fallowfield, where they lived at least from 1941, five doors away from where Ella had lived with her parents. They later moved to 107 Shetland Way, Davyhulme where Geoff is recorded as the telephone subscriber in 1975, and finally to 16 Rosthernmere Drive,

Cheadle Hulme. Ella died 28 March 1974 at Davyhulme.

Geoff was a skilful table-tennis player winning several competitions and medals in south Manchester c1950. He worked for Ferranti for over 25 years and died very suddenly 28 November 1986. Bob and Geoff were inseparable. Bob said 'he wasn't just my brother, he was my best mate.'

So, 150 years after the birth of John Clapham Greaves his surname disappears. There were ten children, nine grandchildren but only five great grandchildren.

Acknowledgements

I am indebted to the staff of the John Rylands Library, Manchester; the Borthwick Institute, University of York; and the Stockport Local History library. Also to Glenda Murphy, Librarian King Williams College I.O.M. and to Rev Ian Mutton for their assistance.

Notes and references

1 Census returns for England and Wales 1841-1911
2 Methodist Recorder. The Who's Who of Methodism. pub Methodist Publications 1933
3 Hill's Arrangements 1819-1988
4 Hall, Joseph et al. The Circuits of Great Britain 1765-1980
5 The Greaves Family Bible
6 The History of Kingswood School. Charles H Kelly 1898.London
7 Withington Methodist Chapel Records per Rev Ian Mutton
8 Slaters and Kelly's directories
9 Patricia Heap – personal communication
10 Peter Mayer (grandson of Richard Greaves) unpublished autobiography and personal
     communication
11 Ruston, Alan. List of Unitarian Ministers. www.unitarianhistory.org.uk
12 St Saviourgate, York Unitarian chapel records   (Borthwick Institute)
13 King William's College IOM Register 1833-1927. Glasgow, Jackson Wylie and Co 1928 and The
Barrovian June 1923
14 Sir Raymond Streat: Lancashire and Whitehall Diary. vol 1. ed. Marguerite Dupree. Manchester University
Press, 1987

18

… AND FINALLY

… this is not the end, merely a pause during which we have tried to capture the history of the family. The generations continue to unfold, the old die, newcomers are added to the family tree, children are born albeit more out of wedlock than in. This was probably no different in William the Founder's time and certainly in the generations before William. Marriages in William's time could only be solemnised and recorded in the Anglican church. Due notice had to be given and banns called. This caused problems for the non-conformists and could mean the family was well established before the marriage took place, baptism of the first child often being delayed until after the marriage.

Mere pause or not, it is an opportunity to look back over the last two hundred and fifty years or so and ask ourselves what has changed. How has this family of ours responded to the many and varied changes in their lives? My immediate thought is that the pace of change in my lifetime has been such that it cannot possibly have been equalled in previous generations. Yet William the Founder and his forebears changed in a remarkably brief period from a predominantly agricultural life in small hamlets and villages to a highly mechanised industrial life in the large cities and towns, thanks largely to the Industrial Revolution. Nothing we have experienced in our lifetimes can even begin to touch that.

We often quote the effects of the last two wars, and particularly the social changes which took place after the 1939-45 war, as one of the factors determining the type of life we live and enjoy today. Yet William and his family lived through the American War of Independence and the loss of the American colonies, and then had to endure thirty years of war with France following the French Revolution. The Napoleonic Wars brought with them hardship, shortages, economic decline and the imposition for the first time of income tax! …but it was not a war that directly involved the people as a whole. The

Army and the Navy were largely made up of 'regulars' and found most of their recruits from amongst the disadvantaged. There were Volunteers but they were few in number. The 1939-45 war involved almost everyone in the country, man, woman and child, as we fought for our very existence. All eligible persons were conscripted to serve in the forces or in some other capacity. Women had to take on the jobs which had previously been done by their men folk. The number of civilian casualties caused by the bombing of our cities was such that the figures were not fully disclosed until many years after the war had ended. This was quite unlike anything we had seen or experienced before, although the prescient who had read of the Spanish civil war and looked again at the horrors in the trenches in the first world war and should have had a fair idea of what was in store for us.

There have of course been great advances in science and technology, the invention of the steam engine, the coming of the railways, the internal combustion engine, the jet engine, the computer age, the discovery of DNA, and remarkable advances in medicine. They seem to have been accepted by William and his generation just as they are today. William and his descendants made use of each new invention as it came along, using them to develop and improve their business and increase the profits for the benefit of the family as a whole.

Social and institutional changes have been no less striking. Take the sphere of religion. William and his descendants were all ardent Wesleyan Methodists, and we looked at possible reasons for this. The position of the Established Church had been seriously weakened by the Toleration Act of 1689 which removed its legal monopoly. Its problems became particularly acute as industrialisation and urbanisation freed people from the bonds of traditional society and brought them together in numbers that overwhelmed existing facilities for public worship. Anglicanism had already forfeited its traditional position as the church of the people, and into this vacuum rushed a wide variety of nonconformist churches, of which the Methodists were but one. The established church had failed to adapt to the growing needs of the industrial north, and a religious census in the middle of the 19thC showed that only about 40% of the population were regular church goers.

As Anglican attendance declined, the Methodists flourished. As we have seen, William and his descendants embraced all the tenets of the new faith. It determined the way he brought up his family, he lived his life according to the edicts of John Wesley, carrying his beliefs through into the way he ran his business.

The position today is very different. Church attendance declines year by year. By and large, the teachings of the church no longer dictate how we should live our lives. We have become a secular society … and, unlike other subjects under discussion in this chapter, this is one area in which the Government of the Day declined to legislate both now and in the past!

Another subject of increasing concern and interest is immigration. It would not have been a problem for William and his descendants since the number of immigrants to this country in his time would have been almost nil. I doubt whether there would have been any employees of African or Asian ethnic origin in William's labour force. Even in my childhood, the sight of a black face was something to be remarked. The only significant ethnic or racial minority in Rochdale were the Ukrainians and Poles who settled in Rochdale after the last war. The position today is very different. Over 10% of the population of Rochdale is of Asian origin and the town has grown enormously in size, with a population of 250,000 in the Greater Metropolitan Borough compared with 80,000 in William's day – although different geographical boundaries make accurate comparisons difficult. It remains a problem, and successive governments have seen the need to legislate to control the number of immigrants allowed into the country and to try and impose equality of opportunity for those who are already here.

Politics … William had to endure the Chartist riots which had begun to interfere with the way he ran his business as well as constant demands for reform of the electoral system. In William's time the right to vote was restricted by the so-called £10 suffrage. I think he would have approved of the universal suffrage that followed over a period of time, as he would have approved the elimination of the 'rotten boroughs' and the creation of the new constituencies which replaced them that gave Rochdale (and the surrounding towns) their own member of parliament. The demands for electoral reform were as bitterly contested in William's time as they are today. How William would have responded to his wife being given the vote is less certain. William's world was very much a male orientated society in which the place of women was very different to today's.

The two main political parties which existed in William's time are still with us with the addition of the Labour party. Whigs have become the Liberals and Tories the Conservatives. William and his descendants were all Liberals although they showed a tendency to become Tories (Conservatives) as they grew rich and occupied a higher place on the social ladder.

Perhaps the biggest changes have been the alteration in the status of women in our society, the death of the 'nuclear family' as we had known it, and the sexual freedom which came with 'the pill'.

We can be sure that William would not have expected, or even allowed, his wife to work although no such restriction applied to women of the working classes. They worked alongside their husbands in the woollen and cotton mills, often as part of a family group that included their elder children. They were paid lower rates than their husbands and had little control over their lives. They owned no property, everything they possessed belonged to their husbands. The situation today is very different. Female entrants to medical school now outnumber their male counterparts whereas in the 1950s they formed less than 3% of the Cambridge University intake. In many professions and other occupations there is no disparity in earnings.

This alteration in the status of women has contributed to the break-up of what we had come to know as the 'nuclear family' consisting of the parents and their children. But of greater import has been the advent of 'the pill' that has given rise to the sexual freedom which we enjoy today, sex has become a recreational pastime to be enjoyed by all. As a consequence, many men and women expect to have two or more partners during their lifetime and families are often made up of children from several unions.

This concept would have been quite foreign to William's way of thinking and I would have expected him to find the whole idea inexplicable. William believed in 'The Family' as the main stable unit within which their lives were organised. With ten children to his name how could he feel otherwise? Indeed this concept of family and its duty towards its members was an essential part of the Wesleyan ethic: your duties towards your family came well up the list of your responsibilities. In subsequent generations, when the family firm was beginning to fail, room was always found for their less competent relations, even to the firm's detriment.

Quite what William would have made of Civil Marriages, same sex marriages, gay sex and the legalisation of homosexuality is not difficult to imagine. I think he would have found the whole idea abhorrent and totally beyond his comprehension.

※

My sympathies lie with anyone who seeks to add further chapters to our history. It has been a difficult enough task as it is to sort out the multiple marriages, how will the family historian of the future cope with single sex marriages where the two male partners produce children of the marriage through the services of a surrogate mother? How will he or she cope with couples who do not marry but have two or more partners in succession with his children, her children, their children, and where the divorce rate of those who do marry is over 50%? Happily I have been enabled to drawn a line across the page before such an event occurs.

Rightly or wrongly we decided to draw that line some time after the 1939-45 war and its immediate consequences, though one or two of the more interesting people have crossed the barrier. Information about the living is surprisingly difficult to come by since many of the records are access-denied for a period of fifty or hundred years. This is as it should be. We all have parts of our lives we wish to keep to ourselves. It has been noticeable that most of our relatives will speak quite freely about those who are long since dead and gone, but they become more reticent when questions are asked about their current lives … assuming our family continues to survive, and as we have seen they are a fecund lot so the odds are in their favour, it would be interesting to speculate about their future. Certainly they will be scattered over the globe, inter-racial marriages or partnerships will be the norm. The days of the tight self-contained family are gone for ever.

Appendix 1

THE HEAP COAT OF ARMS

blazon: Argent a chevron between two crescents in chief, and a dexter arm embowed, couped, fesseways, wielding a sword all gules.
crest: a cross, crosslet, fitchee, gules, between two branches of palm in orle, proper.

The origin of the coat of arms that has been in use by some members of the family since the mid-19thC is unknown. It was used on a signet ring owned by my uncle Michael, it was depicted in stained glass on one of the windows at Chamber House when the latter belonged to my grandfather Walter Heap, it was embroidered by my Aunt Kathleen on a fire screen, and it appears 'painted' on one of the windows in my sitting room at Marsh Mary Cottage. It also appears on the frieze at the Rochdale Town Hall in recognition of the mayoralty of William Tweedale Heap and Charles Heap.

In an attempt to resolve this matter I consulted the College of Arms and commissioned a search of their records. This proved most helpful.[1] They could find no record in the *Encyclopaedia Heraldica* by William Berry (London: no date) which was quoted by Richard and Charles Heape as their main source, although there is a record of the Arms in the first edition (1842) of *The General Armory* by Sir Bernard Burke, and repeated in subsequent editions down to the last in 1884. This last edition has become the standard reference work by purveyors of *Arms for a surname*, including those on the internet, and hence the widespread dissemination of this particular ascription

Unable to find a record at the College of Arms, Charles Heape concluded that it must have been found in a manuscript collection at the British Museum and therefore it is 'ancient' and not a more recent Victorian 'invention'. In support of his argument he quotes a letter from one Thomas Heape of Pilkington, dated 1660, found in the Harleian MSS 2153 fol 62 in which Thomas is writing to the *Lancashire and Cheshire Herald* asking for an appointment as Deputy at Arms. The contents of the letter clearly show he has considerable knowledge of the subject. Alas! There is no record of his being appointed.[2]

The College of Arms carried out a search of their earlier records at my request including The Heralds Visitations, Funerary Heraldry, Register of Pedigrees prior to 1900, registers of Grants of Arms by the College prior to 1900, and numerous other sources, all with negative outcome.

The first official record of a Grant of Arms is that made to Charles Heape of Hartley in 1908 and to Richard Heape of Hedley (does he mean Healey?) Hall in 1910, when the Arms recorded are exactly as we know them and as described above. I think it is clear how this came about. Richard and Charles Heape commissioned a full search of the records at the College of Arms as part of their research into the history of the family and came to the same conclusion as ourselves – namely that no Grant had been made, and there was no record earlier than the 1830 date referred to above. They then set about making a full and proper application for a Grant to bear Arms, using the achievement with which we are all familiar. This was granted to them and their heirs and presumably still exists today.

This is no way gives our side of the family a right to bear Arms or to make use of the Arms granted to the Heape family. Our American cousins clearly suffered under the delusion that the family had a right to bear arms and this is referred to by Edith Mary Stamm in letters written to her cousin in England, Alice Heap Lye.[3] However the use of heraldic shields showing an armorial achievement is widespread today and is no longer governed by the strict regulation used to control such matters in past centuries. No doubt various members of our family, along with countless others, will continue to make use of, and to display, the Heap or Heape coat of Arms as they see fit.

Notes

1 Correspondence with The College of Arms March 2010
2 see also *Records of the Family of Heape* by Charles and Richard Heape. Appendix p.277
3 see Appendix 3: The Lye Stamm Papers final paragraph

Appendix 2

THE FAMILY BIBLE

Note – the words in italics denote direct entries in the Bible

As with many families, the family Bible that belonged to William Heap – the Founder of the firm of Samuel Heap and Son, provides us with an incontrovertible record of the early history of the family. In our case this has proved to be of vital importance.

The only occasion on which I had sight of the Bible was when I visited the mill at Caldershaw some sixty years ago while still a medical student in London. I was just beginning to research the history of the family. Happily, I took copious notes of the various entries in the Bible and other papers attached thereto, and it is the contents of those notes that form the basis of this appendix. The Bible was kept in the mill safe at Caldershaw and Mr Wingfield, the then Secretary to the Board, said that the ownership of the Bible was not clear but it belonged to the mill. And there, so far as I know, the Bible remained until Samuel Heap and Son was taken over by Courtaulds in 1964.

When George Heap, the last Chairman of the Board, left the mill in 1965 he took with him the portrait of William Heap The Founder which used to hang in the Board Room. It is inconceivable that he would have left the Family Bible behind. We know that George had either Willed or given the portrait to his nephew Peter Charles Heap who lives in Vancouver. In turn it was thought he had given the family Bible into the safekeeping of Peter's sister, Denise who also lived in Vancouver. Peter does indeed have the portrait but a recent search of their mother's possessions has failed to reveal any trace of the Bible. So for the time being its whereabouts remain unknown. The notes which I made back in the 1950s therefore become of even greater importance.

Inside the front cover of the Bible on one side was written *William Heap June 1st 1805, Bridge Hall, Heap Bridge, near Bury*. This is presumably the date on which the first entry was made in the Bible. William would have been 35 years of age, he had a growing family and was on his way up in the world. It was time to make a start on recording his family line – hence he starts to record the births, deaths and marriages in a family Bible

Inside the front cover on the other side is inscribed:

William Heap was born 5th July 1769 and died at Spotland in 1833 aged 64yrs
Betty Heap was born 7th September 1765
Isaac Holt   Book Goose Lane , Rochdale 9th May 1840

It is unclear whether this date refers to Isaac's death. Isaac was a Methodist local preacher and had married Elizabeth Heap, third daughter of William and Betty Heap.

On the middle pages of the Bible, pages 336 and 337, are listed the names and dates of birth of:

The children of William and Betty Heap of Caldershaw as follows

Mary born 29 August 1790 Sunday 5.30am [Mary never married and died aged 41 on 8th Aug 1832 and is buried in the same grave as her father in the churchyard of St Chad's Parish Church, Rochdale]

James born 1st May 1792 [died young, hence a later son also called James]

Thomas born 25 May 1793 Saturday 8.30am [Thomas went to Milnrow and   Newhey]

Betty born 24 July 1795 Friday 1.00pm

William born 27th Dec 1797 Wednesday 2.15am

Elizabeth born 18th Nov 1799 Monday 4.40pm

Rachel born 2nd Nov 1802 Tuesday 5.45am

John born 5th July 1805 Monday 12.15am

Samuel born 29th June 1807 Monday 8.00am

Jms [James?] born 5th Nov 1809 Sunday 1.10am

The most vital piece of information is the record of William The Founder's birth. Although we have confirmatory records for his father, Stephen, this entry in the Bible is the only record of William's birth. Diligent search of the Parish Registers of the parishes between Bury and Burnley and to the north of Burnley have failed to reveal any record of William's birth. It is almost certain William was baptised into the Wesleyan Methodist faith. By 1769 the Wesleyans had been in existence for just over 20 years, and many of the chapel registers are ill kept, difficult to read, and often illegible. Many are missing altogether.

Stuck on the inside of the front cover is a further piece of paper which reads as follows:

The Father of William Heap, the owner of this book, was Stephen Heap who was born at Worsthorne near Burnley in 1739. He removed to Heap Bridge near Bury and later left there and died at Ellenrood, Spotland, in 1827 aged 88 years. He was a Fulling Miller. The son, William, came with his father to Spotland and died there in 1833 aged 64. He was also a Fulling Miller. He built Caldershaw Mill and houses and also the reservoirs. The children of William and Betty Heap are given between pages 336 and 337.

'The son, Thomas, born 25th May 1793 settled at Haugh, was a flannel manufacturer and was the father of James, William and Benjamin. The last named is now of Weston Super Mare. The sons of James [Harry and James A B Heap] continue the family business.

The son, William, born 27th Dec 1797 was the father of Joshua JP of Dunster House, Rochdale and managing director of Kelsall and Kemps. William Henry, Samuel, Thomas Edward, John Joseph. William Heap founded a flannel manufactory of William Heap and Sons of Littleborough which was continued by his sons William Henry and Samuel.

'The son, Samuel, born 29th June 1807 seems to have continued the fulling business at Spotland under the name of Samuel Heap and Son Ltd at Caldershaw and elsewhere. It is now carried on by his sons Alderman W T Heap and Charles Heap and his grandchildren. Dr Samuel was another son.

'The son James Secundus was born 5th Nov 1809 and became a flannel manufacturer at Milnrow, afterwards carried on under the name 'Exors of James Heap'. Two of his sons, Jonathon and William, are dead. I think one son, John, is now living at Blackpool. 16th Feb 1914 John Heap died today aged 75.

'The son, John, born 5th Feb 1805 was I think the father of William Edward

Heap of Bentmeadows.

'The daughter, Elizabeth, born 18th Nov 1799 married Isaac Holt, the Methodist Local Preacher for Rochdale. She lived to be 90 or more.'

Signed   RICHARD HEAPE 14th May 1906

This statement is interesting not only for its content, which provides us with a wealth of detail concerning William The Founder's children, but also because it provides us with a link to 'The Records of The Family of Heape' written by the same Richard Heape and his brother Charles Heape. The amount of research carried out by these two brothers was immense and inevitably they would have come across the records and details of our own family, particularly for the years after 1800. Richard recorded the details in this statement which was then incorporated into the family Bible.

Appendix 3

LYE-STAMM PAPERS

The Lye-Stamm papers are one of the enigmas of this family history. Where did they come from? Where have they gone? How reliable are they? As far as I can recall they were among the papers and documents to be found in the safe at Samuel Heap and Son. Negley Harte had the same access when he was writing his history of Samuel Heap and Son, but over forty years later cannot recall how they came to be in the firm's possession. He made several attempts to contact the Stamm sisters by letter but without success.

There are various references to these papers in the main text. They were the work of Marion Isabelle Stamm and Margaret Victoria Stamm of 514 Meadow Road, Winnetka, Illinois who traced their family history through the Fielden family of Todmorden. The latter were linked to our own family when Elizabeth Haslam Fielden married William Heap, son of William The Founder, in about 1827. The papers probably date from about 1926.

William's (son of William The Founder) eldest son, Thomas Edward, had a daughter Alice who married Fred Lye. The Stamm sisters refer to Alice Lye née Heap as their cousin. The correspondence that included the so called Lye Stamm papers was originally between these two cousins. Fred Lye was a relative of the Rigg family who still live in Rochdale today.

The two Stamm sisters appear on the Spensley family tree and trace their connection back to Alice Lye née Heap as granddaughters of Hannah Heap who married William Spensley in 1850. Hannah was the eldest daughter of William Heap (son of William the Founder) and Elizabeth Haslam Fielden, and sister to the Thomas Edward mentioned above.

In addition to the Fielden and the Spensley Family trees, the Stamm sisters provided a wealth of detail about the rest of William Heap's children which is given below. Quite how they were able to collect and collate this information is one of many unanswered questions, as at this time they, and most of their relatives, were in the USA.

The Stamm sisters also produced copies of letters written by William Heap and his brother Thomas to their cousin Richard Howarth in Canada. Richard had served in the army from 1805 to 1815, and took his discharge while serving with the army in Canada. How the letters came into the possession of the Stamm sisters remains a puzzle, unless they had pursued him as another of their relatives. Copies of the letters are featured in Appendix 4. The letters themselves are one of the most fascinating collection of documents to come into my possession. They give a vivid description of the events which were taking place in Lancashire and the rest of the country at that time.

Throughout these papers there is some doubt as to who is 'speaking', a Lye or a Stamm. Relationships when quoted, such as 'my grandfather', should therefore be treated with caution.

Although I have not checked or followed up the Spensley and Fielden data, they are reproduced in full so the information is not lost, and remains available for any future enquiry. The data is reproduced as shown in the originals.

The Stamm sisters begin their account with their Heap relatives:

'THOMAS' FAMILY (Ma's grandfather) had sisters Mary (who died), Rachel, Elizabeth (William Heap) brothers Thomas on this page, John, Samuel and James, Grandpa Thomas Heap had five sons and five daughters – named Thomas, Ann, William, James, Elizabeth, John, Sarah, Rachel, Benjamin, Jane.
Thomas of The Haugh had three daughters and one son named, Jemima, Rachel Ann and Jane Kershaw and the son died. Rachel Ann married a rich Irish Gentleman. Jemima married a Doctor from Shaw and Jane Kershaw married a manufacturer.
Ann married a Mr Butterworth in the leather industry and had a daughter Elizabeth who married a Mr Baron, a woollen manufacturer from Rochdale.
William married but died without family.
James of The Haugh had two sons.
Elizabeth married Mr Mills and had one son and one daughter.
John drank himself to death.
Sarah married Mr Hastings, a manufacturer, and had four children all of whom died young.
Rachel married a Mr Walker and had a boy and a girl.
Benjamin married.
Jane never married.
'JOHN (brother to Thomas) and William, my Grandfather. John lived

at Shepherd Mill, Norden and had 3 children viz....Mary Hannah, William Edward, Elizabeth Ann.

Mary Hannah married twice but had no children.

William Edward married Sir Titus Salt's niece and had two children – Reginald and Jess.

Elizabeth Ann married a Mr Pritchard.

'SAMUEL (brother to Thomas) and William, lived at Caldershaw and had Abraham who died as a child, William Tweedale, Samuel, Henry drowned as a child, Charles, Herbert, Sarah Ann, Alice, Emily, and another child who died of croup. William Tweedale was Mayor of Rochdale. Charles of Caldershaw Mills came to America and returned to Rochdale where he was also Mayor.

Herbert is in Boston and married

Sarah Ann married a Mr Watson of Liverpool

Alice...

Emily...

'JAMES (brother to Grandpa) James had John, Mary, William, Jonathon, Edward, Eliza and Annie. He lived at Milnrow. John lived at Milnrow also and had club feet.

Mary married Robert Lee and had John and Lizzie. John married and lives in Australia, Lizzie is also married and lives in Oldham.

William married and had one child who died.

Edward went to Australia and married someone he met on the voyage there

Eliza married and had one child, I think the husband's name was Holden.

'RACHEL (Grandpa's sister). Rachel married Mr Butterworth and had William, John, Mary, Hannah, Ellis, Rachel Ann, Alfred and James Henry

William had three children, William, Julia and Rachel

John married Betty Collins

Mary married Mr Holt of Liverpool and had no issue

Hannah married Mr Stott and had 2 sons, Fred and Alfred. Fred married an American girl and had 3 children all of whom live in New Orleans. Alfred married Louis Holt

Ellis never married
Rachel Ann married
Alfred was crippled and never married
James Henry…

THE FIELDEN FAMILY

In addition to the Family Tree, the Stamm sisters recorded the following:

'JOSEPH (son of Grandma's brother John) married Aunt Polly, lived at Halifax, and had about a dozen children
Harriet married her cousin William Henry Heap and has 3 daughters and one son living, Annie McFarland, Florence never married, Helena never married, Gerald lives in Wales and ran a mill in Littleborough.
John Henry was blind and never married
Joshua William went to the Cape of Good Hope, married and had 2 sons and 3 daughters, named Oswald Frere and Percy Arthrington.

'JAMES (Grandma's brother) had 2 sons and 3 daughters named William Sutcliffe Haslam Fielden, Alice, Elizabeth, Emily and John Joshua. WSH Fielden married and lived at Gundlice, Northamptonshire.
Alice married a Mr Sugden and had Arnold and Hettie. Hettie never married and died.
Elizabeth married Mr Holden, a cabinet maker of Todmorden.
Emily married a Mr Bayes, an artist living in London, had 4 children – Emmeline, Walter, Gilbert who was a sculptor, Jessie who was an illuminator. Their father was a black and white artist according to Alice Heap Lye in a letter to Marion Stamm in 1922 when Marion saw pieces of their work in an exhibition at Burlington House in London
John Joshua never married

'WILLIAM (Grandma's brother) married and had one daughter Zilla Matilda. He died when Zilla was still a baby

'ALICE (Grandma's sister) married a Mr Herbert Wilson of Cornholm, a bobbin manufacturer, and had 8 sons all named

'ELIZABETH (Grandpa's sister) married Mr Holt and had no children, died aged 95yrs from Diabetes
Grandma (Elizabeth Heap nee Haslam) had Hannah, Samuel, John, William, James, Alice, Thomas. Hannah married Mr Murgatroyd of Sowerby bridge and had Thomas, Eliza Ann, Joseph and one who died as a baby Thomas had one daughter and is dead.
Eliza Ann married Mr Wainwright and had Phoebe, Annie, Agnes and another son who died whilst crossing the water.
Agnes lives in Dululle, married a Lawyer (Fargo N.D.   Mr J J Skus)

Annie married a grocer and lives in Toronto or Montreal
Samuel's descendants are the Humes and the Foxes of Amesbury, Mass.
Thomas' descendants are Frank Fielden etc
John lives at Bradford and had Elizabeth, Thomas, Martha Alice, Joseph, Harry, John Henry, Joseph William.
Elizabeth never married
Thomas married Martha Shaw and had Charles Edward Shaw Fielden and   John William. Thomas married a second time and had 2 daughters and one son
Martha Alice married Mt Blackburn and had Emily, Lizzie, Maria and John Henry
Emily married Teddy Caxon and had no issue
Lizzie died young
Maria …
John Henry married and had no children'

The papers further recorded that (see Appendix 1):

'Edith Marion Spensley Stamm of Chicago has an authentic copy of the Heap coat of arms and the crest as it is in the Town Hall at Rochdale. It was given to her by her cousin, Alice Heap Lye, in June 1934. It was done by Alan Handley … a clever photographer, he got the crest from a cousin of his, Herbert Heap, whose father got it all in an approved manner. Herbert Heap's father, Sam Heap is now dead'

Such is the desired belief of our American Cousins!

APPENDIX 4

LETTERS FROM THOMAS AND WILLIAM HEAP TO THEIR COUSIN RICHARD HOWARTH IN NIAGARA FALLS, CANADA

Richard Howarth would have been the son of one of Betty Howarth's brothers (Betty being the wife of William Heap 'The Founder'). He was born in Bury in 1785 and served in the Army with the Corps of Royal Artillery Drivers for ten years and 231 days before taking his discharge in the Niagara District of Ontario. Whilst in Canada he farmed until his death on 1 April 1871, his address is given as 19 Talbot Street, Southwold, near St Thomas, Upper Canada.

There are ten letters in all covering the period from 14 June 1817 to 22 May 1851. Copies of the letters were found among the papers held in the mill safe at Samuel Heap and Son, and excerpts had been published in the *Rochdale Observer* in 1947. Although there are some subtle differences in the wording of some of the letters in the two versions, it is clear that the Editor of the *Observer* had cut out large sections which he deemed of less interest to his readers.

The letters were sent to the *Observer* by a Miss Jane Howarth of 719 Main Street, Niagara Falls, presumably a descendant of Richard Howarth. This suggests that the original letters had been retained by the recipient. It would have been interesting to have read Richard Howarth's replies but it seems that no copies were retained or they have been destroyed over a period of time.

The letters cover a variety of subjects from an exhortation to keep faith with the Wesleyan Methodists, the price of bread and corn, the Chartists and Civil unrest, their success or otherwise in the flannel industry, the coming of the railway. Family news of births, deaths and marriages is passed on, as is the progress in various law suits and Wills and inheritances of which Richard Howarth was a beneficiary.

The earlier letters are written from the Hamer Mill. Thomas then moves to the Ogden Mill in Newhey and William to Caldershaw and then to Littleborough.

One of the earlier letters is reproduced in part in the chapter on Wesleyan Methodism (see chapter 6). It expounds at great length the writer's religious beliefs and urges his Canadian cousin to put his faith in the Lord and seek guidance and help. The writers religious fervour seems to have diminished somewhat as the years roll by.

The letters are full of family news and have been of help in establishing the relationships between some of the earlier members of the family …

'your uncles and aunts are all well, uncle James' wife is dead, Mary Barnes and her daughter are both wed …'

'Uncle John Howarth has leased Top'path Lee Farm'

'My brother Thomas was married last June and has a child six weeks old'

'Your uncle James Howarth has left his family and we don't know where he is'

'My cousin William is in good health and still lives at Ramsbottom Mill'

'Sister Rachel has married and cousin Rachel of Uncle James is also married to someone in Shuttleworth'

'I am still living at Ogden Mill and my brother and sister are still living at Caldershaw'

'My brother John has one son and two daughters'

The writers also keep Richard fully informed about various monies which he is due to inherit from several Wills although the sums involved are all small, and the legal arguments drag on interminably. The arguments over Thomas Kay's Will even ended up in the High Court of Chancery:

'… the greater part of it was wasted amongst the Lawyers and very little found its way to his heirs, I received 25 shillings as my share and when I deducted my father's expenses in making the claim there is scarcely anything left.'

Nothing changes!

The comments about the flannel trade and the progress they are making in their various businesses, the cost of living and the price of foodstuffs, and the political agitations of the Chartists are among the more interesting parts of the letters and open a window on life in the first half of the 19C:

'In respect of trade in this country, it has been a long time flat and although at present we have plenty of work, provisions are very dear. We have been giving last week for potatoes 25/– per load, meal is selling at 70/– per load, flour 100/– that we have very dear living'

'Trade has been tolerably brisk this year and the harvest plentiful although it has been the driest summer known in the memory of man which however has been the cause of butter rising in price as now is selling at 19d per pound, cheese at 10d, mutton at 8d … potatoes, sheep and wool have taken a rapid advance'

'things in this country are now in a very awkward state at present owing to the dullness of trade and commerce. The woollen weavers have been out for an advance in wages for twelve weeks and this has caused great stagnation … but I think the strike is nearly over now as many workers have returned to work at the lower wage (written in 1830)'

'the flannel trade has been moderately good for the last three years until last Christmas since when there has not been much doing. I now have a good mill for finishing flannels which is within five minutes walk of the Littleborough station of the Lancashire and Yorkshire Railway and still nearer to the Rochdale canal so that I have every convenience for the transport of goods. I have six pairs of fulling stocks and am finishing 450 to 480 pieces a week [written in 1851]'

'the reform party is now quiet as a good trade and plentiful harvest was what we most wanted and now when it is come we sit at ease and enjoy the blessings of peace and I pray that so long as I live I may not behold the horrors of war and discord [this was written in 1818 just three years after Waterloo]'

There was clearly a constant stream of people crossing the Atlantic travelling to and from America and Canada, and there are constant references such as:

' … a man who lives near us is going to America by Fort Georgia
Tembra … there are a great deal of people leaving England for
America among the rest Tom Howarth from Bury'

There are frequent references to the Reformers and the social unrest which
they caused:

'Perhaps you will not know what the Reformers mean. England has
almost been in an uproar for they have had what is rather Reform
meetings in every town in England. At the last meeting in Manchester
there were about 6000 of them to Reform Parliament. A man by
the name of Cobbett had been very active for them until there was
an Act passed which put a stop to them and the Habeas Corpus Act
suspended' [this was written in 1817 just two years before the Peterloo
Massacre]

'There is a prevailing disorder in this country called the Influenza
which has scarce left a family untouched and a great many have gone
to their long home'

'My brother Thomas bought the whole of the Tops of Spotland Estate.
He gave the sum of 1155 pounds for it and it was thought to be not
dear. It makes him £60 per annum for rent. Besides this he has
bought a mill which is now worked by my brother John as a Fulling
mill which I expect will make him £200 a year in rent [this was the
Shepherd Mill in Norden]'

'We are partners in the fulling business and are finishing 400 flannels
a week. We employ 25 men and boys in the business and have a
pretty good run of business since we commenced business on our own
account'

….and a final word from William in Littleborough:

'will probably have seen in the public papers that the Church of
England as established by Law in this country is much agitated.
Different clergymen entertaining different theological opinions, and
a number of them have gone over to the Church of Rome. What the
end of these things can be, perhaps no one can tell. The Wesleyan

Methodists are much agitated here. Thousands of people are not satisfied with the Doings of Conference and the Preachers are not disposed to concede things to the opinion of the people … my opinion is that many thousands of people will separate from them'

The letters are fascinating, but change a few names and words and you might be reading letters written today … nothing changes!

FAMILY TREES and CHART INDEX

INDEX

Numbers in bold refer to figure numbers of illustrations

BIBLIOGRAPHY

Aspin, C, The Woollen Industry: Shire Publications Ltd

Bennett, W, The History of Burnley part 3: Burnley Corpn.1971

Bevan, Amanda, Tracing Your Ancestors in the National Archives, the website and beyond: 7th ed 2007

Brierley, Henry, The Rochdale Reminiscences of Henry Brierley: Rochdale Times Ltd. 1923

Burton, Anthony, The Canal Builders: Tempus 2005

Campbell, Fred, 'Bury's Two Rivers': 1988 Neil Richardson

Champness, E M, The Life Story of Thomas Champness: Kelly, London 1907

Coates, Berwick, Wellington's Charge – a portrait of the Duke's England: Robson Books 2002

Cole, John, Rochdale Revisited, a town and its people: vol I and II: George Kelsall, Littleborough 1990

Cole, John, Down Poorhouse Lane, the diary of a Rochdale workhouse: 2nd Ed 1994

Cole, John, Yesterday's Rochdale: Henderson Publishing co.1983

Davidoff L and Hall, Catherine, Family Fortunes, men and women of the English Middle class 1780-1850

Digby, Anne, The Evolution of British General Practice 1850-1948: Oxford Univ Press

Falkus, Malcolm, Britain Transformed – an economic and social history 1700-1914: Causeway Books

Hall, G D, Congregationalists, Methodists and Lancashire Nonconformists 1790-1907: thesis

Hank, Patrick – Editor, Dictionary of American Family Names.

Harte, Negley B, A History of Samuel Heap and Son 1823–1964: typescript.

Herber, Mark, Ancestral Trails: Sutton Publishing 2004

Higgs, Edward, Making Sense of the Census Revisited: Univ of London 2005

Higgs, E, Domestic Servants and Households in Rochdale 1851-1871: New York 1986

Jenkins DT and Ponting KG, The British Wool Textile Industry: Heinemann 1982

Leary, William, My Ancestors were Methodists: Soc of Genealogists 2005

Loudon, Irvine, Medical Care and the General Practitioner 1750-1850: Clarendon Press 1986

Milne, Jack, Rochdale as it was: Henderson Publishing 1973

Moore, B, History of Wesleyan Methodism in Burnley and East Lancashire.. Gazette Burnley 1899

Mullett, Michael, Sources for the History of English Nonconformity 1660-1830

Ree's Manufacturing Industry 1819-20 vol 5 - Fullery and Fulling: David and Charles reprints.

Rose, Mary B, The Lancashire Cotton Industry– a history since 1700: Lancashire County Books 1996

Smith, Mark, Religion in Industrial Society – Oldham and Saddleworth: Clarendon Press Oxford 1994

Taylor, Rebe P, A Centenary History of Rochdale 1956 – Rochdale Retrospect: Rochdale Corpn.1956

Tillmanns, Martin, Bridge Hall Mills, three centuries of paper manufacture : Compton Press 1978

Tippett, L H C, A Portrait of the Lancashire Textile Industry: OUP 1969

Wadsworth A P and Mann, Julia, The Cotton Trade and Industrial Lancashire 1600-1780: Manchester University Press 1931

Waller, Ralph, John Wesley, a personal portrait: SPCK 2003

Walton, John, Nat Trust Guide to late Georgian and Victorian Britain from the industrial revolution to World War 1: Nat Trust 1989